Exploring the Potentials of Automation in Logistics and Supply Chain Management: Paving the Way for Autonomous Supply Chains

Exploring the Potentials of Automation in Logistics and Supply Chain Management: Paving the Way for Autonomous Supply Chains

Editor

Benjamin Nitsche

MDPI • Basel • Beijing • Wuhan • Barcelona • Belgrade • Manchester • Tokyo • Cluj • Tianjin

Editor
Benjamin Nitsche
Chair of Logistics
Berlin University of Technology
Berlin
Germany

Editorial Office
MDPI
St. Alban-Anlage 66
4052 Basel, Switzerland

This is a reprint of articles from the Special Issue published online in the open access journal *Logistics* (ISSN 2305-6290) (available at: www.mdpi.com/journal/logistics/special_issues/scm_automation).

For citation purposes, cite each article independently as indicated on the article page online and as indicated below:

LastName, A.A.; LastName, B.B.; LastName, C.C. Article Title. *Journal Name* **Year**, *Volume Number*, Page Range.

ISBN 978-3-0365-1905-0 (Hbk)
ISBN 978-3-0365-1904-3 (PDF)

© 2021 by the authors. Articles in this book are Open Access and distributed under the Creative Commons Attribution (CC BY) license, which allows users to download, copy and build upon published articles, as long as the author and publisher are properly credited, which ensures maximum dissemination and a wider impact of our publications.

The book as a whole is distributed by MDPI under the terms and conditions of the Creative Commons license CC BY-NC-ND.

Contents

About the Editor vii

Benjamin Nitsche
Exploring the Potentials of Automation in Logistics and Supply Chain Management: Paving the Way for Autonomous Supply Chains
Reprinted from: *Logistics* **2021**, *5*, 51, doi:10.3390/logistics5030051 1

Evelyne Tina Kassai, Muhammad Azmat and Sebastian Kummer
Scope of Using Autonomous Trucks and Lorries for Parcel Deliveries in Urban Settings
Reprinted from: *Logistics* **2020**, *4*, 17, doi:10.3390/logistics4030017 11

Stavros T. Ponis and Orestis K. Efthymiou
Cloud and IoT Applications in Material Handling Automation and Intralogistics
Reprinted from: *Logistics* **2020**, *4*, 22, doi:10.3390/logistics4030022 35

Masoud Zafarzadeh, Magnus Wiktorsson and Jannicke Baalsrud Hauge
A Systematic Review on Technologies for Data-Driven Production Logistics: Their Role from a Holistic and Value Creation Perspective
Reprinted from: *Logistics* **2021**, *5*, 24, doi:10.3390/logistics5020024 53

Anselm Busse, Benno Gerlach, Joel Cedric Lengeling, Peter Poschmann, Johannes Werner and Simon Zarnitz
Towards Digital Twins of Multimodal Supply Chains
Reprinted from: *Logistics* **2021**, *5*, 25, doi:10.3390/logistics5020025 85

Daisuke Watanabe, Takeshi Kenmochi and Keiju Sasa
An Analytical Approach for Facility Location for Truck Platooning—A Case Study of an Unmanned Following Truck Platooning System in Japan
Reprinted from: *Logistics* **2021**, *5*, 27, doi:10.3390/logistics5020027 97

Wim Lambrechts, Jessica S. Klaver, Lennart Koudijzer and Janjaap Semeijn
Human Factors Influencing the Implementation of Cobots in High Volume Distribution Centres
Reprinted from: *Logistics* **2021**, *5*, 32, doi:10.3390/logistics5020032 113

About the Editor

Benjamin Nitsche

After working in strategic purchasing in consumer electronics, in 2014, Benjamin Nitsche joined the Chair of Logistics at the Berlin University of Technology (TUB). He finished his doctoral thesis in 2018 in the field of volatility management, which has been awarded by the German Association of Industrial Engineers. He is currently heading the Competence Center for International Logistics Networks (ILNET) at the Chair of Logistics at TUB. At ILNET (funded by the Kuehne Foundation), a team of researchers—jointly with researchers from Africa and China—investigates current trends and strategies in international logistics networks by integrating a variety of industry partners and industry working groups (online and on-site). He also serves as a reviewer for international journals and is a member of the editorial board of *Logistics*. He is also a visiting lecturer at ESCP Europe and at FOM University of Applied Sciences and conducts executive education seminars.

Editorial

Exploring the Potentials of Automation in Logistics and Supply Chain Management: Paving the Way for Autonomous Supply Chains

Benjamin Nitsche

Chair of Logistics, Berlin University of Technology, Straße des 17. Juni 135, 10623 Berlin, Germany; nitsche@logistik.tu-berlin.de; Tel.: +49-030-314-26007

Abstract: The world of logistics is changing and entering a new era. The advance of digitalization and technologization enables new business models, increased process efficiencies, novel planning approaches, and much more but, on the downside, there is also the risk of being lost in the maelstrom of developments. Within these developments, the automation of logistics processes and ultimately the design of autonomous logistics systems is one of the most defining trends that has far-reaching consequences for the planning and execution of future logistics processes. This Special Issue aims to contribute to the discussion and to get to the bottom of the question of how the path towards automated and autonomous logistics systems should be designed. This editorial lays a foundation by presenting application areas of automation and discussing the theoretical path towards autonomous logistics systems. The articles that follow provide highly practical insights into current research results on the automation and autonomization of informational and physical logistics processes.

Keywords: process automation; autonomous logistics systems; industry 4.0; logistics 4.0; autonomous driving; internet of things; digital twin; cobots; digitalization

Citation: Nitsche, B. Exploring the Potentials of Automation in Logistics and Supply Chain Management: Paving the Way for Autonomous Supply Chains. *Logistics* **2021**, *5*, 51. https://doi.org/10.3390/logistics5030051

Received: 20 July 2021
Accepted: 29 July 2021
Published: 3 August 2021

Publisher's Note: MDPI stays neutral with regard to jurisdictional claims in published maps and institutional affiliations.

Copyright: © 2021 by the author. Licensee MDPI, Basel, Switzerland. This article is an open access article distributed under the terms and conditions of the Creative Commons Attribution (CC BY) license (https://creativecommons.org/licenses/by/4.0/).

1. Introduction to Automation in Logistics and Supply Chain Management

For years, the digital transformation has probably been the most defining trend in the logistics and supply chain industry, presenting practitioners with significant challenges but also offering enormous opportunities to achieve competitive advantages at various levels [1,2]. The automation of informational and physical processes represents one of the most significant developments in this regard, as it has the potential to have a lasting impact on the planning and control of logistics systems at the strategic, tactical, and operational levels. The motivations for automating processes are multifaceted and range from the desire to reduce costs and strive for productivity increases to the expectation of more independence regarding the decisions of individuals in logistics networks.

The general idea of automating processes originated from the production environment, where manual processes were supported or replaced by machines in the advancing era of mass production. However, the idea of automation evolved from there and, today, it also includes the automation of informational flows across globally dispersed networks [3]. Therefore, today, automation in the context of logistics and supply chain management includes the automation of physical and also informational flows; each of these is equally important, and there is still room for improvement in each. More specifically, Nitsche et al. define logistics and supply chain automation as "the partial or full replacement or support of a human-performed physical or informational process by a machine. This includes tasks to plan, control or execute the physical flow of goods as well as the corresponding informational and financial flows within the focal firm and with supply chain partners" [4].

Although automation of processes is an important trend for logistics and supply chain management today, and will have increasing importance in the near future, companies are still hesitant and experience challenges in developing automation solutions. In the area of automation of physical processes, for example, in warehousing or production logistics, the automation state is more advanced with regard to the automation of informational processes but, even here, high costs and the difficulty of integration into existing systems are still issues. Regarding the automation of informational processes in logistics networks, the complexity even increases, because this often also involves aligning and integrating multiple partners in complex global networks.

Although this had already been an important trend for many years, the COVID-19 pandemic additionally stressed the need for more automation in logistics networks. Straube and Nitsche [5] emphasized the need for more automation to increase responsiveness, and also to gain partial independence from personnel, which was one of the most important trends that logistics and supply chain managers already recognized at the beginning of the pandemic: A trend that manifested and even increased in importance throughout the first year of the pandemic [6]. Many other authors have also stressed that the COVID-19 pandemic eloquently expressed the need for more automation in future supply chains to achieve responsiveness and resilience [7–9].

However, owing to the pressure induced by COVID-19, many promising automation solutions were developed in the short term that proved to be efficient in a wide range of fields. For example, automated emergency response systems have been developed that combine physical and informational automation approaches to automatically supply regions with goods in urgent need [10]. Manufacturing companies, in particular, were quick to develop automation solutions for managing their supply chains more rapidly than would have been the case without the pressure of the pandemic. To give one example, Nitsche and Straube [6] reported that companies developed so-called "supplier risk towers," an automated supplier survey technique that enables greater network visibility through the calculation of vulnerability scores on different levels (supplier, plant, and regional levels). Based on the survey results, this automation solution is a very efficient crisis management approach; however, only a few companies have similar approaches already in place.

Therefore, it can be said that the automation of processes in logistics and supply chain management is advancing rapidly. According to Nitsche and Straube [6], the use of robotic process automation (RPA) will increase within the next five years (by 2026) so that processes will become less error prone and increasingly independent of individuals. Moreover, based on the investigations of Junge et al. [2], it can be assumed that, until 2029, most operational functions in logistics will be handled in near to full autonomy.

Regardless of whether these predictions are accurate, it is already clear that the automation and autonomization of logistics systems is an important trend that is currently gaining in importance. This Special Issue, therefore, aims to contribute to the necessary discussions in selected areas of automation and autonomization. Here, we explain what the path towards autonomous logistics systems can theoretically look like. To this end, the findings of a recent review on application areas and antecedents of automation projects in logistics are first summarized. Subsequently, evolutionary stages towards autonomous systems are briefly explained and the concepts of automation and autonomy are distinguished from each other. Finally, an overview of the content of the articles in this Special Issue is given before heading into the concrete articles.

2. Paving the Way for Autonomous Supply Chains

2.1. Application Areas and Antecedents of Automation in Logistics and Supply Chain Management

In order to provide an overview of potential application areas of automation as well as the antecedents of successful automation projects, Nitsche et al. [4] conducted a meta-analysis that combined a systematic literature review with a structured group exercise among logistics and supply chain experts. As a result, ten application areas (including multiple sub-areas) were condensed and four dimensions of antecedents (including ten antecedents in total) were defined. The resulting conceptual framework of this study is displayed in Figure 1.

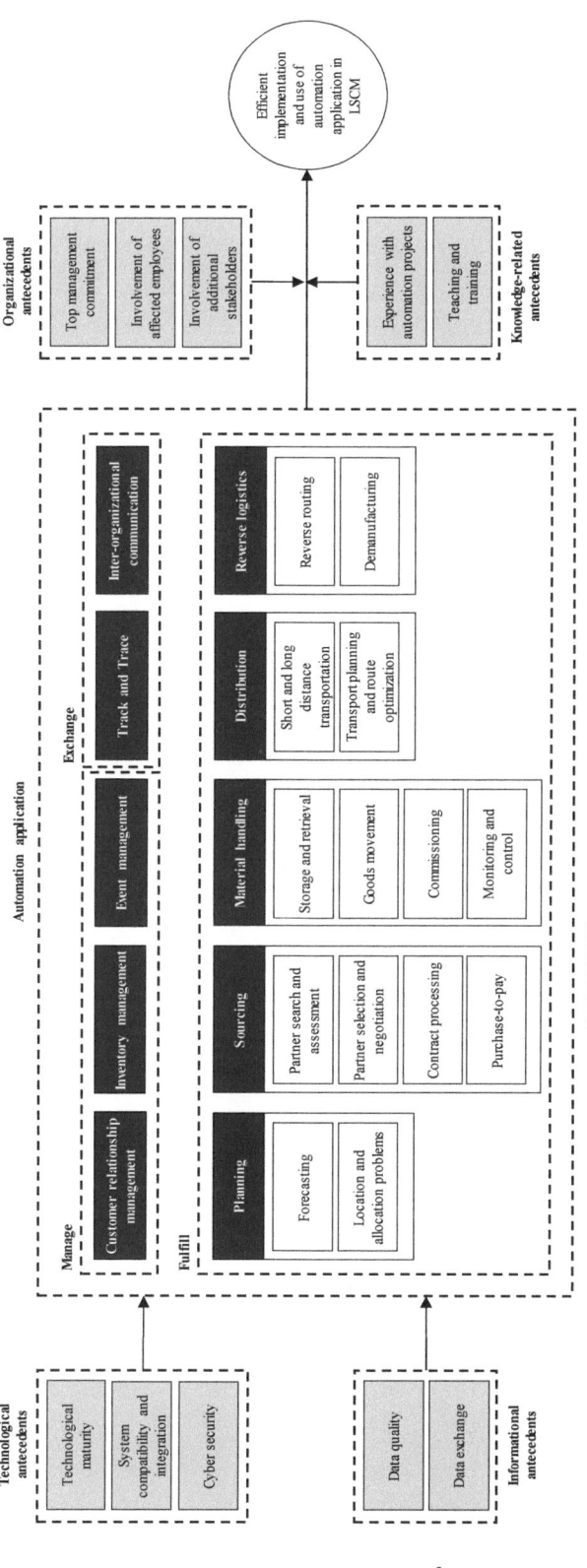

Figure 1. Conceptual framework of automation in logistics and supply chain management [4].

2.1.1. Application Areas of Automation

As can be seen in Figure 1, the application areas of automation are subdivided into three main dimensions, i.e., fulfill, exchange, and manage. Automation areas belonging to the "fulfill" dimension are automation applications that mainly seek to support the fulfillment of the main customer order process. More specifically, this includes the application areas planning, sourcing, material handling, distribution, and reverse logistics. Of all the application areas surveyed, Nitsche et al. [4] identified the most literature on automation applications in the areas of sourcing and material handling. Although applications in sourcing often aim at the automation of the informational processes of the purchasing department—such as payment processes, partner search, and negotiations—automation applications in material handling mostly include the automation of physical processes through automated and autonomous vehicles and robots. Moreover, in the field of planning, the automation of the forecasting process provides the dominant research field.

Applications related to the "exchange" dimension mostly seek to facilitate the automated collection and exchange of data within the supply chain. More specifically, this includes the automated collection and monitoring of data to improve materials management and also the automated data exchange between supply chain partners through platforms.

Applications in the "manage" dimension mostly focus on management functions indirectly related to the fulfillment process. More specifically, this includes applications from the application areas inventory management, customer relationship management, and event management that range from automated replenishment approaches through automated customer service applications to autonomous multi-agent approaches to automatically identify risks and autonomously change logistics plans accordingly.

On the basis of this very generic classification of application areas of automation in logistics and supply chain management, it can be observed that the field is very broad and includes several substreams of research and literature. Additionally, the classification subdivides automation applications into several areas, although it might be the case that a particular automation application in practice touches several application areas at the same time. Especially when it comes to autonomous logistics systems, where multiple actors communicate and decide autonomously, multiple application areas are being touched upon.

2.1.2. Antecedents of Automation

Although the concrete antecedents of an automation application in one of the areas described above might be case specific, analyzing them on a meta level provides certain insights into how to handle the implementation of automation solutions in practice. According to the analysis of Nitsche et al. [4], there are four dimensions of antecedents that influence the efficient implementation and use of automation applications.

"Technological antecedents", including "technological maturity", "system compatibility and integration", as well as "cyber security", in addition to "informational antecedents", including "data quality" as well as "data exchange", have a direct influence on the efficiency of the implementation and use of an automation solution. This means that the technological and also the data-related quality of the solution is of decisive, though not sole, relevance. This in itself is unsurprising, but it does show how complex it is to either purchase or develop a solution that fulfills all these factors, i.e., a solution that is technologically mature, compatible with existing systems, and takes security aspects sufficiently into account, but also that the necessary data for the automation solution is available and can be exchanged. However, there are also other factors that influence the successful implementation. More precisely, "organizational antecedents", including "top management commitment", "involvement of affected employees", as well as "involvement of additional stakeholders", and "knowledge-related antecedents" moderate the effects of technological and informational antecedents. This finding emphasizes that the human factor in the implementation of automation solutions plays a vital role and cannot be neglected. This effect has also been seen with other technology implementations and underlines that automation might enable increases in productivity and reduce dependence of personnel but, more importantly, it is still people who plan and steer the project, develop the solution, use the application, etc. This being said, the human factor in automation is also one of the more dominant topics of this Special Issue, in addition to other, equally important discussions.

2.2. Moving from Automated to Autonomous Processes in Logistics and Supply Chain Management

The automation of physical and information processes in logistics and supply chain networks is not the end of developments. The vision of not only automating processes, but also gradually equipping them with decision-making powers, and thus enabling those processes to run autonomously, is driving scientists and practitioners and is already a reality in some use cases. Therefore, the step toward automation is to be understood as the next logical step on the way to autonomous logistics systems. Dumitrescu et al. [11,12] proposed five development stages of technical systems towards autonomous systems, which are shown in Figure 2. Although this classification describes the automation and autonomization of technical systems (especially robots, vehicles, and machines, but also software) and would perhaps need further refinement for the purposes of technical processes that are mostly the norm in logistics systems, the classification distinctly shows the necessary evolution of those systems and clearly distinguishes between automated and autonomous systems. The five stages are defined as follows [11,12]:

(1) Remotely controlled systems: For these technical systems, humans take over the major control of the apparatus and no automation or autonomy is present.
(2) Systems with assistance function: For these systems, predefined processes are implemented that seek to assist the user. Although such systems can be argued to be automation applications, all steps of the system are predefined and no intelligent reconfiguration of the system is implemented to react to unforeseen changes.
(3) Semi-automated systems: These systems can perform automated steps in a predefined way and also react to predefined situations with if–then relationships. This means that this is an important intermediate step towards self-learning autonomous systems, but these systems recognize and process events only based on already gained knowledge and not through learning by themselves.
(4) Semi-autonomous systems: These systems are highly automated and efficient and also have self-learning capabilities, while the knowledge base is constantly expanding during ongoing operations. In some cases, these systems can already control themselves and make decisions independently on the basis of the knowledge they have acquired, but human intervention is still necessary in more complex problems.
(5) Autonomous systems: Here, systems have full self-learning capabilities and are able to decide autonomously without human intervention for most situations, even if a particular situation is not known. The system is fully integrated into other relevant systems and can adapt to, but also anticipate, certain events. They run autonomously for longer periods of time and human intervention is sparse.

Even though the concrete assignment of an existing system to one of the levels may not always be possible, undoubtedly, in individual cases, some necessary system characteristics become clear with increasing levels. Whereas automated systems tend to perform predefined, known tasks, autonomous systems are about being equipped with decision-making capabilities and competencies and becoming able to adapt to the situation intelligently. This means that, with increasing level, more complex problems are solvable with less and less human intervention. The ability to make decisions is indispensable for autonomous systems. In the context of logistics, however, this means that owing to the interdisciplinarity and, above all, the high number of stakeholders often involved, the development of autonomous systems that enable running complex logistics processes without human intervention is extremely complex, and their development has not yet reached the level of autonomous technical systems such as autonomous vehicles. The differentiation of the evolutionary stages of autonomous technical processes in logistics on the basis of existing findings is certainly necessary in the context of further research. However, it also makes sense to investigate when these evolutionary stages are likely to be reached or when they will become industry-wide practice, and what prerequisites will have to be created for this in logistics.

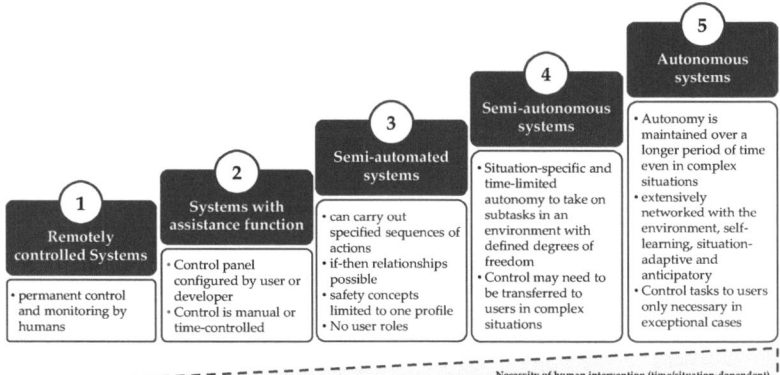

Figure 2. Development stages of technical systems towards autonomous systems according to Dumitrescu et al. [11] (p. 18).

3. Summary of Articles in this Special Issue

3.1. Scope of Using Autonomous Trucks and Lorries for Parcel Deliveries in Urban Settings

With urbanization rates increasing at a massive pace, population densities in cities are on the rise and supplying those urban areas with goods in a sustainable manner is becoming more and more challenging. Courier, express, and parcel services (CEP) are taking up this challenge and have to find new methods and approaches to deliver goods faster than ever before. What is already a tough task is further exacerbated by a massive driver shortage in many industrialized countries. Thus, future city logistics is one of the main problems that the industry has to solve. Here, automation and especially autonomous vehicles will play an important role in satisfying the future needs of cities. The authors of this article [13] investigated the future role of autonomous trucks and lorries for parcel deliveries in urban areas. To do that, they investigated current implementation barriers and future delivery opportunities while taking into consideration, through interviews, the views of several actors in the CEP industry. Autonomous delivery concepts were compared to traditional concepts and recommendations were given regarding how autonomous can become advantageous. Additionally, cost implications were discussed and potential use cases were illustrated. With their study, the authors advanced knowledge in this field and triggered important future discussions on what logistics innovations are needed to be better prepared for the future.

3.2. Cloud and IoT Applications in Material Handling Automation and Intralogistics

In the wake of digitalization, concepts such as Industry 4.0 have become indispensable and already play a decisive role in the development of new logistics and manufacturing concepts. Especially in the field of logistics automation, material handling in warehouses is often among the first physical processes to be automated by using several technological solutions. Therefore, these physical assets have to be integrated with the digital world, which often leads to problems. Through a literature review, the authors of this article [14] highlighted the main fields of research but concluded that there is a lack of real-world automation applications documented in the literature; to account for that, the authors developed and explained a cloud-based IoT application that could be integrated into a real-life distribution center by using autonomous material handling technologies such as automated guided vehicles, conveyors, shuttles, and others. The case study was situated in a distribution center for home furniture and sporting goods, and they outlined, in an impressive way, how beneficial the integration of the cloud-based IoT solution with material handling automation solutions could be. This is a field that will surely receive more attention in practice in the near future.

3.3. A Systematic Review on Technologies for Data-Driven Production Logistics: Their Role from a Holistic and Value Creation Perspective

The automation of informational as well as physical production logistics processes is among the most dominant fields when it comes to automation. In this regard, several data-driven information technologies have arisen that support this development and contribute to the future vision of smart autonomous factories. To add significant value to a necessary discussion in this field, the authors of this article [15] conducted a sound systematic literature review of 142 articles to outline the current state and future role of technologies for data-driven production logistics. By systematically analyzing those articles, first, the authors identify ten technology groups (and multiple technologies belonging to those groups) that enable data-driven production logistics. Subsequently, the identified technologies were mapped to three production logistics activity clusters (shopfloor and operational activities, planning and scheduling-related activities, as well as control and track and trace related activities) and their concrete processes within those clusters. Concrete use cases and the value of the technologies were discussed. Moreover, the authors explained how the technologies surveyed could contribute to value creation in production logistics.

3.4. Towards Digital Twins of Multimodal Supply Chains

In several logistics and supply chain trend studies, the development of digital supply chain twins has been identified as among the most important trends in the industry, as it offers new ways for planning, managing, and controlling logistics networks on the basis of up-to-real-time data; however, additional simulation opportunities can also become reality. These new ways of exchanging and processing data also make the digital twin technology a promising one for the automation of informational processes. The authors of this article [16] outlined the necessity of digital twins in future supply chains and dove deeper into the conceptualization of a framework for a holistic digital supply chain twin of multimodal supply chains that seeks to include an entire multimodal supply chain and enables new simulation and evaluation opportunities. The intended approach would also enable early risk detection and mitigation in order to create more robust networks. In this article, the enablers of this digital supply chain twin approach are outlined, the information flow within such multimodal transport chains is investigated, and a framework for a digital supply chain twin application is developed. By doing so, the authors shed light onto an area that will receive more attention in the near future. While digital twins of single assets are already being developed, twins of whole supply chains are still in their early stages. Therefore, discussions and findings such as those in this article are highly relevant.

3.5. An Analytical Approach for Facility Location for Truck Platooning—A Case Study of an Unmanned Following Truck Platooning System in Japan

Autonomous and semi-autonomous driving not only plays an important role in the design of future city logistics concepts and last-mile solutions; particularly, in long-distance transport, autonomous concepts can solve safety problems and, at the same time, address the driver shortage that exists in many places. In this context, platooning, one of the main concepts for more efficient long-distance transport, is already being tested in various industrialized countries. The authors of this article [17] investigated the case of truck platooning in Japan and developed a facility location model. By so doing, the authors clearly demonstrated the advantages that platooning can bring as compared with scenarios without this approach. Finding the concrete centers from where multiple unmanned trucks could simultaneously drive in platoons on the same track is a challenging and important task that was addressed by this study. The study outlined the current state of truck platooning in Japan and the developed model was applied to the case of Japan to derive several recommendations for multiple scenarios.

3.6. Human Factors Influencing the Implementation of Cobots in High Volume Distribution Centres

Even if the automation and autonomization of processes in logistics brings various advantages and can give rise to completely new logistics systems, the human factor in this development must not be ignored. On the one hand, it is people who use automation solutions, but, on the other hand, above all, the question arises of what the role of people in logistics systems will be in the future, and when will it be possible to carry out most processes autonomously, i.e., without human intervention, i.e., in a decade or so. In this article [18], the authors put a spotlight on the human factor in logistics in the context of automation. More specifically, they investigated the role of the human factor when implementing cobots for collaborative order picking in high-volume distribution centers. Four in-depth case studies were conducted and analyzed and included multiple interviews with representatives from the case study companies that had already tested and implemented cobots for order picking in their environments. Throughout this process, a multitude of human-related factors were identified that influenced the successful implementation process from project kick-off until actual use. On the basis of this work, recommendations are given for a more human-inclusive approach for implementing such automation solutions while also considering the personal traits of employees.

Funding: This research received no external funding.

Institutional Review Board Statement: Not applicable.

Informed Consent Statement: Not applicable.

Data Availability Statement: Not applicable.

Conflicts of Interest: The author declares no conflict of interest.

References

1. Kersten, W.; Seiter, M.; von See, B.; Hackius, N.; Maurer, T. *Trends and Strategies in Logistics and Supply Chain Management: Digital Transformation Opportunities*; DVV Media Group GmbH: Hamburg, Germany, 2017.
2. Junge, A.L.; Verhoeven, P.; Reipert, J.; Mansfeld, M. *Pathway of Digital Transformation in Logistics: Best Practice Concepts and Future Developments*, Special Edition; Straube, F., Ed.; Scientific Series Logistics at the Berlin Institute of Technology; Universitätsverlag der TU Berlin: Berlin, Germany, 2019; ISBN 978-3-7983-3094-8.
3. Viswanadham, N. The Past, Present, and Future of Supply-Chain Automation. *IEEE Robot. Autom. Mag.* **2002**, *9*, 48–56. [CrossRef]
4. Nitsche, B.; Straube, F.; Wirth, M. Application Areas and Antecedents of Automation in Logistics and Supply Chain Management: A Conceptual Framework. *Supply Chain Forum Int. J.* **2021**, 1–17. [CrossRef]
5. Straube, F.; Nitsche, B. Heading into "The New Normal": Potential Development Paths of International Logistics Networks in the Wake of the Coronavirus Pandemic. *Int. Transp.* **2020**, *72*, 31–35.
6. Nitsche, B.; Straube, F. Defining the "New Normal" in International Logistics Networks: Lessons Learned and Implications of the COVID-19 Pandemic. *WiSt-Wirtsch. Stud.* **2021**, in press.
7. Wuest, T.; Kusiak, A.; Dai, T.; Tayur, S.R. Impact of COVID-19 on Manufacturing and Supply Networks—The Case for AI-Inspired Digital Transformation. *SSRN Electron. J.* **2020**. [CrossRef]
8. Hobbs, J.E. Food Supply Chain Resilience and the COVID-19 Pandemic: What Have We Learned? *Can. J. Agric. Econ. Can. Agroeconomie* **2021**, *69*, 189–196. [CrossRef]
9. Belhadi, A.; Kamble, S.; Jabbour, C.J.C.; Gunasekaran, A.; Ndubisi, N.O.; Venkatesh, M. Manufacturing and Service Supply Chain Resilience to the COVID-19 Outbreak: Lessons Learned from the Automobile and Airline Industries. *Technol. Forecast. Soc. Change* **2021**, *163*, 120447. [CrossRef] [PubMed]
10. Khan, I.; Javaid, M. Automated COVID-19 Emergency Response Using Modern Technologies. *Apollo Med.* **2020**, *17*, 58–61. [CrossRef]
11. Dumitrescu, R.; Westermann, T.; Falkowski, T. Autonome Systeme in Der Produktion. *Ind. 40 Manag.* **2018**, *2018*, 17–20. [CrossRef]
12. Dumitrescu, R.; Gausemeier, J.; Slusallek, P.; Cieslik, S.; Demme, G.; Falkowski, T.; Hoffmann, H.; Kadner, S.; Reinhart, F.; Westermann, T.; et al. *Studie "Autonome Systeme"*; Studien zum deutschen Innovationssystem; Expertenkommission Forschung und Innovation (EFI): Berlin, Germany, 2018; p. 90.
13. Kassai, E.T.; Azmat, M.; Kummer, S. Scope of Using Autonomous Trucks and Lorries for Parcel Deliveries in Urban Settings. *Logistics* **2020**, *4*, 17. [CrossRef]
14. Ponis, S.T.; Efthymiou, O.K. Cloud and IoT Applications in Material Handling Automation and Intralogistics. *Logistics* **2020**, *4*, 22. [CrossRef]

15. Zafarzadeh, M.; Wiktorsson, M.; Baalsrud Hauge, J. A Systematic Review on Technologies for Data-Driven Production Logistics: Their Role from a Holistic and Value Creation Perspective. *Logistics* **2021**, *5*, 24. [CrossRef]
16. Busse, A.; Gerlach, B.; Lengeling, J.C.; Poschmann, P.; Werner, J.; Zarnitz, S. Towards Digital Twins of Multimodal Supply Chains. *Logistics* **2021**, *5*, 25. [CrossRef]
17. Watanabe, D.; Kenmochi, T.; Sasa, K. An Analytical Approach for Facility Location for Truck Platooning—A Case Study of an Unmanned Following Truck Platooning System in Japan. *Logistics* **2021**, *5*, 27. [CrossRef]
18. Lambrechts, W.; Klaver, J.S.; Koudijzer, L.; Semeijn, J. Human Factors Influencing the Implementation of Cobots in High Volume Distribution Centres. *Logistics* **2021**, *5*, 32. [CrossRef]

Article

Scope of Using Autonomous Trucks and Lorries for Parcel Deliveries in Urban Settings

Evelyne Tina Kassai, Muhammad Azmat * and Sebastian Kummer

Welthandelsplatz 1, Institute for Transport and Logistics Management, WU (Vienna University of Economics and Business), 1020 Vienna, Austria; evelyne.tina.kassai@s.wu.ac.at (E.T.K.); Skummer@wu.ac.at (S.K.)
* Correspondence: mazmat@wu.ac.at

Received: 17 June 2020; Accepted: 21 July 2020; Published: 7 August 2020

Abstract: Courier, express, and parcel (CEP) services represent one of the most challenging and dynamic sectors of the logistics industry. Companies of this sector must solve several challenges to keep up with the rapid changes in the market. In this context, the introduction of autonomous delivery using self-driving trucks might be an appropriate solution to overcome the problems that the industry is facing today. This paper investigates if the introduction of autonomous trucks would be feasible for deliveries in urban areas from the experts' point of view. Furthermore, the potential advantages of such autonomous vehicles were highlighted and compared to traditional delivery methods. At the same time, barriers that could slow down or hinder such an implementation were also discovered by conducting semi-structured interviews with experts from the field. The results show that CEP companies are interested in innovative logistics solutions such as autonomous vans, especially when it comes to business-to-consumer (B2C) activities. Most of the experts acknowledge the benefits that self-driving vans could bring once on the market. Despite that, there are still some difficulties that need to be solved before actual implementation. If this type of vehicle will become the sector's disruptor is yet to be seen.

Keywords: self-driving trucks; autonomous vans; CEP companies; CEP sector; autonomous delivery; urban logistics; logistics

1. Introduction

Due to the complexity of urban areas, planning and execution of transport and logistics are among the most challenging tasks faced by private organizations and public authorities. Nowadays, the last-mile problem generates significant issues for delivery service providers, and to remain competitive, these companies must deal with several challenges [1]. This research presents a comprehensive overview of autonomous trucks or lorries (T&L), as upcoming developments that could alter the customer experience and the logistics behind urban deliveries. While a decade ago, driverless vehicles seemed unimaginable; they are getting closer to become a reality. According to the "DHL Logistics Trend Radar," self-driving vehicles have a high probability of fundamentally transforming the way businesses are executed today, creating new possibilities in different sectors [2]. Moreover, driverless cars could reshape our society and have such an enormous impact on humanity as the first automobiles. The expression "driverless car" will maybe sound similar to the anachronism "horseless carriage" in the future [3].

The importance of autonomous vehicles (AVs) for future urban logistics development has been stated by a handful of journal articles or institutions. Researchers have highlighted that these advancements in the automobile sector have the potential to significantly reduce the transport and logistics-related challenges in complicated urban settings [1,4]. However, most of the articles in the field either hold a general description of autonomous trucks without distinguishing an industry, or they present various logistical innovations in the field of courier, express, and parcel (CEP) companies, such as drones, light electric freight vehicles, self-driving parcels or droids [5,6]. Few of the papers have already suggested examining the potential of using autonomous trucks in urban areas for last-mile deliveries, stating that "specific areas such as last-mile logistics would be of interest" [7]. It is still not known how to "assess the benefits of self-driving vehicles for city logistics", so more research is needed in this area [1].

Finding the possible use cases, advantages, and barriers is crucial to establish a better understanding of the topic as the "challenges of urban logistics change continually" [1]. Thus, a single paper cannot bring the overall solution to this problem, but it could be a good starting point when it comes to autonomous trucks and their implications. The significance of the innovation in the mobility sector with autonomous vehicles is undeniable. Therefore, this paper aims to examine what autonomous T&L could offer in comparison to traditional delivery methods and to what extent these vehicles could be used in the future. This will be answered by presenting the current perception and opinion of the experts working in CEP companies. It leads to the primary research question of this paper:

1. How is the introduction and implementation of self-driving trucks currently viewed by the experts of the CEP segment?

In order to answer this question as precisely as possible, the article has two other sub-questions which should enable to examine the main question stated above from two different angles:

1a. How could autonomous T&L be more advantageous than traditional delivery methods when it comes to urban areas?
1b. What are the possible barriers that could hinder or slow down the implementation of autonomous T&L in urban settings?

Without formulating research objectives, the "same level of precision" cannot be achieved, as they help to specify and detail the research questions even more [8]. Therefore, this study presents a three-fold research objective:

1. To sketch use-case scenarios for driverless T&L in urban settings;
2. To investigate the feasibility of a potential autonomous delivery implementation from different viewpoints;
3. To review the possible logistical changes this implementation could bring for the CEP sector.

2. Literature Review

The purpose of this section is to create an excellent theoretical understanding of the topic and present the state of the art. To achieve this, the chapter will be divided into four different subtopics. The first part will define urban delivery and CEP companies as significant players on the market while elaborating on the challenges related to last-mile delivery. After that, autonomous trucks will be presented as potential solutions for this problem. Lastly, the paper will examine the implications on logistics.

Most of the information presented derives from secondary literature, for example, scholarly journal articles. The topic of autonomous trucks is relatively new in the academic field, so a considerable part of the literature review is also based on trend reports or blog posts of consulting firms, companies involved in transportation, logistics or supply chain management, and experts in the field. Besides, the paper has made beneficial use of primary sources found, such as patents. These types of sources were essential to show real-life examples of autonomous vehicles.

Last but not least, two events organized by the Institute for Transport and Logistics Management of WU (Vienna University of Economics and Business) were also attended. The first event was a roundtable discussion entitled "KEP-Dienstleister im Schatten der Online-Giganten." At the same time, the second was an online lecture held by Mr. Jakob Puchinger called "Urban Deliveries with

Autonomous Vehicles." Both events helped to gather more information, dig deeper, and gain additional knowledge about the topic.

Thus, investigating different kinds of source has ensured a robust and reliable background for a topic which is still open for discussions.

2.1. Urban Delivery

2.1.1. Domains of Urban Logistics

The concept of city logistics has gained popularity in the last few years but is not by any means a new phenomenon. One way to describe city logistics could be as "finding efficient and effective ways to transport goods" [1]. Cardenas et al. [9] state that there is a lack of consensus when it comes to the terminology used for different areas of urban logistics. In order to achieve a certain level of transparency, the authors have created a framework with three urban logistics domains and present two different scopes: first, the geographical scope describes the boundaries of each domain while specifying their space of activity and second, the functional scope explains what the focus of the domain is [9].

Urban goods distribution (macro-level) and last-mile delivery (micro-level) will represent the dominant fields in the case of this article, as it will analyze how would autonomous trucks alter the design of distribution networks and how they would affect logistics services [9]. Furthermore, it will also give a detailed overview of the final product delivery under those new circumstances. However, AVs can also be recognized as innovation examples in a "smart city" context. These initiatives try to enhance the performance of urban environments with the help of information technologies in order to "provide more efficient services to citizens" and "to encourage innovative business models" [10].

2.1.2. Courier, Express and Parcel (CEP) Companies

Since this paper will investigate the topic of autonomous trucks and vans from the perspective of CEP companies, it is crucial to present these vital market players. The CEP service providers have a particular significance in urban logistics. This sector can be examined based on two dimensions: time-certainty or speed and weight [11]. The maximum weight of parcels is around 31.5 kg [12]. Couriers deliver lightweight shipments usually on the same day, while express delivery is defined by a fixed time window (within one or two days). Finally, parcel providers consolidate lightweight parcels [11–13]. Express is also called integrator because it covers almost every market segment [11]. Figure 1 presents this classification. Some parts of these services are overlapping; hence most of the CEP players offer all of them [12].

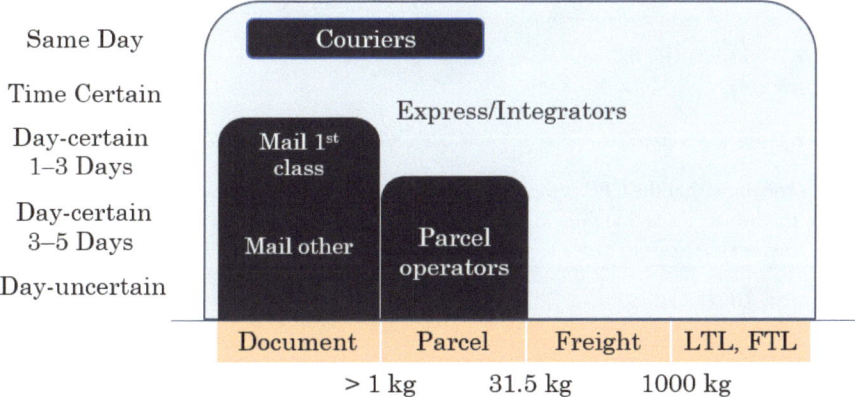

Figure 1. Courier, express, and parcel (CEP) company definition based on TNT [11] and Ducret [12].

2.1.3. Challenges of Urban Deliveries and the CEP Sector

As mentioned in the introduction, there is a vast number of drivers that shape the process of urban distribution. The difficulty of performing urban deliveries derives from a series of challenges that CEP companies must face. Accessing certain areas of a city, the distance and space are just a few problems mentioned by Cardenas et al. [9]. Because of the complexity of urban areas, delivering on time is a crucial challenge as well [9]. Furthermore, policy regulations like parking or truck size restrictions, time-windows, or a ban on night deliveries can also represent an immense hurdle to delivery companies [14].

On top of that, current trends also have a massive impact on urban logistics. Population growth and urbanization are continuously increasing the demand for goods and services [1]. Savelsbergh and Van Woensel [1] highlight that by 2050 two-thirds of the world's population will live in cities. The expansion of emerging markets and globalization are other megatrends that give rise to urban delivery challenges [11]. Another crucial driver is e-commerce, which has given a substantial boost to the business-to-consumer (B2C) sector in recent years [1,11]. Consequently, CEP companies also started to offer same-day delivery options or, in some extreme cases, even instant deliveries in order to "compete with brick-and-mortar retailers" [1]. The desire for speed, instant gratification, and the loss of patience is not a new phenomenon, and companies are trying to build their services around those needs [15]. As a result, consumers are accustomed to real-time services and favor those over regular delivery times [15].

Interestingly, the majority of customers would not pay additional fees when it comes to extra services [1]. McKinsey and Company [6] have found that only about a quarter of customers are willing to pay for a same-day delivery, which shows how cost-sensitive are the end-customers. Figure 2 illustrates the percentage of people that would pay a premium to benefit from a select delivery option.

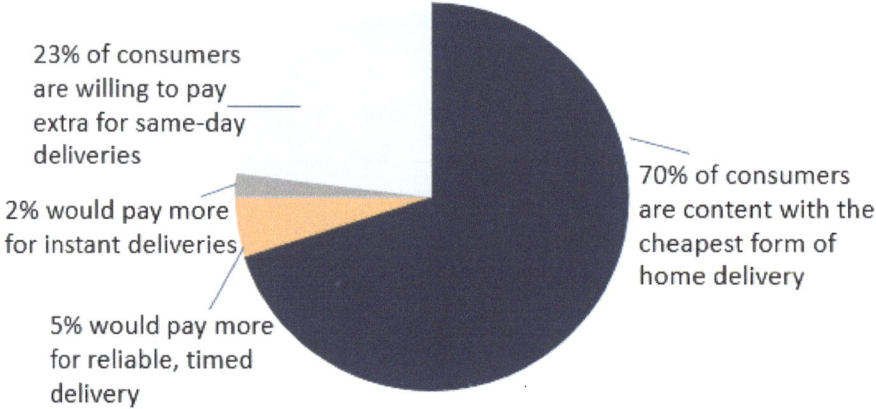

Figure 2. Share of consumers choosing different delivery options based on McKinsey and Company [6].

We can conclude that the CEP company plays a crucial role in urban areas and will get even more attention in the future. To tackle the market challenges, CEP players must find suitable solutions and design innovative strategies in order to remain competitive and execute high-quality services.

2.2. Autonomous Trucks

2.2.1. A Promising Solution

When it comes to urban deliveries, several future models are envisioned. However, automotive technology is mentioned by several different papers. Savelsbergh and Van Woensel [1] underline that the actual introduction of self-driving cars might be close in the next few years. Based on three distinct aspects (financial value, social value, and feasibility), McKinsey and Company [16] have found six promising approaches, which have the most significant potential to mitigate the urban delivery problems. It turns out that one of the best transportation solutions could be autonomous ground vehicles with parcel lockers [16].

McKinsey and Company [6] also published a matrix with two essential dimensions, one being general customer preferences (regular parcel, high reliability of timing, same-day, and instant delivery) and the second dimension being drop density. The result shows that autonomous ground vehicles (AGVs) with parcel lockers will dominate urban areas with average to high densities (excluding instant deliveries) in the anything-to-customer (X2C) sector [6]. Based on this report, the use of drones is only cost-efficient in rural areas, while droids might be applicable just in case of instant deliveries in dense cities [6]. Figure 3 depicts those findings.

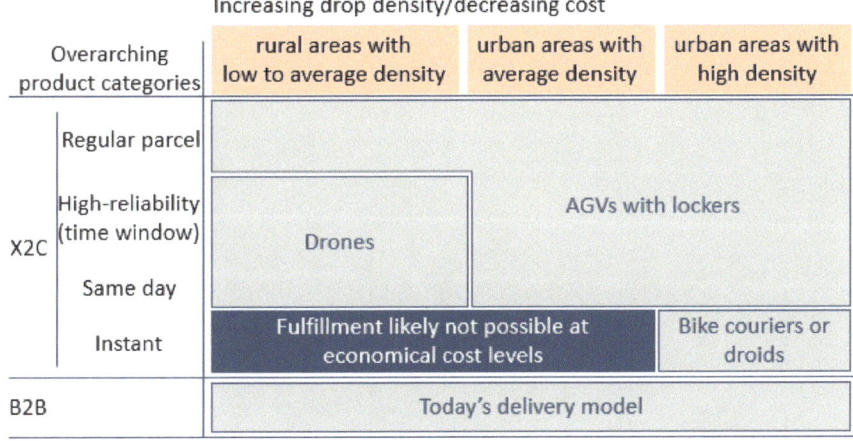

Figure 3. Future delivery models (author's rendition: adopted form McKinsey and Company [6]).

2.2.2. Autonomous Driving

To understand what impact AGVs could have on the CEP industry, we first have to define what is autonomous driving. "Automated driving," "autonomous driving," and "cooperative driving" are terminologies often used in a general sense, even though these have different meanings [17]. Based on the definition of smart [17], automated driving means that a specific autonomous (sub)system runs and supports the driver, who is in control of driving. The highest degree version of automated driving is autonomous driving, in which case no human intervention is necessary. Meanwhile, cooperative driving focuses on different technologies, which are important to gain information and communicate in road traffic systems. There are two types of communication: "vehicle-to-vehicle" and between "vehicle and road infrastructure" [17]. Figure 4 shows how the three types of driving overlap.

Furthermore, Society of Automotive Engineering (SAE) International [18] offers a taxonomy that describes the various levels of automation, presenting five various stages. We can see this distinction in Figure 5. Level 0 or "no automation" serves as a starting point or "point of reference." According to SAE International [18], the first 3 levels need a human driver to monitor the environment. In contrast, in the case of levels 3, 4, and 5, this is the task of the automated driving system, as stated in Figure 5. The classification of the Federal Highway Research Institute (BASt) and the National Highway Traffic Safety Administration may slightly differ but approximately correspond to each other [18]. This study will mainly focus on automation levels 4 and 5 because the principal advantages of the implementation could only unfold under the circumstances created by fully autonomous trucks (i.e., no human driver behind the wheel).

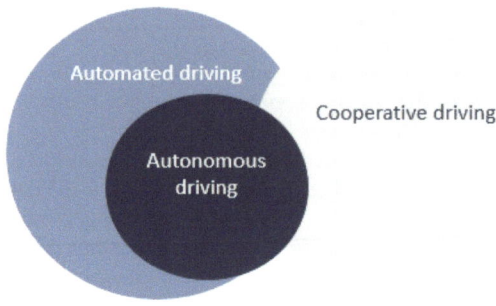

Figure 4. Areas and overlap for three types of driving based on SMART [17].

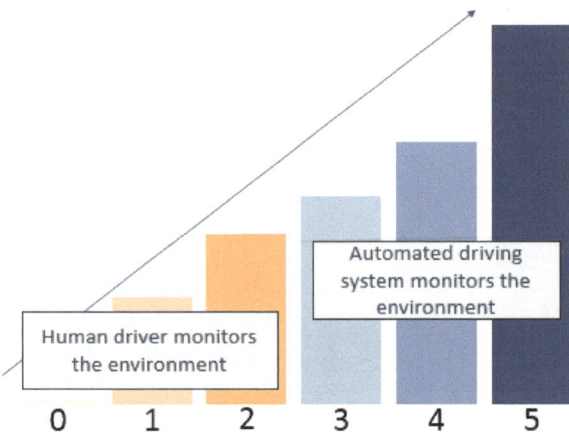

Figure 5. SAE automation levels based on SAE International [18].

2.2.3. Autonomous Truck Patents and Examples

As we can conclude from the previous explanations, AGVs are basically "land-based robots," which do not need the presence of a human in order to operate [19]. Thus, this category involves autonomous trucks, lorries, and vans as well. There is a lengthy list of companies that are involved in manufacturing the best concepts for urban deliveries. These innovative vehicles all have different futuristic features and attributes, which could immensely improve parcel deliveries. Table 1 contains a wide range of these plans.

Table 1. Company investments into self-driving vehicles.

Company	Name/Type of Vehicle	Description	Reference
Google	Autonomous van with built-in parcel lockers	A so-called "box truck" could have several different compartments each secured with a code	[20]
Ford	"Autolivery" autonomous van	A self-driving van combined with drones that could transport parcels or everyday items	[21]
Daimler	Mercedes-Benz Vision Van	The van has a fully automated cargo loading system and can launch self-driving robots or drones to transport the parcel to the doors of the customer	[22]
Charge	Self-driving, electric delivery van	The vehicle is lightweight and can be assembled in only 4 hours by one person	[23]
Next	Mobile parcel locker	A customizable automated modular vehicle solution which can be used as a parcel locker	[24]
Renault	EZ-PRO electric transport platform	A robot-vehicle designed for urban deliveries	[25]

2.2.4. Future Use Cases of Autonomous Trucks

Autonomous trucks with parcel lockers could be used in two different ways. In the first version, the vehicle could drive itself to the address of the customer. If a truck is scheduled to deliver packages, a compartment could be reserved, and a package could be placed in it [20]. The truck would drive autonomously to the address, and the addressee could open the compartment using a personal identification number (PIN) code [20]. That is the so-called "direct" or "door-to-door" delivery [16]. In the second, cheaper version, AGVs could function similarly like regular parcel lockers and serve as pick-up points. The autonomous truck would inform the customers in the area, and for a prolonged time, they could collect their packets. The most significant advantage in contrast with today's parcel lockers would be the opportunity to move the whole truck to another area. Thus, a truck could always park in the proximity of customers or "easy-to-access locations" [16]. Besides, the examples mentioned above show that autonomous trucks could be united with other methods of deliveries, like drones, droids, or robots, that could significantly improve the last-mile delivery.

2.3. Implications for Logistics

Implementing autonomous T&L will drastically restructure the logistics network, in terms of processes, stages of delivery, or distribution network. It is the case when it comes to same-day deliveries, as these need to be fulfilled within a short amount of time. Urban consolidation centers (UCCs), which are "large facilities usually located within the suburban area of big cities," might not be enough in the future to perform these services [26]. It will be more reasonable to locate the logistics center closer to the recipient [6].

Furthermore, McKinsey and Company [6] accentuates the fact that autonomous trucks will be smaller than regular trucks and thus will need to be reloaded more times. This is one of the reasons why CEP companies could decide to use so-called "city hubs" or "micro-distribution centers" to deliver parcels [12]. Based on Ducret [12], this solution sees widespread usage amongst innovative new players on the market (e.g., last-mile deliveries done with tricycles or mini-vans). It could also be implemented in the case of (electric) AGVs. An urban micro-consolidation center (UMC) or micro distribution center (MDC) would primarily focus on the package sorting (barcodes), loading/unloading of cargo, short-term or overnight storage, delivery scheduling and vehicle maintenance [27]. Figure 6 shows how could UMCs be integrated into the delivery circle of CEP companies.

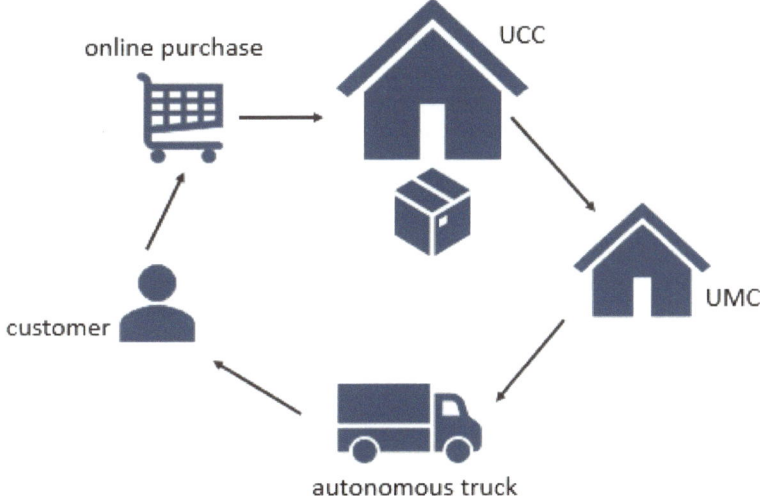

Figure 6. The integration of urban micro-consolidation center (UMCs) into the delivery circle.

3. Methodology

Investigating the secondary literature about the main topic has not only helped to draw up the research questions and to construct the literature review, but it was also the starting point for the research approach and design. Once the research questions and objectives were clear and defined, the "research onion" of Saunders et al. [8] has helped immensely to point out the right direction for this paper. This chapter will present the decision-making process regarding the methodological approach and data analysis.

3.1. Research Philosophy and Research Approach

Saunders et al. [8] state that a research question usually cannot be categorized that easily into a particular research philosophy. Undeniably, the subject of AGVs required a high degree of flexibility. As the research strategy and design can influence the understanding and the results of the research, choosing an appropriate research philosophy at the very start of the research was crucial. The topic of autonomous vehicles is future-oriented, and at this stage, generalizations are nearly impossible. Furthermore, the outcome of this trend is shaped in the present by different social actors through their decisions, actions, and belief. This is particularly true when it comes to the business world and management. Thus, interpretivism, as research philosophy, was chosen to answer the research questions in as detailed a way as possible [8].

The paper aimed to capture data about the perception of AGVs in the field of CEP or postal companies and to report these in a way that gives a rich and systematic insight. Because of the missing theoretical framework, this was done with an inductive approach—rather than testing a hypothesis, and the end goal was to develop a theory [8]. Based on the opinion of several researchers, qualitative data are more suitable for induction [8,28]. It must be stated that due to the qualitative character of the research building, a theory in this context purely means "internal generalizability" instead of a statistical one. However, this can still provide valuable insights, for example, by posing "a general but articulated question" [28]. Generally speaking, in the case of qualitative research, it is harder to guarantee the validity and reliability of the data which is why the checklist containing different criteria (such as ethics, worthy topic, credibility, meaningful coherence, contribution, etc.) of Easterby-Smith et al. [28] was used as a guideline to ensure the quality of this paper.

3.2. Data Collection Method

As mentioned above, the paper should explore many different aspects of the topic (within the boundaries of the research questions) and detail these in depth. Because of the investigative nature of the research and since induction uses mostly qualitative data and small samples, a single qualitative data collection technique was chosen to collect primary data, namely semi-structured interviews. In the case of semi-structured interviews, the researcher will try to cover a list of predetermined themes, but questions can be omitted/added or asked in a different order [8]. It gives more flexibility than highly structured interviews and, at the same time, offers some sort of system in contrast to unstructured interviews [28].

Keeping in mind the research questions, the most appropriate form of information collection was to conduct expert interviews. Bogner et al. [29] define experts as individuals who acquired specialized knowledge through their specific functions, e.g., their professional role. This type of interview is exceptionally efficient in the case of projects which are in the exploratory phase—such as the implementation of autonomous trucks—because they can serve as "crystallization points" [29].

3.3. Selecting Samples and Creating Access

The limitation of the topic and the research questions to a particular type of company explain the use of non-probability and purposive sampling, as these will enable selecting experts who can answer the research questions specifically related to these firms [8].

Choosing specific experts in the CEP industry, who have an adequate insight and necessary experience or knowledge to form a solid opinion about this topic, was of high importance, as the results were deducted from the current viewpoints of these persons. This approach has also ensured the comparability of the different interviews. As a result, experts with a secure connection to the field, either by being an employee at a CEP company or working closely with these types of company, were chosen as interview partners. Moreover, they needed to be up to date with innovative logistics solutions and trends.

The process of finding the right people for this research was a multi-stage process. First, it was cardinal to limit the geographical location of the experts to Austria in order to locate and contact them at the authors' convenience. Second, reading newspapers (e.g., "Verkehr"), transportation magazines (e.g., "Delivered."), and research papers have helped to identify professionals with enough expertise. In some cases, the contact details of these persons could be found online. In other cases, it was necessary to network on different professional platforms or websites such as LinkedIn. At this point, the goal was to reach out to them and explain the aim of the research. Some researchers suggest sending an introductory letter which "should outline in brief (...) how the person contacted might be able to help and what is likely to be involved in participating" [8]. Additionally, potential interview candidates were sent a sample interview questionnaire to familiarize themselves with possible questions. Many authors also suggest the use of topic guides in the case of semi-structured interviews, which "can be used as a loose structure for the questions" [28]. The topic guide created for the interviews can be found in the Appendix A.

3.4. The Interview Process

After searching for potential candidates, the next step was to conduct the interviews. In total, 17 international CEP organizations that were involved in international logistical activities and had a significant share in B2C services were selected for this study. Out of 17, 4 companies agreed to the interview. However, one company prohibited us from using the information provided by them due to some internal issues; therefore, the authors could only account for three interviews with four interviewees. The interviews were conducted in the English language with experts in the CEP sector in Vienna, Austria. All of the CEP companies are big players on the market, offering parcel transport and a wide range of B2C services (express delivery, postal services, etc.). One of the interviews was conducted face to face at the headquarters of the company, and two were the telephonic interviews. According to Saunders et al. [8], this type of interview can be used effectively where the distance or the accessibility of interview partners raises issues. Moreover, Easterby-Smith et al. [28] highlight that managers can even prefer remote interviewing to face-to-face interviews because it is more flexible. Specifics and information about the interviews conducted are presented in Table 2, which details the duration, date, type of interviews, and gives a piece of overall information about the organizations and interviewees.

Table 2. Information about respondents and organizations (Adopted from [4]—Author's rendition).

Organisation Type	Operations in Countries	Number of Interviewees	Interview Mode	Interview Time	Position Held	Experience in Years	City, Country
CEP A	23 countries	1	Telephone	35 Minutes	General Manager	25 years	Vienna, Austria
CEP B	9 countries	2	In person	25 Minutes	Head of Innovation	7/10 years	Vienna, Austria
CEP C	220 countries	1	Telephone	40 Minutes	Global Head of Quality	20 years	Vienna, Austria

In the research where comments and opinions of the professionals and experts are assessed, several different ethical issues can arise, such as the privacy and anonymity of the participants or the problem of maintaining confidentiality [8]. Therefore, for the sake of impartiality and to avoid any biased opinions, the identity of the CEP organizations and interviewees is kept anonymous. At the start of the interviews, it was always explained that the interviewee could withdraw from the process, and it was ensured that they agreed to the conditions. For example, the participants were asked to give verbal consent to record the interview and to produce a transcript. It was later used to quote some of the answers directly.

3.5. Data Analysis

Considering the small sample size and the richness of the data, thematic analysis was chosen as a data analysis method. Based on the definition of Braun and Clarke [30], thematic analysis is "a method for identifying, analyzing, and reporting patterns (themes) within data." Nowell et al. [31] present in great detail the six phases of the thematic analysis, which is depicted in Figure 7. In this paper, the purpose of the data analysis was to recognize emerging themes and detail these in-depth. This means that particular data gain attention (by being labeled as a code) not because of the number or frequency they appear, but because they capture the information relevant to the overall research question [30]. Of course, the findings were compared to each other, so similarities and differences across the interviews were elaborated to find critical themes and depict different opinions even better. However, this was not done to quantify the initial data, like in the case of content analysis [30].

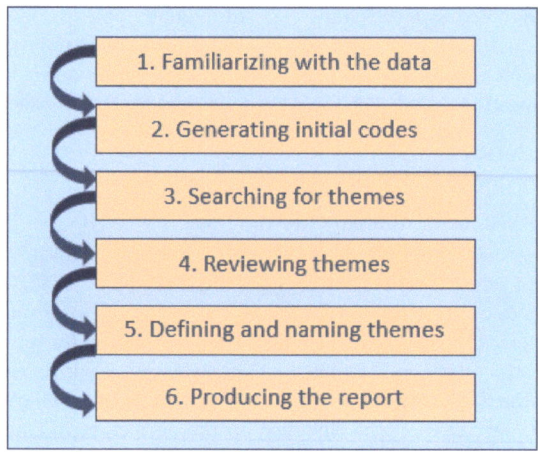

Figure 7. Phases of thematic analysis based on Nowell et al. [31].

The codes were selected inductively, without a "pre-existing coding frame," so any topics that might have been identified during previous research done by others did not get more attention than an entirely new piece of information [30].

3.6. Reporting the Findings

Producing a transparent and rich extract of the findings is the essence of the whole research. That is why one of the most critical parts of this research was to write the following chapter to be as intriguing as possible. First of all, the goal was not a simple description of the answers gathered, but rather to present the information as part of a whole, complex system. Otherwise, the results will not serve its purpose correctly and "will only offer a flat descriptive account with very little depth" [31].

In order to achieve this complexity and to create an "overall story," several methods presented by Nowell et al. [31] were used. Firstly, the report contains short quotes and lengthier passages as well. This way, the more succinct answers can ground the "understanding of specific points", while the more extensive quotations can "give readers a flavor of the original texts" [31]. Secondly, the report refers to the literature to confirm the research findings or to challenge them, which can expand the knowledge by adding new interpretations. Thirdly, all of the relevant information, even unexpected ones, are discussed to ensure credibility [31].

4. Results and Analysis

The following chapter will summarize the findings of the interviews held with the experts and will answer the research questions defined in the introductory part of the article. This chapter will also compare the answers of the participants to the current literature findings.

4.1. How Is the Introduction and Implementation of Self-Driving Trucks Currently Viewed by the Experts of the CEP Segment? (RQ 1.)

During the interviews, the experts were shown to have a profound understanding of the topic and a positive attitude toward logistical innovations. In general, CEP companies are aware of the sector's changes, and some of them have started to invest in pilot projects and research as a response to the market's push. However, based on their answers, using a fully automated vehicle for B2C processes is still not anticipated for the next several years due to the risks associated with this new form of delivery. To investigate the attitude of the experts toward innovative trends and to answer the research question precisely and accurately, the interviewees were asked to state their opinion on some of the actual megatrends. Thus, subtopics like autonomous vehicles, logistical innovations in the CEP industry, potential use cases of self-driving trucks, and changes in the delivery process were brought to the discussion.

4.1.1. Autonomous Driving and Autonomous Vehicles

The experts had a good basic understanding of the term autonomous vehicle, and they were describing it similarly. E1 mentioned different steps of the autonomous driving stating that "[in case of] semi-autonomous driving, you still have a driver, but there is some sort of technique which enables the autonomous driving" and "fully autonomous driving is when you have a truck or a van completely driving on its own." E2 gave the following definition: "a vehicle which is capable of moving around completely on its own without the need of somebody to use any kind of remote control or even any kind of route planning because this is something the vehicle is ideally capable of doing on its own." Last but not least, E3 stated that "there is no need for somebody who holds the wheel and physically controls the vehicle." Obviously, these answers are not as precise as the SMART definition, but this had no adverse effects on the results because every expert understood the meaning of a fully autonomous vehicle.

4.1.2. Logistical Innovations (in the CEP Industry)

E1 highlighted the importance of logistical innovations for the CEP industry: "in the B2C sector, you have to constantly offer new things because that is what enables the company to gain additional business". E1 also mentioned that "because of e-commerce, the prices are always under pressure." Thus, innovation in different areas like "customer service, online tools, communication with customers, and consignees" is of great importance. E2 claimed that autonomous delivery is something the company is looking at "just to figure out if it is usable or not," but right now, the firm does not have any specific business model for that. E3 highlighted the importance of logistical innovations in the following way: "[in our company] we always try to approach problems by using digitalization (...) we do not call this innovation but rather we ask how could we digitalize the whole system, how can we integrate artificial intelligence into our procedures either by using specific robots or technologies".

4.1.3. Potential Use-Cases

When asking to describe potential use-cases for autonomous vans in the B2C sector in urban areas, the ideas mentioned were mostly similar to the box truck concept mentioned in the second chapter of the paper. An autonomous van having multiple lockers that could drive to a specific place, and once arrived, the recipient could pick up the parcel. E1 brought up the fact that the company already had this idea: "we thought about this without autonomous driving, we call it a mobile parcel shop (...) but we could also do that with a van that drives around autonomously". E2 also spoke briefly about this type of delivery, stating that "it could work, it is something that maybe we are implementing, I am not sure." E3 also tried to describe this as "post boxes where you can pick up your parcel or return a parcel", stating that "it does make sense to try to automate it and it could be executed".

Another mentioned use-case of E2 was a "kind of semi-automated assistance for the employee," in which case "the autonomous van might be driving around the street, and the employee has the time to look for the parcel" or "maybe the employee has to go from one door to the next door, and the vehicle would be waiting already there."

As the paper examines fully autonomous vehicles, alternative solutions where a driver is still part of the delivery will not be detailed further. So, the next sections of the results will only refer to the box truck scenario.

4.1.4. Alteration of Logistical Processes

Everyone agreed that a fully autonomous delivery would change at least some of the logistical processes. E1 pointed out that "there will be areas where you would need to alter processes." According to E2, "if a company would plan to fully automate the delivery, then a completely new delivery process is required." E3 affirmed that "the whole technological system would need to be adapted."

When asking for possible changes in the logistical processes, most of the experts compared the present delivery process with the future one. E2 described this in the following way: "It would make the process completely different because at the moment an employee has a delivery area and has a daily average of parcels for a tour. If the delivery is completely autonomous, this average will change because the vehicle has to stop and has to wait for a certain amount of time until the person comes to the meeting place to pick up the parcel. So, this is something that would change the productivity."

Moreover, E3 also presented some parts of the process which should be changed, for instance, liability ("the liability passes on from the warehouse to the driver after loading the van, in case of autonomous vehicles this have to be reconsidered, because there is no one to take over the responsibility"). Similarly, the role of distribution centers ("distribution centers will probably become more important") and the loading/unloading activities ("if the van returns empty or with a few parcels you would have to decide what to do with those parcels, how do you want to load the vehicle again and at which gate"). E1 accentuated the importance of a control system as well: "even if you do not have drivers anymore, you still need to have a control system to control the trucks."

The necessity of a micro hub concept was not answered in detail, but this subtopic was also mentioned briefly. E1 disclosed that "this would sure be a possibility" as they already use these types of hubs with electric tricycles: "we call these city hubs (...), and of course, we could deliver from the city hubs using autonomously driving trucks too". E2 reflected on this question stating that "[the company] is trying out a new concept for urban areas and it is actually not a matter of vehicles but a matter of different approach to the last mile challenge (...) at the end of the day you can change the vehicle for a self-driving one, and it will probably still work".

As we can see, the answers covered only a part of the possible changes which could happen because at this stage it is hard to say if autonomous vehicles will somehow be integrated into the existing design and only some parts must be changed or companies will have to model the new processes from scratch.

4.1.5. Estimated Timeframe

The interviewees were also asked to estimate how many years it would take to introduce self-driving trucks on the market. Every expert said that this type of delivery would take several years or even a decade to be fully implemented. This also corresponds with the findings of other researchers. Estimating the transition period and specific implementation time is crucial because this will allow companies "to plan for the upcoming future in a better way and adjust their business dynamics" [32]. Because of the complexity of urban settings and logistical processes, a fully autonomous (level 5) delivery is not expected to enter the market soon. However, the experts have stated that experimenting with different types of new technologies is the right direction for the CEP industry. It is also important to recognize early enough, which are the suitable technologies for different areas of the sector. E1, for example, believes that "autonomous driving is definitely one solution which is interesting for the CEP industry because other innovations like drones are only a marketing idea (…) it will not be used on a bigger scale, especially in urban areas".

4.2. How Could Autonomous Trucks or Lorries (T&L) Be More Advantageous Than Traditional Delivery Methods When It Comes to Urban Areas? (RQ 1a.)

Research on the implementation of autonomous trucks for urban deliveries is limited. Nevertheless, AGVs are getting even more attention, and the existing literature indeed identifies the positive impacts of autonomous trucks. In order to answer this research question appropriately, the first part of the subchapter will describe the advantages found in the literature. In contrast, the second explains the answers given by the experts.

4.2.1. Cost Advantage

As B2C last-mile delivery is the most cost-expensive part of the supply chain, therefore autonomous trucks could have a substantial positive impact on the industry [33]. Delivering a parcel in an average city includes fuel or energy, vehicle and equipment, and labor costs [34]. The highest expenses are labor costs; in some rare cases, they can even reach 80% of the total costs [35]. Accordingly, based on network density, geography, and labor costs, autonomous trucks could significantly reduce delivery costs by 10% to 40% compared to the traditional delivery method, based on a study of McKinsey and Company [34].

As we can see in Figure 8, implementing autonomous trucks would increase capital costs, but these would remain cost-efficient [33]. Moreover, such a considerable saving would equal a "15 to 20 percentage point increase in profit margin" [16]. If we compare AGVs to other forms of deliveries, the outlook is the same. Van Pelt [35] claims that due to economies of scale, a drone could not compete with an autonomous delivery truck in urban areas, even if its lifespan would double or its capital costs would decrease by 50%. Considering that vehicle costs represent only 15% of all costs, electric vehicles could not cause an immense cost reduction [34]. However, cost advantages might be even higher if autonomous vehicles were fully electric and could be combined with other solutions, like night deliveries or consolidation centers [16].

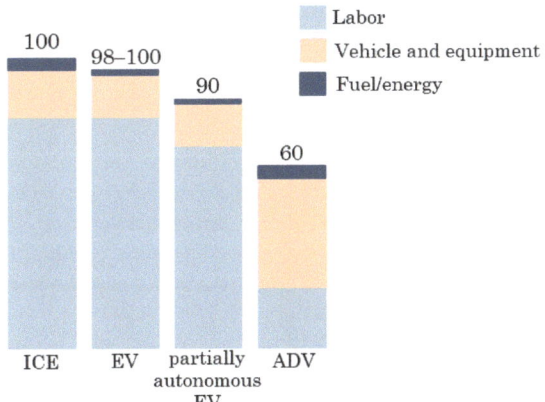

Figure 8. Last-mile delivery cost per parcel in an average city (author's rendition: adopted form McKinsey and Company [34]).

4.2.2. Enhanced Customer Service

Without a doubt, autonomous trucks would improve the customer service of CEP companies in diverse ways. AGVs would probably open the door to new opportunities, such as new service options and unique selling points. For example, "overnight pickup" and "Sunday delivery," two services with "superior value for customers" [16]. At the moment, these services are impossible to execute because labor laws do not allow it in most of the countries or due to residential noise concerns [16]. Identifying customers' requirements is crucial when it comes to urban deliveries. Table 3 presents the new trends among customers.

Table 3. Consumers' wish list based on Accenture [36].

Delivery Options and Choices	Examples
Delivery control	<ul><li>package tracking</li><li>control last-mile service</li><li>when and where will parcels be delivered</li></ul>
Delivery location	<ul><li>pick-up or lockers</li><li>anonymous delivery options</li><li>secure locations</li></ul>
Delivery timing	<ul><li>range of delivery times at different prices</li><li>24/7 options</li></ul>

Based on Google's patent, autonomous trucks could offer a higher level of convenience to end consumers. First of all, better communication and experience will ensure that customers' needs are satisfied. The autonomous truck would send the estimated arrival time in text and another message when it is actually at the place of pick-up; delays (e.g., traffic) could also be communicated in the same way [20]. After arriving at the address, the truck will remain at the destination for a while ("dwell period"), which could also be extendable. Customers will have the opportunity to share the PIN code with other family members or persons to collect the parcel, which is another notable feature [20].

Another critical factor to mention is returnability. These days a vast number of parcels are returned as an effect of e-commerce. Thus, CEP companies should not forget about revised logistics [37]. Customers want a convenient way to return their orders, and so far, parcel lockers have proven to be very popular [38]. This trend could continue and probably gain more attention once AGVs with parcel lockers are implemented.

4.2.3. Competitive Advantage

It is worth examining how autonomous trucks would represent a competitive advantage in the CEP market. The theoretical framework of Wong and Karia [39] describes four stages of achieving competitive advantage using "resource-based view": in the first step, a CEP company has specific resources in its portfolio; in the second stage, the firm acquires "strategic resources," which are "valuable, rare, inimitable and non-substitutable"; after that, these strategic resources should be bundled with other resources to achieve a competitive advantage, and finally, the company could create a new portfolio for future resource acquisitions.

Autonomous trucks and lorries are road vehicles, thus physical resources. Wong and Karia [39] claim that physical resources are crucial to "create network coverage." If a company cannot access specific physical resources, it could become challenging to fix new contracts. If autonomous trucks are bundled together appropriately with other types of resources, this could lead to a competitive advantage.

Wong and Karia [39] present different strategies used by companies. For example, trucks could be integrated easily with the information system of the company thanks to their technological development. Process automation, track, and trace, or route optimization are just a few possibilities that could be realized.

Another integration strategy would imply "relational resources" [39]. This is also highlighted by McKinsey and Company [34], stating that traditional CEP companies could maintain their role on the market and gain competitive advantage through partnering up with commercial vehicle (CV) firms. A successful alliance would undoubtedly create a new business model and strengthen the position of both players [34]. Cooperation in city logistics is an essential key to success as it can lead to "a higher and efficient utilization of resources" [1]. Wong and Karia [39] mention this form of strategy as complementing "the value of a resource with another resource."

4.2.4. Negative Externalities

As a transport, activities have a direct impact on the environment; specific adverse effects will inevitably occur. If the transport users do not take into consideration these consequences and do not cover the external costs, we talk about negative externalities [40]. There are different categorizations when it comes to negative externalities. For the last-mile logistics, these are the "air pollution, climate change, noise pollution, congestion, accidents, and infrastructure wear and tear" [41].

Due to the high number of vehicles, the high rate of deliveries, and the traffic volume, the issues of transportation can be multiplied in cities, especially in the case of last-mile deliveries in which the numerical data also suggest that, for producing 25% of the total CO_2 and 35% of the NO_x emissions of the whole transport sector, the urban transport of goods should definitely be taken into account when it comes to greenhouse gases [42]. Gonzalez-Feliu [42] accentuates the fact that end-consumer movements (including home-deliveries, B2C services, pickup points development, etc.) have a great significance, as they are also accountable for 50% of the road occupancy issues. The importance of the urban areas is also highlighted by the "Handbook on the external costs of transport" [40].

In order to place a limit on the adverse side effects of transport and reduce the costs in urban areas, several models are envisioned. One of these is autonomous delivery vehicles, which could bring a remarkable result [33]. If we examine the report of McKinsey and Company [16], we can see that AGVs are compatible with several other logistical solutions. Based on Ranieri et al. [41], the positive effects of AGVs on negative externalities would be even higher by combining these solutions and creating a "smart logistics system".

One of these solutions is to use autonomous electric vehicles for deliveries. At the moment, it is not certain whether AGVs will be hybrid, electrically powered, or fuel-run. However, companies can easily experience a push for fully electric vehicles. This can come from three different sides: the first is stakeholders' preferences (e.g., partners, customers) who focus on sustainability and desire such products; the second is the decreasing cost of innovative technologies (e.g., batteries, charging stations); the third is an emission or efficiency regulation policy [6,11]. The latter is already a discussion, as some suggest a policy that would prescribe fully electric autonomous vehicles [43]. Electric vehicles also have the significant potential to reduce noise; hence they are suitable for night-time deliveries. This is another excellent solution that can be combined with autonomous vehicles. Moreover, electric trucks could gain access to the city centers as it is restricted for internal combustion engine-based vehicles to enter those areas [37].

All in all, Berns et al. [44] claim that addressing sustainability would not only be helpful for our environment but could improve the image and the brand of the company and create unique selling propositions.

4.2.5. Most Significant Advantages

In comparison to the literature findings, the answers of the interviewees can be categorized into five different types of advantage. Some advantages were similar to the literature, like the increased cost-effectiveness, the possibility of new services, and the positive impacts autonomous trucks might have on the environment. Moreover, the experts accentuated the problems related to human resources. In their opinion, the autonomous delivery might solve the human errors which appear during a traditional delivery process and also provide a solution to the demand growth and driver shortage problem of the CEP industry. These are shown in a systematic way below. Table 4 lists some of the answers given by the interview participants.

Table 4. Most significant advantages.

Derived Advantage	Response
Elimination of human errors • punctuality/predictability • constant performance • safety	"if you program the technology behind this vehicle really well, it will execute its job perfectly" (E3) "[the autonomous vehicle] does not need further instructions or training, it does not get sick, it does not have bad days, it will always perform consistently well" (E3) "many of the accidents happen because the driver was tired" (E1)
A solution to the driver shortage and demand growth	"I think for our industry that it is a very positive development because we already suffer from having not enough drivers for our trucks" (E1) "there are periods when CEP companies have to deliver more parcels because the demand is really fluctuating, this solution can also help in those situations" (E3)
Cost reduction	"because there will be no driver, the company will not have to pay loans, sick leave or any kind of these costs (...) of course, there will be some maintenance costs, but you can plan with these fix costs and it will be way less than the costs you have to pay to an employee" (E3) "if there is no need for a driver anymore it will reduce the costs" (E1)
Environmental factors	"it will have a positive effect on the CO2 reduction (...) driving autonomously means actually less pollution because there is more technology behind the truck, you have the right speed and a reduced amount of fuel" (E1) "there could also be some environmental advantages if the vehicles would be electric (...) maybe solar panels could be mounted on the top of them" (E3) "the full capacity could be used to store more parcels because you would not need a driver seat and wheel (...) so the whole delivery process could be established in a more efficient way, which could be environmentally friendly" (E3)
New services • instant delivery • scheduled delivery • night-time delivery • weekend delivery	"it opens the possibility for different services depending on the customer's needs, for example, the customer could contact the van, by sending a message that he/she is at home and this way the van could arrive in the area in a timeframe which is suitable for the recipient" (E3) "instant delivery, night-time delivery or deliveries on some kind of scheduled basis could work" (E2) "when you drive on a Sunday, you normally have certain rules which lead to problems when it comes to the labor law (...), so yes, maybe that is a possibility to enlarge the service" (E1)

Figure 9 illustrates a radar chart of the derived advantage categories and assigns a certain point (from 1 to 5, 1 being the lowest) to the results, based on the experts' elaboration and opinion. This shows which one of the advantages seems to be of greater importance for a particular company. The dotted average curve represents the final average values of all CEP companies.

4.3. What Are the Possible Barriers That Could Hinder or Slow Down the Implementation of Autonomous T&L In Urban Settings? (RQ 1b.)

Besides having numerous positive effects and benefits, challenges, and barriers will possibly slow down the implementation of autonomous lorries. The change of fleets could even have temporary downsides. Despite that, the following challenges will most likely not hinder the switch to fully autonomous vehicles, and companies will try to overcome those difficulties. During the interviews, the experts were also talking carefully about the use-cases mentioned above, always listing potential risks and factors which can slow down the implementation. E2, for example, expressed some of these concerns in the following way: "This is something we have to look at carefully because maybe there are some risks too."

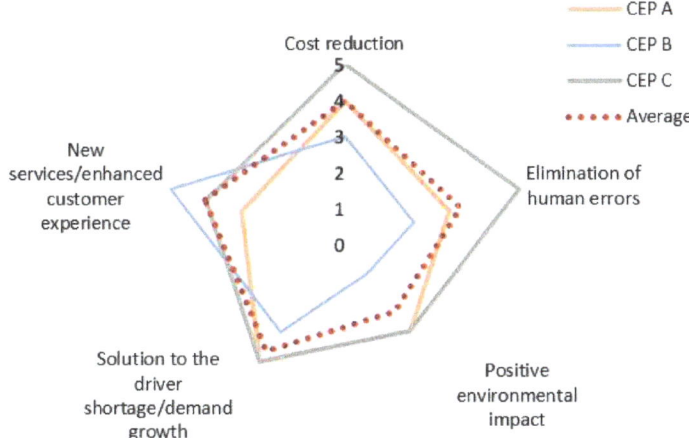

Figure 9. Radar chart—assessment of different advantages based on the experts' opinion.

4.3.1. Legislative Issues

Right now, the most cardinal challenges for companies are the legislative issues and regulations [45]. Currently, the Vienna Convention on Road Traffic restricts autonomous driving on public roads [45]. This was also brought up by E3: "The legal, regulatory environment would play a huge role because we will have to examine if the law of that particular city enables these types of autonomous delivery or not." E1 also accentuates the fact that "autonomous driving needs special legal requirements," especially in case of accidents ("you need to know who is responsible for that").

However, in 2016 a new regulation was added, which states that transferring driving tasks to the vehicle is permitted if the driver can stop the system at any time [46]. In contrast, the United States has recognized the necessity of legislation. California, for instance, allows companies to test their fully autonomous cars on public roads without a safety driver [47]. This could be a massive step in the development of autonomous vehicles.

4.3.2. Infrastructure and Technology

Two other widely recognized factors by the experts during are infrastructure and technology. In this context, E3 mentions "the quality of the roads" and the possibility of "technological break-downs in the system." E3 states that "the implementation will really depend on the presence of vehicle producers who can produce AGVs with an almost error-free technology." Furthermore, E1 mentions the importance of the real-time information share: "there is the need to transfer data to those trucks, so you must have all technical things in place ready to work."

Based on the literature, in the case of a real implementation of an autonomous vehicle fleet, companies would certainly need a sophisticated IT technology and infrastructure to optimize route choices [6]. Autonomous vehicles would require continuous monitoring and guidance in daily traffic. Plus, due to the interconnection of digital systems, security risks should not be neglected [3,48]. This would pose a considerable danger both to the customers and the companies, as hackers could collect personal data, sensitive information or try to take over the control of autonomous trucks [3,48].

4.3.3. Restructured Workforce

Although the interviewees did not mention it, recruiting the necessary experts and the restructuring of the workforce are other challenges that companies should consider [6]. In the stage of early adaptation, employees could work on administrative tasks. However, autonomous trucks will eventually reach full maturity, and drivers will possibly lose their jobs. There is a question as to whether retraining would help this issue or not. From another perspective, autonomous delivery vans could also create new job opportunities: CEP companies will need supervisors for their fleets [6]. It is still unforeseeable if these supervisors or fleet managers will have the same responsibilities as today. Fleet managers will most likely play a vital role, "providing a distinct and needed function (...) being managers of control centers" [49]. They will have to make sure that the deliveries are made on time by monitoring for delays. Another crucial task might be to examine if the vehicle is operating correctly. All in all, they will "need to understand trucks, but will also need to be a logistics expert" [49].

4.3.4. Altered Customer Experience

Furthermore, the participants have put an immense emphasis on the altered customer experience and the acceptance of this type of new delivery. Even though failing to meet the customer's expectations can have severe negative impacts on a company, this issue is not addressed in detail in most of the literature. E2 highlights the importance of the topic, stating that autonomous delivery "is changing the whole customer experience completely." These barriers are enlisted systematically in Table 5 as an overview of many different aspects all connected to the recipient. To sum it up, E3 explained that the implementation "could be solved, but this would mean that the customer has to do more."

Table 5. Most significant barriers.

Derived Barrier	Response
The general acceptance of the customers	"there might be risks of how the economy accepts or sees technology" (E2) "[autonomous vehicles] might scare the customer because this something they are not used to see" (E2)
Increased inconvenience for the customers • Distance • Weather conditions • Parcel size and weight	"in order to receive your parcel, you have to plan your way to the vehicle" (E2) "most of the customers want to get the parcel in their hands or see the parcel on the doorstep" (E3) "Is the customer willing to come and pick up the parcel in every situation? (...) it could be raining or snowing" (E2) "other factors could disturb the whole process, for example, the weather" (E3) "maybe I ordered a really heavy parcel which I would like to see in front of my door" (E3)
Communication with the customers	"How will the communication be established? How could you follow where your parcel is at the moment?" (E2) "I can see a huge obstacle when it comes to B2C e-commerce deliveries in urban areas, and that is the communication with the recipient. So, if an autonomous van will stop before my house, how will the vehicle notify me? How will I get my parcel?" (E3)
Missing human interaction	"I think the B2C sector right now is defined by this human-human interaction" (E3) "the customer expects a certain delivery experience which is connected to the interaction between the postman and the recipient (...) if our employee rings the bell to hand over the parcel to you, this is something that is typically noticed as a very nice interaction with the postman, because you receive something" (E2)

Researching customer experience should be crucial for CEP companies in order to determine "an effective customer experience strategy" [50]. Firms have to find the right balance by delivering the necessary customer expectations but not exceeding them, as these could generate high costs and could lead to a profit loss [50].

4.4. Strength, Weakness, Opportunity, and Threat (SWOT) Analysis

Based on the findings from the literature and interviews, the following strength, weakness, opportunity and threat (SWOT) analysis in Table 6 summarises the strengths, weaknesses, opportunities, and threats related to a hypothetical introduction of a fully autonomous, electric, self-driving truck (used for B2C services) in a CEP company.

Table 6. Strength, weakness, opportunity and threat (SWOT) analysis.

Strengths	Weaknesses	
1. reduced labor costs 2. competitive advantage/unique selling proposition 3. new possible CEP services 4. enhanced company image 5. can be an integral part of corporate social responsibility (CSR)	1. full reliance on technology 2. delivery processes might need to be changed or modeled from scratch 3. requires information technology (IT) infrastructure and connectivity 4. restructuring of the workforce 5. increased capital costs	INTERNAL
Opportunities	Threats	
1. new business cooperation types 2. increased investments in research and development (R&D) 3. push for environmental sustainability and green city logistics 4. promising new technologies and logistic trends	1. competition between different delivery modes 2. customer acceptance 3. legislative issues 4. technical capabilities of autonomous ground vehicles (AGVs) might be overestimated 5. cybersecurity and data protection 6. economic and market conditions	EXTERNAL

5. Discussion

5.1. Reflection on Findings

At the moment, the concept of using autonomous vehicles for urban deliveries is in an introductory phase. Currently, only a few companies are trying to test these vehicles under real conditions and circumstances. As we can see, the topic of logistical innovation seems to be of great interest to experts working in the field, especially if we talk about the B2C sector, which represents a significant challenge for CEP companies. Nevertheless, even considering this colossal interest and all the information available, right now, we cannot draw certain conclusions. We can only examine the possible effects it could have on the CEP industry. Because the logistics of the future is dependent on the decisions of the present, this paper had the primary goal of understanding how key players of the market perceive this innovation. Derived from the answers of the experts, it was assumed that autonomous vans would surely enter the market sooner or later. Of course, there are still open questions, and there is still controversy regarding AGVs, specifically autonomous vans.

On the one hand, we see a negative attitude toward this concept, which stems from the missing technology and legal environment, the complexity of last-mile delivery processes, and the needs of the customers. Primarily, this last component was brought into the center of the discussion several times during the interviews. Most of the experts used anecdotal descriptions and placed themselves in the shoes of the customers, proving that ultimately the focus point of the delivery process is the customer. E3 also mentioned the importance of the market or demand research: "I think it would be essential to do customer research to identify if the recipients are inclined toward this new form of delivery." The literature reveals some findings regarding the customer's reaction to new delivery concepts. For example, a study has found that 60% of customers would "be in favor of or indifferent to drones" [6]. However, there is not much research about the demand and openness of customers in the context of autonomous vans, which represents a considerable gap. The paper of Wintersberger et al. [51] examines the general attitude of consumers towards the daily and private usage of autonomous cars. Similar research could be undertaken to analyze the concerns of customers regarding autonomous vans and their overall willingness to change the process of urban delivery. Right now, companies are not questioning the technology but rather the attitude of the consumers. Once this is proved to be positive, the companies will most likely start to introduce autonomous vehicles.

On the other hand, we can also see that CEP companies are already heavily involved in logistical innovations and would like to reshape this whole sector. In a few years' time, their resources might not be enough to serve the increasing market. The general attitude of Austrian and German experts is decisive when it comes to AVs. This is also in line with other research findings, which state that the majority of experts have a favorable opinion when it comes to business projects related to AVs [52].

The experts highlighted several advantages during the interview. For example, autonomous vehicles could open the door to a wide range of new services (e.g., night-time or scheduled delivery), which are not possible right now. As a result, autonomous vans have a huge chance to become a disruptor.

To conclude, there is still a dilemma regarding autonomous delivery. E2 condensed this idea as a "trade-off, which has two sides: it is nice, it is efficient versus it is dangerous and there are risks behind it (…) we have to find the right balance".

5.2. Unanswered Questions

Questions about possible cooperation with vehicle producers, tech companies, or consultancies could not be answered at this stage. E1 had the following response: "they still have to work on technology, gain experience, capture data, and I think it is still too early for us as a company to step into that (…) you need to have a solution on the market already". Future research might investigate the different cooperation possibilities and the possibility of a relational competitive advantage, also mentioned by Wong and Karia [39].

Another topic that was not brought up by any of the experts is the possibility of using autonomous vans for returning parcels. As mentioned in the literature review, this would be a real chance to revolutionize the way of sending back packets, providing easy access and a simple process for customers.

Moreover, some of the questions remaining can only be answered by conducting case studies. For example, in a particular company, it could be analyzed how significant is the percentage of small or medium-sized packages (defined by weight or the shape of the parcel) among the total of B2C orders, in order to find out whether the introduction of box trucks could cover a large part of the deliveries. Similarly, questions about possible fleet size or cost reductions will depend on a particular business case.

In other words, it is still undefined whether autonomous vans could once be used on a larger scale or if they will remain a solution that will be utilized only in case of increased demand. If a CEP company were interested in implementing such a solution, it would be imperative to work out these details meticulously.

6. Conclusions

The primary purpose of this paper was to give a general overview of the implementation of autonomous lorries. This was undertaken by investigating different perspectives of the topic, all supporting the central question, which dealt with the perception of experts regarding a possible self-driving truck introduction. However, at this stage, it is hard to say whether the positive features of AGVs will outweigh the challenges that companies will undoubtedly face as autonomous vehicles are still under ongoing developments. Using expert interviews as a data collection method proved useful for gaining insights about the attitude of market players specialized in urban deliveries, more specifically CEP service providers. The literature review and findings undoubtedly underline the importance of the topic. Gaps in current knowledge have also been revealed.

Of course, the first definitive results in the topic of autonomous vehicles will only be available in the next few years. Thus, the papers' current aim is to provide an academic basis and a better understanding of the topic. Hopefully, the results of the research will be beneficial for both the industry and the academic world. Undoubtedly, it will be fascinating to see if these predictions are going to be correct.

Limitations of the Research

This study is designed to bring attention to the topic of using autonomous trucks in urban settings. Other autonomous vehicles like robots, droids, or drones might be mentioned at some point in the paper but do not represent the basis of the research. A combination of autonomous trucks or vans with some of these solutions was also omitted. It is necessary to mention that the topic was not investigated from a technological point of view. Instead, it describes feasibility from economic, environmental, and useability standpoints through thematic literature review and the experts' opinion. Limited technological details were included only to understand the concept of autonomous trucks better. Because of the complexity of this topic, it was necessary to circumscribe this broad concept and put emphasis on a single type of vehicle: a fully autonomous box truck or van, which works as an autonomous pick-up station.

Moreover, the paper brings to light only international CEP or postal companies (with B2C activities) from Vienna, Austria, as an essential market player when it comes to urban deliveries. Last but not least, this paper provided a qualitative inside into the topic and not a quantitative one. Even though the number of interviews required for qualitative analysis is subjective, the authors of the study understand that three interview companies with four interviews might not sound much. However, the experts' combined experience in CEP sector of more than 50 years gave us enough information necessary to lay out the qualitative outlay for the CEP and autonomous trucking sector for the future. Furthermore, it is evident from business and management disciplines that there are studies which have been published in reputable peer reviewed journals with as few as 3–5 interviews [53].

It is just the beginning of the research in this direction, and there is a lot more qualitative and quantitative data that are needed to nurture this area to its perfection. As these experts, most of the time, work in the top management and hold critical roles in CEP companies, they were rarely open for such a collaboration. Due to the time constraints and the current pandemic (COVID19) situation, it was not possible to reach more companies within the limits of this research paper. Nonetheless, given the actual population (i.e., the total number of international CEP companies with B2C services operating from Vienna, Austria) the selected sample size represents almost 30% of the entire population.

Of course, it would have been intriguing to work with a bigger sample size in order to gain additional empirical findings, generalize the results, and make them acceptable for a broader audience. However, opinions collected through the interviews are a good reflection of the cities with 20 or fewer CEP companies. The interviews involved three gigantic CEP organizations and experts with an ample amount of experience. Thus, the data are not only credible but also give a thorough insight into the topic under discussion. Future studies related to the same project would definitely consider conducting more interviews, increasing the data set, and undertake more quantitative analysis, especially for the impact of autonomous trucks in last-mile urban deliveries.

Author Contributions: Authors Contributed in this manuscript on an overall workload basis: E.T.K. (50%), M.A. (30%) and S.K. (20%) All authors have read and agreed to the published version of the manuscript.

Funding: This research received no external funding.

Conflicts of Interest: The authors declare no conflict of interest.

Appendix A

Table A1. Interview guide.

	Subtopics	Sample Questions
Part 1	• demographic questions • position and responsibilities • information about the company	Tell me something about the company you are working at? What is the focus of the company? Could you describe your position and your responsibilities in the company?
Part 2	• general trends • autonomous vehicles • logistical solutions • attitude of the CEP company toward innovations • challenges of the last-mile delivery	What do you understand under the "autonomous trucks" term? Is your company interested in the topic of autonomous trucks? Do you think postal or CEP companies are suitable for implementing driverless trucks or lorries? (Why?) Are there any barriers?
Part 3	• possible use cases and introduction in the CEP sector • advantages • disadvantages • implications on logistics • new services	Could you describe one (or more) specific use(s) case of the autonomous truck in the CEP industry? What would be the advantages and disadvantages of autonomous trucks in your opinion? Which prominent issues could autonomous trucks mitigate and which not? Would the implementation alter any logistical processes? Which one? Is there a new service which could be provided?

References

1. Savelsbergh, M.; van Woensel, T. 50th Anniversary Invited Article—City Logistics: Challenges and Opportunities. *Transp. Sci.* **2016**, *50*, 579–590. [CrossRef]
2. DHL. Logistics Trend Radar 2018/19. Available online: https://www.logistics.dhl/global-en/home/insights-and-innovation/thought-leadership/trend-reports/logistics-trend-radar.html (accessed on 10 June 2020).
3. Davies, A. The WIRED Guide to Self-Driving Cars. 2018. Available online: https://www.wired.com/story/guide-self-driving-cars/ (accessed on 10 June 2020).
4. Azmat, M.; Kummer, S. Potential applications of unmanned ground and aerial vehicles to mitigate challenges of transport and logistics-related critical success factors in the humanitarian supply chain. *AJSSR* **2020**, *5*. [CrossRef]
5. Slabinac, M. Innovative solutions for a "last-mile" delivery—A European experience. In Proceedings of the 15th international scientific conference Business Logistics in Modern Management, Osijek, Croatia, 15 October 2015.
6. McKinsey and Company. Parcel Delivery. The Future of Last Mile. September 2016. Available online: https://www.mckinsey.com/~{}/media/mckinsey/%20industries/travel%20transport%20and%20logistics/our%20insights/how%20customer%20demands%20are%20reshaping%20last%20mile%20delivery/parcel_delivery_the_future_of_last_mile.ashx (accessed on 10 June 2020).
7. Neuweiler, L.; Riedel, P.V. Autonomous Driving in the Logistics Industry: A Multi-Perspective View on Self-Driving Trucks, Changes in Competitive Advantages and Their Implications. Master's Thesis, Jönköping University, Jönköping, Sweden, May 2017. Available online: https://www.diva-portal.org/smash/get/diva2:1129922/FULLTEXT01.pdf (accessed on 10 June 2020).
8. Saunders, M.; Lewis, P.; Thornhill, A. *Research Methods for Business Students*, 5th ed.; Pearson: Essex, UK, 2009.
9. Cardenas, I.; Borbon-Galvez, Y.; Verlinden, T.; de Voorde, E.V.; Vanelslander, T.; Dewulf, W. City logistics, urban goods distribution and last mile delivery and collection. *Compet. Regul. Netw. Ind.* **2017**, *18*, 22–43. [CrossRef]
10. Albino, V.; Berardi, U.; Dangelico, R.M. Smart Cities: Definitions, Dimensions, Performance, and Initiatives. *J. Urban Technol.* **2015**, *22*, 3–21. [CrossRef]
11. TNT. Supplementary Report 2010. Available online: https://www.tnt.com/content/dam/corporate/archive/Images/TNT-Express-Report-2010_tcm177-540070.pdf (accessed on 10 June 2020).
12. Ducret, R. Parcel deliveries and urban logistics: Changes and challenges in the courier express and parcel sector in Europe—The French case. *Res. Transp. Bus. Manag.* **2014**, *11*, 15–22. [CrossRef]
13. Kumar, S. Courier, Express and Parcel (CEP) Industry and How E-Commerce is Helping the Growth of CEP Industry? 29 December 2015. Available online: https://www.linkedin.com/pulse/courier-express-parcel-cep-industry-how-e-commerce-helping-kumar/ (accessed on 10 June 2020).
14. Verlinde, S.; Macharis, C.; Witlox, F. How to Consolidate Urban Flows of Goods Without Setting up an Urban Consolidation Centre? *Procedia Soc. Behav. Sci.* **2012**, *39*, 687–701. [CrossRef]
15. Edwards, S. Companies Using Speed as a Competitive Advantage. 5 January 2016. Available online: https://www.entrepreneur.com/article/253372 (accessed on 10 June 2020).
16. McKinsey and Company. An Integrated Perspective on the Future of Mobility, Part 2: Transforming Urban Delivery. September 2017. Available online: https://www.mckinsey.com/~{}/media/mckinsey/business%20functions/sustainability/our%20insights/urban%20commercial%20transport%20and%20the%20future%20of%20mobility/an-integrated-perspective-on-the-future-of-mobility.ashx (accessed on 10 June 2020).
17. SMART. Definition of Necessary Vehicle and Infrastructure Systems for Automated Driving. SMART 2010/0064. Available online: https://knowledge-base.connectedautomateddriving.eu/wp-content/uploads/2019/12/SMART_2010-0064-study-report-final_V1-2.pdf (accessed on 10 June 2020).
18. SAE International. Taxonomy and Definitions for Terms Related to Driving Automation Systems for On-Road Motor Vehicles. 14 January 2014. Available online: https://www.sae.org/standards/content/j3016_201806/ (accessed on 10 June 2019).
19. Chen, Y. Autonomous Unmanned Ground Vehicle (UGV) Follower Design. Master's Thesis, Ohio University, Athens, OH, USA, August 2016. Unpublished.
20. Myllymaki, J. Autonomous Delivery Platform. U.S. Patent No. 9,256,852 B1, 9 February 2016.

21. Curtis, S. Ford reveals 'Autolivery' Concept for Delivering Packages Using Drones and Self-Driving Vans at MWC 2017. 27 February 2017. Available online: https://www.mirror.co.uk/tech/ford-autolivery-concept-envisions-using-9925046 (accessed on 10 June 2020).
22. Smith, L.J. Mercedes Vision Van Debuts at CES 2017—Futuristic Van Comes with Drones and Robots. 18 January 2017. Available online: https://www.express.co.uk/life-style/cars/749337/Mercedes-Vision-Van-2017-concept-CES-electric (accessed on 10 June 2020).
23. Geddes, T. Charge: The Self-Drive Delivery Van That Can Be Built in Four Hours. 4 November 2016. Available online: https://dispatchweekly.com/2016/11/charge-self-drive-delivery-van-built-four-hours-set-uk-streets/ (accessed on 10 June 2020).
24. Symonds, D. Tech Startup Next Unveils Automated Parcel Locker Transportation System. 13 September 2018. Available online: https://www.parcelandpostaltechnologyinternational.com/news/automation/tech-startup-next-unveils-automated-parcel-locker-transportation-system.html (accessed on 10 June 2020).
25. Audebert, T. EZ-PRO, Linking Urban Mobility with the Future City. 19 September 2018. Available online: https://group.renault.com/en/news/blog-renault/ez-pro-linking-urban-mobility-with-the-future-city/ (accessed on 10 June 2020).
26. Gogas, M.A.; Nathanail, E. Evaluation of Urban Consolidation Centers: A Methodological Framework. *Procedia Eng.* **2017**, *178*, 461–471. [CrossRef]
27. Conway, A.; Fatisson, P.E.; Eickemeyer, P.; Cheng, J.; Peters, D. Urban Micro-Consolidation and Last Mile Goods Delivery by Freight-Tricycle in Manhattan: Opportunities and Challenges. In Proceedings of the Transportation Research Board 91st Annual Meeting, Washington, DC, USA, 22–26 January 2012.
28. Easterby-Smith, M.; Thorpe, R.; Jackson, P.R.; Jaspersen, L.J. *Management and Business Research*, 6th ed.; SAGE: London, UK, 2018.
29. Bogner, A.; Littig, B.; Menz, W. *Interviewing Experts*, 1st ed.; Palgrave Macmillan UK: London, UK, 2009.
30. Braun, V.; Clarke, V. Using thematic analysis in psychology. *Qual. Res. Psychol.* **2006**, *3*, 77–101. [CrossRef]
31. Nowell, L.S.; Norris, J.M.; White, D.E.; Moules, N.J. Thematic analysis. *Int. J. Qual. Methods* **2017**, *16*. [CrossRef]
32. Azmat, M.; Kummer, S.; Moura, L.T.; Gennaro, F.D.; Moser, R. Future Outlook of Highway Operations with Implementation of Innovative Technologies Like AV, CV, IoT, and Big Data. *Logistics* **2019**, *3*, 15. [CrossRef]
33. Gevaers, R.; Voorde, E.V.; Vanelslander, T. Cost Modelling and Simulation of Last-mile Characteristics in an Innovative B2C Supply Chain Environment with Implications on Urban Areas and Cities. *Procedia Soc. Behav. Sci.* **2014**, *125*, 398–411. [CrossRef]
34. McKinsey and Company. Fast Forwarding Last-Mile Delivery—Implications for the Ecosystem. 27 August 2018. Available online: https://www.mckinsey.com/industries/travel-transport-and-logistics/our-insights/technology-delivered-implications-for-cost-customers-and-competition-in-the-last-mile-ecosystem (accessed on 10 June 2020).
35. Van Pelt, T. Not drones, but AGVs will Forever Change Last-Mile Parcel Delivery. 24 September 2018. Available online: https://m3consultancy.nl/blog/not-drones-but-agvs-will-forever-change-last-mile-parcel-delivery (accessed on 10 June 2020).
36. Accenture. Adding Value to Parcel Delivery. 2015. Available online: https://www.accenture.com/t20170227T024657Z__w__/us-en/_acnmedia/Accenture/Conversion-Assets/DotCom/Documents/Global/PDF/Dualpub_23/Accenture-Adding-Value-to-Parcel-Delivery.pdf#zoom=50 (accessed on 10 June 2020).
37. Schöder, D.; Ding, F.; Campos, J.K. The Impact of E-Commerce Development on Urban Logistics Sustainability. *Open J. Soc. Sci.* **2016**, *4*, 1–6. [CrossRef]
38. United States Postal Service. Riding the Returns Wave: Reverse Logistics and the U.S. Postal Service. (RARC-WP-18-00). 30 April 2018. Available online: https://www.uspsoig.gov/sites/default/files/document-library-files/2018/RARC-WP-18-008.pdf (accessed on 10 June 2020).
39. Wong, C.Y.; Karia, N. Explaining the competitive advantage of logistics service providers: A resource-based view approach. *Int. J. Prod. Econ.* **2010**, *128*, 51–67. [CrossRef]
40. European Commission. CE Delft. Handbook on the External Costs of Transport. 2019. Available online: https://ec.europa.eu/transport/sites/transport/files/studies/internalisation-handbook-isbn-978-92-79-96917-1.pdf (accessed on 10 June 2020).
41. Ranieri, L.; Digiesi, S.; Silvestri, B.; Roccotelli, M. A Review of Last Mile Logistics Innovations in an Externalities Cost Reduction Vision. *Sustainability* **2018**, *10*, 782. [CrossRef]

42. Gonzalez-Feliu, J. Traffic and CO_2 emissions of urban goods deliveries under contrasted scenarios of retail location and distribution. In Proceedings of the Research and Transport Policy International Conference, Lyon, France, 18–19 March 2010.
43. McMahon, J. Expert: Require Autonomous Vehicles To Be Electric. 8 October 2018. Available online: https://www.forbes.com/sites/jeffmcmahon/2018/10/08/expert-require-autonomous-vehicles-to-be-electric/ (accessed on 10 June 2020).
44. MIT Sloan Management Review. The Business of Sustainability. 9 September 2009. Available online: https://sloanreview.mit.edu/projects/the-business-of-sustainability/ (accessed on 10 June 2020).
45. DHL. Self-Driving Vehicles in Logistics. 2014. Available online: http://www.dhl.com/content/dam/downloads/g0/about_us/logistics_insights/dhl_self_driving_vehicles.pdf (accessed on 10 June 2020).
46. UNECE. UNECE Paves the Way for Automated Driving by Updating UN International Convention. 23 March 2016. Available online: https://www.unece.org/info/media/presscurrent-press-h/transport/2016/unece-paves-the-way-for-automated-driving-by-updating-un-international-convention/doc.html (accessed on 10 June 2020).
47. Hawkins, A.J. Waymo Gets the Green Light to Test Fully Driverless Cars in California. 30 October 2018. Available online: https://www.theverge.com/2018/10/30/18044670/waymo-fully-driverless-car-permit-california-dmv (accessed on 10 June 2020).
48. PwC. Connected Car Study 2015: Racing Ahead with Autonomous Cars and Digital Innovation. 2015. Available online: https://www.pwc.at/de/publikationen/connected-car-study-2015.pdf (accessed on 10 June 2020).
49. Neckermann, L.; LeSage, J. The Mobility Revolution: A Primer for Fleet Managers. 2018. Available online: https://www.neckermann.net/wp-content/uploads/2018/10/NAFAFoundation_MobilityWhitepaper_Neckermann-1.pdf (accessed on 12 July 2020).
50. KPMG. How Much is Customer Experience Worth? Mastering the Economics of the CX Journey. September 2016. Available online: https://assets.kpmg/content/dam/kpmg/xx/pdf/2016/11/How-much-is-custerom-experience-worth.pdf (accessed on 12 July 2020).
51. Wintersberger, S.; Azmat, M.; Kummer, S. Are We Ready to Ride Autonomous Vehicles? A Pilot Study on Austrian Consumers' Perspective. *Logistics* **2019**, *3*, 20. [CrossRef]
52. Azmat, M.; Schumayer, C.; Kummer, S. Innovation in Mobility: Austrian Expert's Perspective on the Future of Urban Mobility with Self-Driving Cars. In Proceedings of the Quality and Business Management Conference, Dubai, UAE, 7–9 March 2016; Hbmsu Publishing House: Dubai, UAE, 2016.
53. Kunz, N.; Wassenhove, L.N.; Besiou, M.; Hambye, C.; Kovács, G. Relevance of humanitarian logistics research: Best practices and way forward. *Int. J. Oper. Prod. Manag.* **2017**, *37*, 1585–1599. [CrossRef]

© 2020 by the authors. Licensee MDPI, Basel, Switzerland. This article is an open access article distributed under the terms and conditions of the Creative Commons Attribution (CC BY) license (http://creativecommons.org/licenses/by/4.0/).

Article

Cloud and IoT Applications in Material Handling Automation and Intralogistics

Stavros T. Ponis *[ ] and Orestis K. Efthymiou

School of Mechanical Engineering, National Technical University Athens, Heroon Polytechniou 9, Zografos, 15780 Athens, Greece; orestisefthymiou@mail.ntua.gr
* Correspondence: staponis@central.ntua.gr; Tel.: +30-210-7722384

Received: 15 July 2020; Accepted: 12 August 2020; Published: 21 September 2020

Abstract: During the last decade, digitalization has borne tremendous changes on the way we live and do business. Industry 4.0, the new industrial revolution, is merging the physical, digital and virtual worlds through emerging technologies that collide with each other and create a distinctive paradigm shift. Even though the topic of Industry 4.0, has attracted significant attention during the past few years, literature in this subject area is still limited. The main objective of this paper is to study the current state of the art and identify major trends and research shortcomings. To that end, the authors conducted a methodological literature review based primarily on the SCOPUS bibliographic database. The review returned 49 relative papers dealing with the paper's subject area. Through a thorough study of the selected papers, four dominant literature categories were recognized and discussed in detail. According to the literature reviewed, it is evident that massive changes are underway for warehouses and intralogistics facilities. Still, despite the intense discussion and appeal of the subject, one of the most important challenges in the scientific area under study, as the literature highlights, is the absence of a matching, to its significance, number of real-life applications. To that end, this paper provides a detailed description of a Cloud-based IoT application drawn from a Distribution Center (DC) that supplies retail home furnishing and sporting goods products to stores in Greece and the Balkan region, with the objective to showcase the feasibility of such an investment, highlight its potential and provide motivation to practitioners to evaluate and proceed in similar technological investments.

Keywords: cloud computing; Industry 4.0; Internet of Things; logistics; material handling systems; smart factory

1. Introduction

Digitalization has caused enormous changes on the way we work and live over the last ten years. Industry 4.0, the new industrial revolution, is blending the physical, digital and virtual worlds through numerous trends that collide with each other and create a huge transformation. Internet of Things (IoT) and Cloud Computing (CC) are two of these trends, which have also infiltrated logistics and material handling. Material handling involves the movement, storage and control of products and materials within the premises of a building or between a building and a transport vehicle, during the entire production, warehousing and disposal life cycle. Material handling processes play a vital part in logistics and supply chains, and usually involve a great deal of both manual labor and automated processes. Usually, material handling systems and processes are designed to enhance customer service, minimize inventories, shorten delivery times and reduce overall production, distribution and transportation costs. IoT and CC have been described as key developments in business technology that will reshape industries around the world [1]. IoT refers to the interaction between objects and other devices and systems, which are Internet-enabled, and has largely emerged due to the powerful introduction of wireless technologies, sensors and the internet. According to [2], the term IoT refers to robust connectivity between the digital and physical worlds, and is a technology that provides possible solutions to alter processes and functions of manufacturing, supply chain and logistics industries. Within the field of Material Handling, IoT provides extensive solutions for the operators and their customers. Integration of technologies such as Mobile and IoT contribute actively to linking devices through distributed logistics and supply chain processes to improve operational, efficiency and profitability-related solutions [3]. Such solutions make products and services 'smart', which in turn frees humans from unnecessary work, since controlling many logistics activities is not needed anymore due to various automation solutions and systems that can plan and execute their workflow without human intervention or assistance. Cloud architecture on the other hand, is intended to provide users with on-demand tools such as storage, servers, network, software and services, through a network [4]. CC usually provides services that are known with acronyms such as SaaS, PaaS and IaaS [5]. SaaS (Software as a Service) offers software or applications to users. PaaS (Platform as a Service) provides a platform for the creation and delivery of software in the suitable programming languages, based on the organization's processes. IaaS (Infrastructure as a Service) refers to the entire Information Technology (IT) infrastructure that includes the storage, servers and network [6].

Although there is an increasing interest in Industry 4.0 technologies, such as IoT and CC, literature on how these affect material handling automation and intralogistics has been restricted up to now, especially when it comes to real-life application cases. Several reasons are deemed responsible for this underdevelopment. According to [7], the lack of digital culture and training, clear digital operations vision and support and the unclear economic benefit of digital investments seem to be the most common inhibitors for companies to move towards the digital capabilities offered by IoT and Industry 4.0 technologies in general. As a result, previous studies highlight that Industry 4.0 is currently populated by small-scale test installations that try to depict real-life situations, thus lacking large-scale applications of its technologies in material handling and in-house logistics. Therefore, the impact of Industry 4.0 in the studied areas in terms of efficiency, flexibility and availability has not yet been tested in detail [8]. This paper seeks to determine the present status of Cloud and IoT applications in material handling automation and intralogistics, analyze their impact and potential consequences and contribute with an actual case study of their application in an industrial setting, thus improving the practical knowledge of Industry 4.0, Cloud and IoT applications in relation to material handling and intralogistics.

This paper is organized in five discrete sections. The current one introduces the basic concepts and states the objectives of this paper. Section 2 presents the detailed analysis of the collected material. Section 3 discusses the review of collected material, Section 4 presents the case study by providing an overview of the installation and its systems, and Section 5 concludes the paper, by presenting the research contributions and limitations of this study.

2. Analysis

This paper attempts to provide an analysis and discussion of the impact and potential consequences of IoT and cloud applications on material handling automation and intralogistics. In doing so, the authors focus on material handling and discuss how IoT technologies and cloud applications affect its different elements through the reviewed literature. As far as methodology and statistics of this study is concerned, the initial sample of publications was selected through two discrete literature searches. The first one was made on the academic database of SCOPUS, but since the number of papers returned was rather small, a second search was decided to be made on Google Scholar. The search on SCOPUS database was divided in two parts and 131 papers were returned in total. For the first search, the language was set to English and all accessible records, such as reviews, journals and conference papers with no time constraints were included in the search space. The actual search was made using the following combinations of terms "Material Handling" AND "Cloud", document type "ALL" and restricted in English language. The search returned 94 papers. The second search was made using the terms "Material Handling" AND "IoT" for year >2009, document type "ALL" and restricted in English language. The search returned 37 papers.

Since the total number of papers returned, constituted an insufficient representative sample for our study, an additional search was decided, which took place on Google Scholar. Two sub-searches were also made, with the first one combining the terms "Material Handling" AND "Cloud", for year > 2009 and restricted in English language. This returned 4220 results. The second search was made combining the terms "Material Handling" AND "IoT", for year >2009 and restricted in English language. This returned 1640 results.

Following the searches, a screening method was implemented, with the exclusion criteria being, (a) duplicate papers, such as conference papers subsequently transformed into journals, (b) contributions that had the keyword string requirements but did not directly deal with the topic, and (c) papers that contribute marginally to this study. For this final category, the writers debated each paper judiciously and then either excluded it from the final sample or retained it for further assessment. Finally, forty-nine (49) papers were chosen for further in-depth assessment due to this process, which will be analyzed below and further discussed in the following section. The literature reviewed showed that main topics of discussion, regarding IoT and cloud technologies that we investigate, were usage on products and warehouse equipment such as Automated Guided Vehicles (AGVs), smart bins and racking, fault detection and performance analysis of warehouse systems, and shared services through the cloud.

According to [9], integrating embedded devices into current systems is the first move towards transforming classic warehouses into flexible modular systems with improved performance. However, the full potential of IoT will be achieved when these systems will be able to communicate with each other and carry out their activities autonomously, without any middle or central management units. Based on [10], with advancements in IoT and cloud, every component within warehouses, such as forklift trucks, industrial robots, and operators via their smart tablets or PDAs, will be represented as individual software agents in the cloud. By being interconnected, they will be able to make their own decisions and, therefore, existing hierarchical control systems will eventually be replaced by decentralized network-like control architectures. The works of [11] mention that cloud architecture provides many advantages on robotics and automation systems and can be split into two complementary levels, which are machine-to-cloud (M2C) and machine-to-machine (M2M). Computing and storage resources can be transferred to servers in the cloud at the M2C communication level, which on one hand minimizes costs, but also provides almost infinite power to the robots since central processing power can be used, and stored information can be shared with other robots for training and learning purposes. On the M2M communication level, robots interact via wireless links to form a collaborative computerized smart factory with computing capabilities pooled from individual robots and creating a virtual ad hoc cloud infrastructure and information exchanged among the collaborative computing units for synergetic decision generation.

According to [12], IoT technology can be of significant aid to enable a 'smart' AGV system. Smart factory requires efficient and accurate monitoring of objects, so IoT technologies such as RFID (Radio Frequency Identification) is widely used in warehouse shop-floors. This allows for real-time status input from each AGV unit that offers an opportunity to improve accuracy and time efficiency in logistics scheduling and inventory management tasks. Based on [13], a cloud robotics architecture that provides multiple functionalities to enable enhanced collaboration of AGV groups used in industrial logistics is presented. According to this architecture, a global live view of the environment is established, containing information about all entities in the industrial setting, which is then used to improve the local sensing capabilities of AGVs, thereby the efficiency and flexibility of AGV motion coordination. It is evident that the essence of cloud and its advantages is gathering data from various sources and providing global information to local devices.

Maintenance of machinery and warehouse equipment plays an important role in today's automated warehouse environments, which directly affects the service life and efficiency of the equipment [14]. Modern intralogistics systems tend to be complex in operation and large in scale. Therefore, a principal concern is to enhance system robustness and consistency. This could be achieved by a context-aware supervision system, as mentioned in [15], where an intelligent system with integration of semantic web and agent technology is proposed that aims at offering Condition Based Monitoring and Condition Based Maintenance (CBM) decisions to the relevant user. According to [16], IoT technology is found to be more effective in maintaining Material Handling Equipment (MHE) in the warehouse due to an array of capabilities such as real-time visibility, smart decision through reacting to errors and faults and therefore reducing or even preventing downtime, and customizable KPI's that support timely decision making. Based on [17], maintainability and sustainability of systems and processes in logistics and manufacturing can be improved by cloud services and resource virtualization. These two, are vital parts for implementing Cyber Physical Systems (CPS) and Industrial IoT (IIoT), which are the main building blocks of Industry 4.0. Effectively, combining local computing capabilities with global computing capabilities is possible through resource virtualization of shop-floor devices enabled by IIoT technology, which seamlessly incorporates smart connected objects into the cloud.

Another theme often discussed in the literature is the Physical Internet (PI) or Physical Web. PI is referred to devices that are part of the IoT and that are directly accessible, tracked or regulated by web technologies [18]. In the PI, individuals, locations, and objects have web pages for providing user experience information and mechanisms. For instance, with web search engines, where a user query returns links to related material, the PI will also return search results, ranked not only by traditional ranking algorithms, but also by proximity, and therefore results may be shown as lists, enhanced charts, or even floor plans, since the Physical Internet is something that one can see, hear, and touch, like for example a TV, a thermostat, a router or a home audio system. The concept of PI and its connection to Industry 4.0 is also addressed in other papers. According to [19], PI involves interconnected logistics in the context of creating an effective, sustainable, responsive, adaptable and scalable open global logistics network based on physical, digital and operational interconnectivity via encapsulation, interfaces and protocols. Therefore, the key word for the concept of PI is universal interconnectivity. This denotes complete collaboration between all supply chain members, complete compatibility with all relevant technical-technological tools and solutions and optimal execution of all operations. Physical interconnectivity is achieved when each object has a unique worldwide identifier and smart tag as an element of the IoT [20].

3. Discussion

Through a detailed assessment process of the selected papers, four dominant literature categories were recognized. A discussion for each one of these categories follows in this section.

3.1. IoT/Cloud and Smart Warehouse Framework

Material Handling and especially warehousing environments are ideal for IoT applications to thrive, since several different assets such as forklift trucks, pallets, products, machines, racking and building infrastructure are within a single space and can be easily interconnected with each other [3]. Therefore, if all these assets could be linked through IoT, then visibility within the plant could provide the ability for several actions to be triggered autonomously and only at the time it is necessary. For example, when an order arrives for a customer on the Warehouse Management System (WMS), then the system will be able to know where the products are located within the warehouse, and could arrange automatically to send the forklift truck that is closest to them, to pick them up. The movement of the truck and products would be easily visible from a control system, so that the warehouse staff could see the progress of the order picking up until the dispatch ramp. According to [21], IoT will change the way logistics systems are designed and operate. Working models will change from hierarchical to mesh-like structures. Entities will be autonomous and self-controlled, permitting higher flexibility and swarms of autonomous devices will rise and cloud-based administration will be implemented. Human workers will also be further integrated with machines, by using Production Assistant Devices (PADs). The PAD is an interface tool that allows the worker to connect to and interact with virtual machine parts, which will become more and more common within the warehouses. Finally, based on [21], the use of CC could provide efficiencies in the whole supply chain through increased visibility and collaboration, and more specifically for warehousing and intralogistics, inventory management and order processing could be greatly aided. According to [22], IoT applications could also assist at increasing safety in warehousing environments. A Communicating Object (CO) is a key element of the IoT to transform a perceptible real world into a digital virtual environment, known as the CPS. By adding COs on people or equipment, automatic decision-making processes could allow or deny actions in case of hazard consequences. Another topic that was observed on the literature reviewed and fits this category, is the Cloud-Assisted Smart Factory (CaSF). Based on [23], the use of CC and Artificial Intelligence (AI) improves smart factories' performance in terms of perception, communication, data processing and analysis. The CaSF architecture that is proposed consists of a smart device layer, a network layer, a cloud layer and an application layer that create a highly dynamic, extensible and reconfigurable system that can meet the constantly changing market demands.

3.2. Material Handling Equipment

This category of papers is related to equipment that is used within the warehouses, such as lift trucks, conveyors, storage and retrieval systems and automation systems, and it was the largest out of four categories that were recognized. As one can understand, material handling equipment is an area that can vastly be benefited from improvements in IoT and cloud technologies. According to [24], a management system for controlling the forklift trucks in a warehouse that is based on IoT devices is presented. The IoT devices of the system are mounted on each forklift and include an Android microsystem which has an application that manages all connected modules, and an RFID device that is used to read the operator's identity on the forklift. To the management system, this knowledge is rather significant, since it delegates the recorded tasks to the operators rather than to the machines. The information from the trucks to the management system is transmitted via various Wi-Fi access points (APs). Overall, the system proposed says that it increases working efficiency, reduces dead times, and raises efficiency of the forklift. Based on [25], an IoT concept for controlling and inspecting an Automatic Storing and Retrieval System (ASRS) is presented. Activities are synchronized via an online cloud database and, therefore, remote access to operation is possible via the internet, but analyzing, controlling and storing data is also possible. According to [26], cloud technologies, such as CC and Cloud Storage (CS), can be very beneficial for robotics. The robot nodes can access knowledge by communicating with the cloud, effectively overcoming the knowledge and learning limitations on the robot. Furthermore, the cloud server's powerful computing power can make up for the robot system's reduced computational power. Therefore, we see that problems faced by industrial robots, such as (a) limited calculation and storage resources, (b) constraints of information and learning capacity, and (c) limits of communication capacity, could be solved by the use of cloud technologies. The same concept is also proposed by [27] where an approach for implementing cloud technologies and cloud services in robots is presented. The paper explores how cyber-domain cloud technology can be used to build robots in the physical world with more functionalities, which will help solve many of the problems that conventional approaches are facing. Based on [28], Smart Connected Logistics (SCL) systems are systems of smart connected products such as AGVs for example, that are orchestrated through the cloud, whereas the cloud based solution is also able to access information from other data sources that exist within the intralogistics area. These systems will change the way today's internal logistics systems operate, i.e., plenty of manual operations executed by workers, and will make them more advanced and complex, more automated, and more intelligent and adaptive. The development of SCL systems will come in steps of advancement. First step is the ability of monitoring, then move to controlling, thenceforth to optimizing, then to being autonomous and finally to being reconfigurable.

3.3. Performance and Preventive Maintenance

System failures are undesirable to any logistics organization as they lead to low levels of customer service. For this purpose, it is important to implement an effective failure management system to ensure smooth system operation in every company [29]. Knowledge of all failures, whether major or minor, is used as a valuable feedback for the creation of an efficient and successful maintenance program. Warehouse operations, especially material handling (e.g., storage, picking etc.), are constructively strengthened through the adoption of IoT solutions [28]. According to [30], technologies such as IoT yield a significant reduction in failures, increase efficiency and make processes more productive. Therefore, concerns should be based on avoiding critical failures, identifying the cause of failures and creating an active framework for predictive failure management rather than prevention. Using IoT for measuring warehouse performance, according to the findings of [16], indicate that it is a suitable technology which ensures proper equipment and asset usage, improves reliability, provides the best return on assets and extends the equipment service life. The above is achieved by using sensors or intelligent devices for data acquisition, networking for communications and cloud or web applications with analytics as the three major components. Thus, for example, a sensor attached to a forklift truck records and sends messages to a gateway that transmits to the cloud or web platform. Subsequently, these messages are routed via a predefined workflow to the interface for tracking and updating. Finally, based on rules that are set on the system, actions are triggered automatically. The works in [31] present a similar view, by mentioning that IoT technology, with the help of data analytics, can usually identify the root-cause of component failures, reduce failures of production systems due to predictive analysis, eliminate costly unscheduled shutdown maintenance and therefore improve productivity as well as quality. According to [32], IoT has helped organizations reduce by 25% their maintenance costs, and by 50% their unplanned downtime. Performance availability evaluation is also another area that IoT technology could be supportive within material handling. Based on [33], a simulation platform is proposed that can enable the evaluation and optimization of material handling systems via the use of IoT technology. A real-world application with autonomous smart devices is explained, with the use of smart bins within a warehouse.

3.4. Physical Asset Sharing

This category of papers is related to the use of IoT technology for locating objects, but in a much broader and general sense compared to a similar use that was witnessed to a degree in the previous sections. The papers that we classified in this category speak of the extensive use of IoT in order to create a physical web, where all things can be tracked and located. For the time being, this thought may still be a vision, but a great potential lies within it and therefore it is being pursued by several programs. The Physical Internet is a paradigm-breaking vision that enables physical goods to be transferred and deployed seamlessly, while logistical networks such as data packets travel through heterogeneous infrastructure that compliments the Digital Internet's TCP/IP protocol in a way that is obvious to the user [34]. Therefore, the Physical Internet represents an open, interconnected, global, and sustainable logistics network that establishes a path-breaking solution to the inefficiencies of existing models [20]. This type of business model is currently very complicated to execute, as it is extremely difficult to achieve global uniqueness in a way that is commonly understood. However, within a smaller scale, such as a warehouse installation, several projects have been executed and operate. Smart labels are a noble solution for physical asset sharing. According to [35], smart labels go beyond the act of identifying and are able to detect and respond to the world around them. Furthermore, if the industrial IoT model is extended to smart labels attached to objects, they can be remotely detected and discovered by other Industry 4.0 systems, which enables these systems to respond in the presence of smart labels, thus triggering specific events or taking a range of actions on them. Therefore, we see that smart labels can provide human-centered industry 4.0 applications with recognition, monitoring, sensing, event detection and interaction, thus making the first steps towards the Physical Internet.

4. An Industrial IoT Application

As noted in the introduction, the reporting in literature of real-life applications of IoT and cloud systems to support material handling and intralogistics in general, is rather limited. This paper attempts to contribute by presenting the case study of a large Distribution Center that supplies retail home furnishing and sporting goods products to stores in five countries in the Balkan region. This DC runs two different automation systems with AGVs, shuttles and conveyors that are equipped with IoT technology. For the retail home furnishing part of business, a pallet automation system is used with 600 m of conveyors, two input stations, four transfer cars, five pick and delivery stations, eight automated Very Narrow Aisle (VNA) forklifts and three sets of flow racks with 108 gravity lines in total. A general layout of the plant is seen on Figure 1 below.

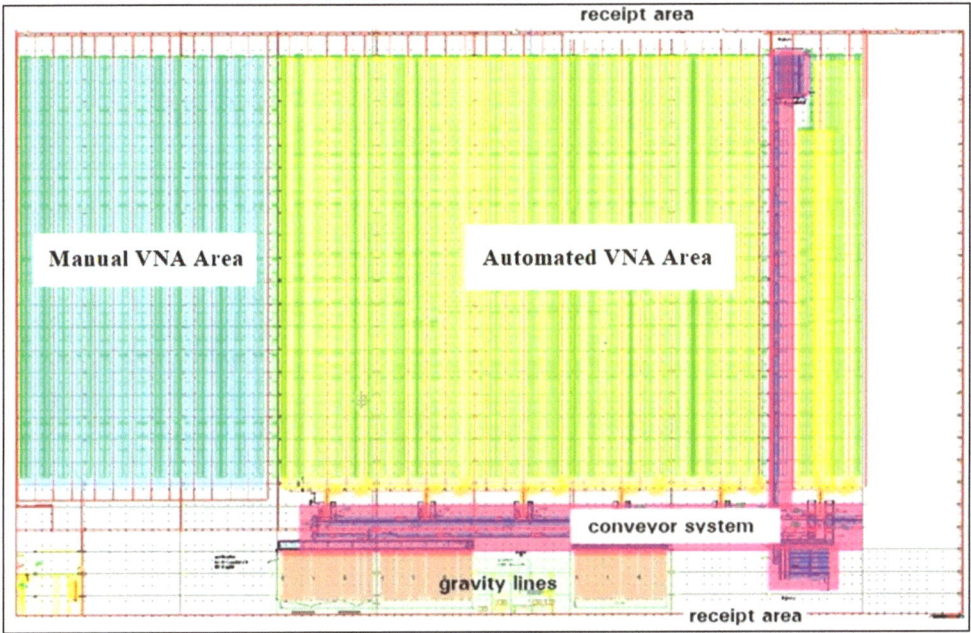

Figure 1. Plant general layout.

On the manual VNA area, VNA trucks operate on typical back-to-back pallet racks and are supported by the main WMS of the plant. On the automated VNA area, similar back-to-back pallet racks exist, but the operation is handled by eight fully automated VNA trucks. The trucks are fitted with a Wi-Fi antenna that communicates via TCP/IP protocol with the Material Flow Controller (MFC) system. A rough system overview can be seen on Figure 2 below.

Each truck and conveyor section of the system communicates via Industrial Ethernet with the MFC/WMS and receives and sends all automatic instructions. The floor of the installation is fitted with five different frequency cables that are connected to a frequency converter, which allows the trucks to move in automatic mode with active enable frequency. Each truck is also fitted with fourteen different sensors in order to be able to pick up and deposit a pallet without causing damage to the products. The operation of the automated VNA area is divided in two types of pallet size. One is the normal EURO pallet (1200 mm × 800 mm) and the other is a EURO-Long pallet (2000 mm × 800 mm), which is a special type of pallet used for longer furniture. In the installation, there are eight automated forklifts installed in total, six for EURO pallets and two for EURO-Long pallets. Regarding the picking process, orders are picked by the forklifts, according to specific priorities and algorithms. Pallets are placed by the forklifts to the Pick and Delivery stations, which are in turn connected to the conveyor system. The conveyor system will then shift the pallet to the allocated gravity line and a stock movement message will be reported to the WMS, when the pallet arrives at the gravity line. A view of an automated truck and a Pick and Delivery station can be seen in Figure 3 below.

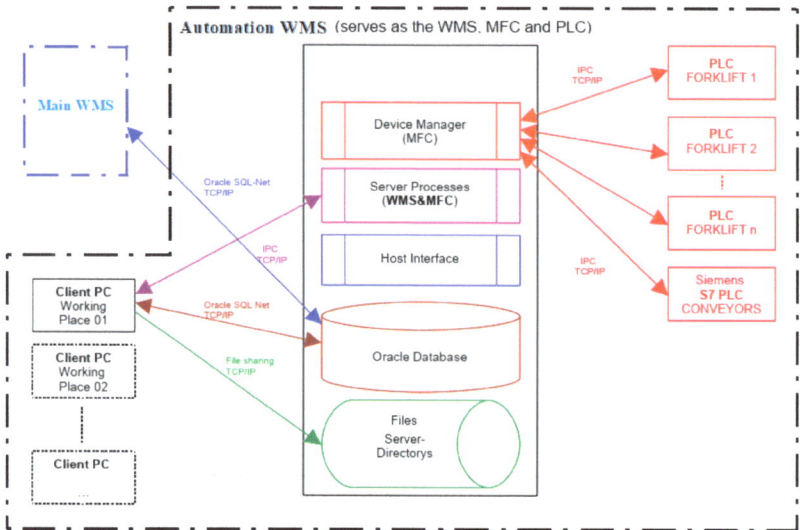

Figure 2. Pallet automation system overview.

Figure 3. View of AGV and Pick and Delivery station.

For the conveyor system, which is responsible for shifting pallets in and out of the warehouse, a Siemens control system (PLC) type S7 CPU416-2DP is used. Live plant information is shown through WinCC, a plant visualization software by Siemens S.A. Access to the control system is made through TCP/IP. Peripheral equipment such as light barriers, frequency converters, control panels, etc., are connected to the control system via AS-Interface and Profibus-DP. Actuator Sensor Interface (AS-Interface) is an industrial networking solution with physical layer, protocol and data access methods that is used in PLC-based automation systems, for connecting devices such as rotary encoders, sensors, actuators, push buttons and analog inputs and outputs. Profibus Decentralized Peripherals (Profibus-DP) is used in automation applications in order to operate actuators and sensors via a centralized controller. Data exchange with the automated trucks in the pallet warehouse is made by the internal Wireless LAN (TCP/IP), directly with the Siemens standard functions. A Scalance WLAN Access-point is installed in all trucks and communication with the WMS is achieved by internal network, through protocol RFC 1006. A visual representation can be seen in Figure 4.

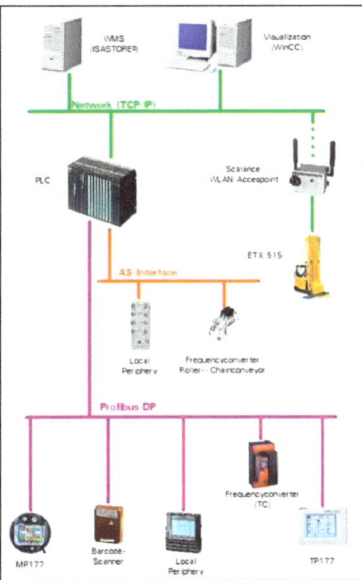

Figure 4. Pallet Automation System Network Diagram.

The output of the system is three sets of flow racks (gravity lines). This is the area, where all the pallets arrive after being retrieved from the automatic warehouse. Each gravity line represents one location in the warehouse modelling. The maximum number of pallets which can be stored into the gravity lines is 972. Plant Visualization is realized with the WinCC visualization software, as mentioned earlier. Plant visualization represents an image of the plant, with several pictures being used to get useful partial views of the plant. The status, automatic and manual mode, of all conveyor elements is visualized, and also all pallets moving on the system are displayed, together with their respective information, such as ID number, transport destination, transport status, etc. Fault messages are presented together with their status and everything is logged in an archive. In Figure 5, some examples of the plant visualization are presented (Figure 5a), together with the interface that is used by the users (Figure 5b).

In order to describe the real flow of goods and the various interactions, communications and control among the various elements of the system, when a pallet enters the system through one of the input stations and has passed the required size and weight criteria, the system transports it towards the corresponding area (i.e., EURO or EURO-Long). On specific points of the conveyor in these areas the WMS decides on the exact storage location of the pallet on the automated racking, according to workload and availability of the automated trucks. The pallet then enters the Pick and Delivery Station of the section that it will be stored and the truck receives a signal from the conveyor to come and pick it up. When the truck picks up the pallet, it transports it to the required location and deposits it. As soon as the movement is completed correctly, the WMS is informed and the truck continues towards its next assignment (i.e., to pick up a pallet from the rack and move it to the conveyor, or pick up another pallet from the conveyor for storage on the pallet rack). Communication for the movement of pallets throughout the conveyors is achieved by light sensors and barcode scanners. That means that when a pallet moves on the conveyor, the system knows its location by the light-barriers attached every few meters, and when there is a change in direction, then a barcode scanner exists that reads the barcode of the pallet and decides where to move it.

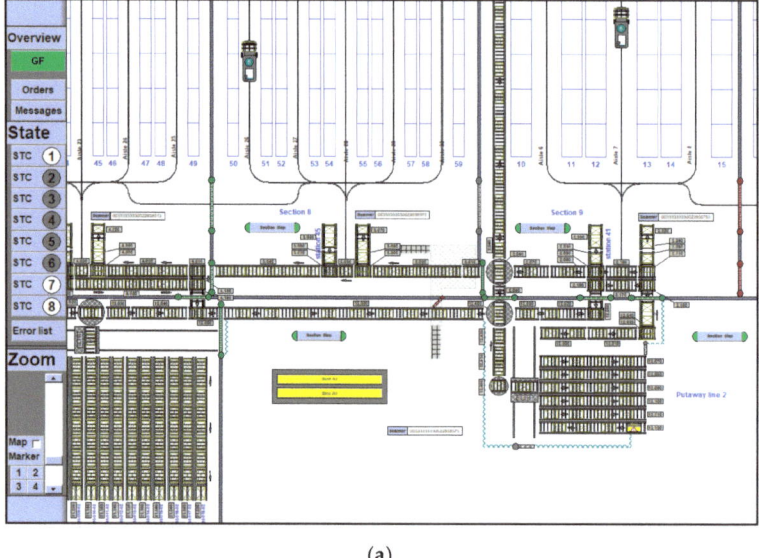

(a)

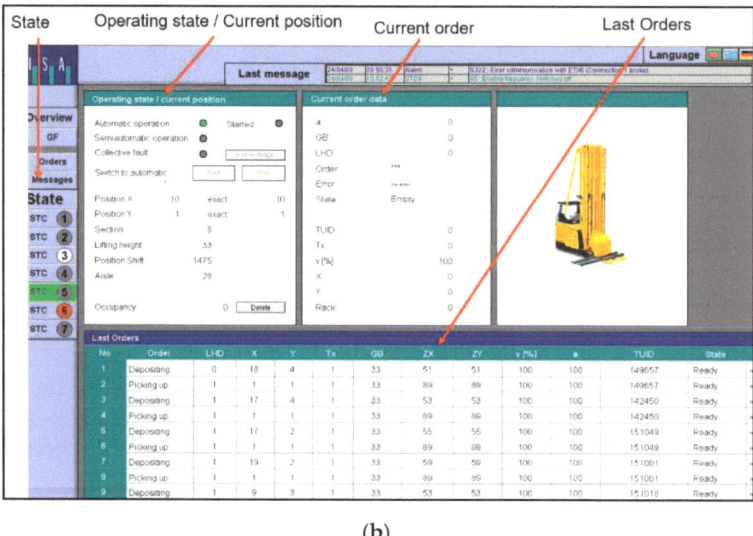

(b)

Figure 5. Human Machine Interface (HMI) WinCC. (**a**) some examples of the plant visualization, (**b**) the interface that is used by the users.

Regarding the retail sporting goods part of business, a box automation system is used, that is comprised from (a) an automated racking system of 22,000 box locations that operates with 6 high speed lift platforms and 51 automated shuttles, (b) five Goods-to-Person stations with 150 flow rack (store) locations and pick-to-light operation, and (c) 500 m of conveying system for transporting boxes between automated racking and Goods-to-Person stations. A general layout of the system can be seen in Figure 6 below.

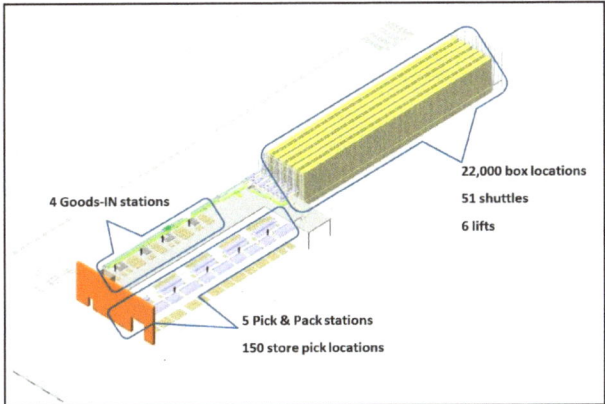

Figure 6. Box automation system general layout.

KiSoft WCS serves as the Warehouse Control System (WCS). The storage procedure is performed by filling plastic system containers and placing them on the conveyor system at the Goods-IN workstations. A storage order containing all information (i.e., order number, container number, articles, quantity, etc.) is transmitted by the WMS to the WCS for the storage containers to be stored in the shuttle system. The storage of the container into one of the rack lines is carried out by the shuttles. For the picking procedure, containers are automatically transported from the stock locations within the racking of the shuttle system to the pick and pack stations. Orders are transmitted from the WMS to the WCS, and as soon as the containers reach the pick stations, the pick-to-light displays indicate the number and target position of the products for picking to the warehouse worker.

The visualization of the automation system is performed by the SCADA software. With this software, the entire warehouse can be monitored, and individual warehouse areas can be started and stopped. SCADA is used for actions such as starting and stopping the conveyor system and electronics for individual warehouse areas, displaying and exporting active and archived messages, confirming error messages, and displaying and exporting statistics. It is installed on a server or computer that assumes the function of the server. The user calls up its GUI through a client. Any hardware device in the warehouse that connects through a web browser to the SCADA server is referred to as a client. The client must have a network connection to the SCADA server. Working with SCADA is possible with every hardware device that has a functioning web browser (Internet Explorer, Firefox, Chrome, etc.). OPC-UA comprises the interface between SCADA and the systems that are visualized on the GUI. Through the SCADA's GUI, all error messages of conveyors are displayed, which are then used by the company for further analysis, as is explained later on. Figure 7 shows the communication interfaces.

Service Client is the system used for checking and manually controlling the shuttles and lift platforms of the storage and picking system. This is a web-based client server application that permits actions such as monitoring the system status and the execution of processes, testing and referencing shuttles and lifts, enabling, disabling or suspending individual components or areas and accessing information concerning previous actions and states. The Service Client is called up through a web browser and is therefore available wherever a connection to the web server is possible. It is installed on the server of the storage and picking system. Figure 8 indicates the communication interfaces at the shuttle. The interface to the master control system is realized with the Storage and Retrieval Controller (SRC).

Through the Service Client software, all error messages of shuttles and lifts are displayed, which are then used by the company for further analysis. Finally, there is one other program, SRC Reports that visualizes warehouse data and is used to influence work process of the warehouse system controlled by SRC. The software is a web application, installed on the SRC server and runs in combination with a database. It is mainly used for actions such as statistics and reports, displaying orders, products, system containers and storage locations with all the associated information, creating picking and inventory orders and displaying operational states.

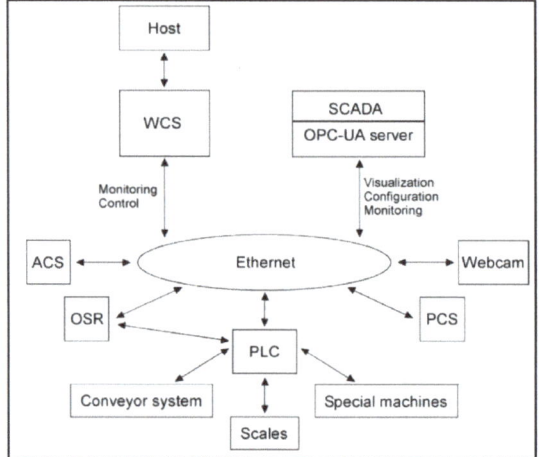

Figure 7. System hierarchy for retail sporting goods operation.

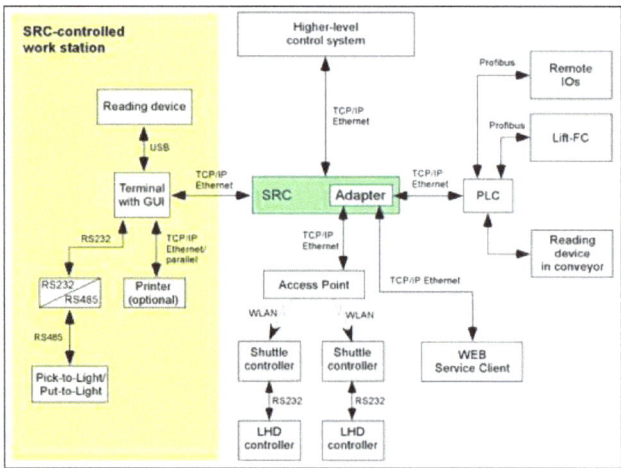

Figure 8. Shuttle interface diagram.

As mentioned previously, the system uses shuttles and lifts in order to move storage containers within the automated racking system. Each level has a shuttle that moves containers horizontally within the level. Overall, there are 51 shuttles operating in the system. For the movement between the different levels of shuttles, there are six lifts installed. Each lift can move one container at a time to the corresponding level. Figure 9a depicts an example of the racking system structure, while the shuttle used for moving the containers within the same level, is depicted in Figure 9b. The orders are transmitted through WLAN from the SRC to the shuttles. Within the racking system, there are access points on specific locations.

For measuring performance and keeping track of the maintenance needs of both automation systems, all error messages from VNAs, shuttles, lifts and conveyors are recorded and analyzed through Kibana, a data analytics and visualization platform. Within this platform, system messages are categorized according to the system and division they belong to, and, therefore, it is easy for the technical team of the company to observe abnormalities and possible problems on the various system components. Visualization of the error messages is done either with pie charts, graphs, or simply list of messages, as seen on examples on Figure 10. Through this data analysis, reacting to errors and faults on the systems, according to specified monitored parameters, is quick, and therefore the overall performance of the system is maintained at a high level.

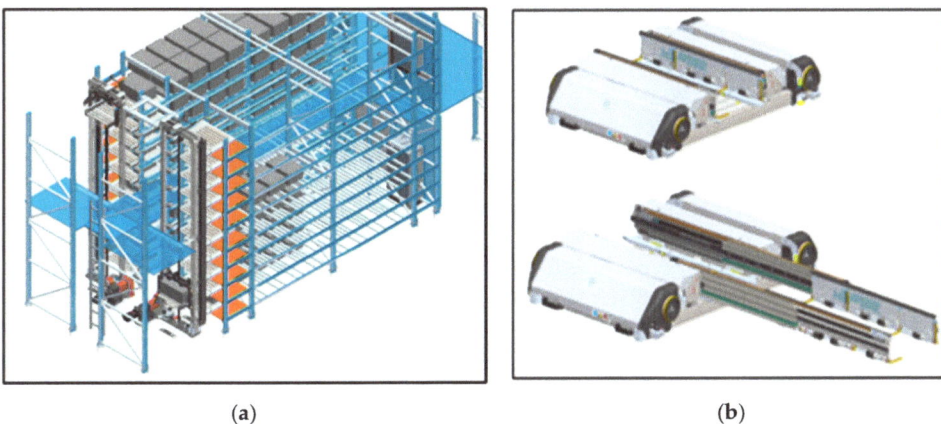

Figure 9. Box automation racking and shuttles. (**a**) an example of the racking system structure, (**b**) the shuttle used for moving the containers within the same level.

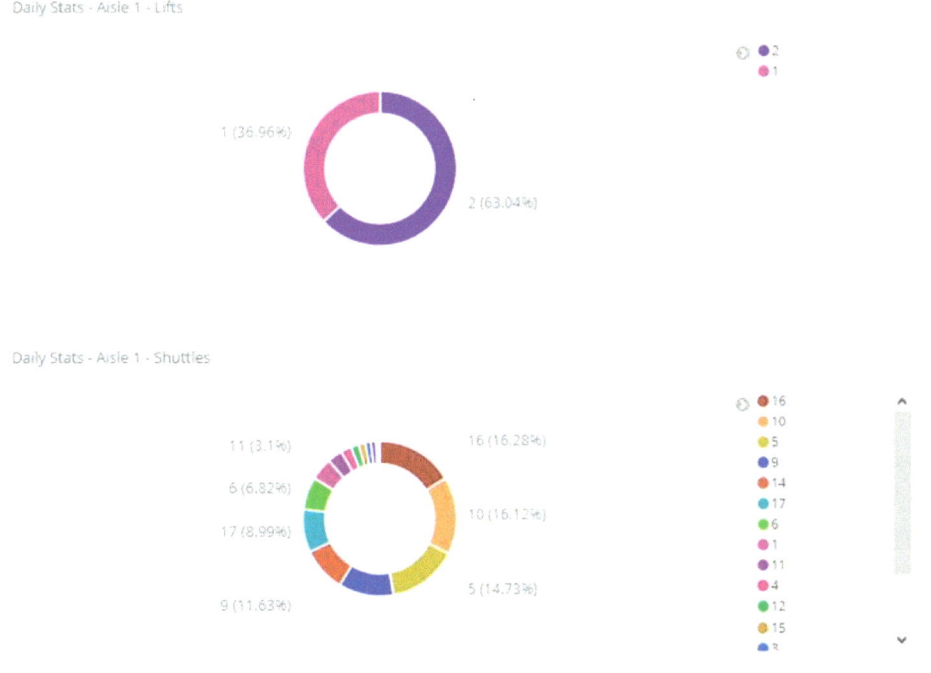

Figure 10. Visualization of system error messages.

5. Conclusions

Industry 4.0 and its technologies are rapidly reshaping our world today. Our daily routines are very different to what they were ten years ago. The way we live and consume is constantly enriched with additional digital and virtual aspects. The same change takes place in our working environments. Logistics, including material handling and intralogistics, both as a science and an economic sector, not only does not lack behind, but rather drives the application and development of basic methods, algorithms and technologies. According to the literature reviewed, we comprehend that massive changes are underway for warehouses and intralogistics facilities. Intelligent automation is gradually replacing monotonous and strenuous activities, mainly due to the need for speed and precision, but also due to the lack of blue-collar workforce, especially in developed countries. Advancements in the areas of goods movement and order picking within warehouses have been substantial within the last decade, with fleets of AGVs becoming more autonomous in their movement around the warehouse space, and picking robots and robotic arms becoming more and more capable of handling various types of goods and materials. Cloud computing has also greatly assisted in improving the performance of AGV fleets and robots by allowing them to share their knowledge outside the four walls of the warehouse and reach similar types of installations worldwide. Furthermore, the ability to handle more complicated activities is made possible due to the fact that stand alone machines do not need to have large processing power to analyze collected data, since central processing devices can do it for them through the cloud and then provide the solution/action which is needed to be performed. Swarms of intelligent AGVs and robots is the foreseeable future for intralogistics and warehousing, with almost no need for human interference between goods-in and goods-out, since all activities will be assigned automatically to the most suitable device within the installation. However, there is still some distance to be covered in order for such a state to become the mainstream. Prototypes need to be further tested in regard to both complexity and size, but most importantly they need to become durable enough in order to be able to withstand the harsh environment and treatment that exists within a warehouse space.

In this paper, an analysis of Cloud and IoT technologies is presented in an attempt to understand their effect on material handling automation and intralogistics. The literature study shows that the subject area is currently dominated by small-scale research facilities that aim to represent real-life scenarios and thus lack large-scale implementations of their innovations in material handling and intralogistics. Consequently, the current status of cloud and IoT technologies in the areas under review in terms of performance, flexibility and availability has not yet been thoroughly tested. This lag between theoretical advancements and practical implementations, as discussed earlier, is not exclusively the result of the technology complexity and poor or underdeveloped prototyping. There is still much road to be travelled when it comes to 'softer' issues, such as the management culture, the workforce expertise and investment mindset and behavior. This paper attempted to showcase an actual successful implementation of an IoT-Cloud application in an international logistics company with two set objectives. The first was to provide an adequate level of details on technical information in order to prove that the complex nature of such installations can be decomposed in actual manageable chunks, which are logically interconnected into a quite straightforward system. The second objective was to highlight a successful case study of an IoT-Cloud implementation in the area of Intralogistics, in order to create the necessary motivation capable of alleviating management reservations and trigger an initial interest on the subject, which eventually will lead to an increased number of technology adaptors.

Finally, this study has some inherent limitations. First of all, evaluating the inclusion/exclusion criteria was a rather cumbersome and copious process. As a result, it is possible that there are several useful publications that have been excluded from the sample. For this, the authors a priori apologize to their colleagues if such an eventuality has occurred. Second, we must notice that the choice of language limits the findings of our research, as it is anticipated that a significant number of publications would use a language other than English, especially in German or Chinese, where a considerable number of authors have been identified. Lastly, the presentation of a single case study permits the authors from generalizing identified phenomena and firmly connecting the case results with the theoretical findings. Actually, recording and debriefing more practical IoT implementations is one of the items the authors have on their future research agenda, which also includes the development of a technology and process reference model for supporting Industry 4.0 implementations in contemporary logistics and the authoring of a roadmap document, providing methods, tools and technologies to guide lagging or hesitant companies through their inevitable journey towards Industry 4.0 enhanced digitalization.

Author Contributions: Writing—original draft, O.K.E. and S.T.P. All authors have read and agreed to the published version of the manuscript.

Funding: This research has been co-financed by the European Union and Greek national funds through the Operational Program Competitiveness, Entrepreneurship and Innovation, under the call RESEARCH–CREATE–INNOVATE (project code: T1EDK-01168).

Conflicts of Interest: The authors declare no conflict of interest.

References

1. Bughin, J.; Chui, M.; Manyika, J. Clouds, Big Data, and Smart Assets: Ten Tech-Enabled Business Trends to Watch. Available online: https://www.mckinsey.com/industries/technology-media-and-telecommunications/our-insights/clouds-big-data-and-smart-assets-ten-tech-enabled-business-trends-to-watch (accessed on 21 December 2019).
2. Manavalan, E.; Jayakrishna, K. A review of Internet of Things (IoT) embedded sustainable supply chain for industry 4.0 requirements. *Comput. Ind. Eng.* **2019**, *127*, 925–953. [CrossRef]
3. Jabbar, S.; Khan, M.; Silva, B.N.; Han, K. A REST-based industrial web of things' framework for smart warehousing. *J. Supercomput.* **2016**, *74*, 4419–4433. [CrossRef]
4. Kawa, A.; Ratajczak-Mrozek, M. Cooperation between logistics service providers based on cloud computing. In *Intelligent Information and Database Systems*; Lecture Notes in Computer Science; Selamat, A., Nguyen, N.T., Haron, H., Eds.; Springer: Berlin/Heidelberg, Germany, 2013; Volume 7803, pp. 458–467. [CrossRef]
5. Dixit, V.S.; Chhabra, S. Logistics business under the cloud computing framework. In Proceedings of the 15th International Conference on Computational Science and Its Applications, Banff, AB, Canada, 22–25 June 2015; pp. 96–99. [CrossRef]
6. Arnold, U.; Oberlander, J.; Schwarzbach, B. LOGICAL—Development of cloud computing platforms and tools for logistics hubs and communities. In Proceedings of the 2012 Federated Conference on Computer Science and Information Systems (FedCSIS), Wroclaw, Poland, 9–12 September 2012; pp. 1083–1090.
7. Ślusarczyk, B. Industry 4.0: Are we ready? *Pol. J. Manag. Stud.* **2018**, *17*, 232–248. [CrossRef]
8. Falkenberg, R.; Masoudinejad, M.; Buschhoff, M.; Venkatapathy, A.K.R.; Friesel, D.; Hompel, M.T.; Spinczyk, O.; Wietfeld, C. PhyNetLab: An IoT-Based Warehouse Testbed. In Proceedings of the 2017 Federated Conference on Computer Science and Information Systems, Prague, Czech Republic, 3–6 September 2017; pp. 1051–1055. [CrossRef]
9. Efthymiou, O.K.; Ponis, S.T. Current Status of Industry 4.0 in Material Handling Automation and In-house Logistics. *Int. J. Int. Man. Eng.* **2019**, *13*, 1370–1374.
10. Martin, J.; May, S.; Endres, S.; Cabanes, I. Decentralized robot-cloud architecture for an autonomous transportation system in a smart factory. In Proceedings of the SEMANTiCS Workshops, Amsterdam, The Netherlands, 11–14 September 2017.
11. Hu, G.; Tay, W.; Wen, Y. Cloud robotics: Architecture, challenges and applications. *IEEE Netw.* **2012**, *26*, 21–28. [CrossRef]
12. Theunissen, J.; Xu, H.; Zhong, R.Y.; Xu, X. Smart AGV system for manufacturing shopfloor in the context of industry 4.0. In Proceedings of the 25th International Conference on Mechatronics and Machine Vision in Practice (M2VIP), Stuttgart, Germany; 2018; pp. 1–6. [CrossRef]
13. Cardarelli, E.; Digani, V.; Sabattini, L.; Secchi, C.; Fantuzzi, C. Cooperative cloud robotics architecture for the coordination of multi-AGV systems in industrial warehouses. *Mechatronics (Oxf)* **2017**, *45*, 1–13. [CrossRef]

14. Wan, J.; Tang, S.; Li, D.; Wang, S.; Liu, C.; Abbas, H.; Vasilakos, A.V. A Manufacturing Big Data Solution for Active Preventive Maintenance. *IEEE Trans. Industr. Inform.* **2017**, *13*, 2039–2047. [CrossRef]
15. Feng, F.; Pang, Y.; Lodewijks, G. Towards context-aware supervision for logistics asset management: Concept design and system implementation. In *Information Technology for Management: New Ideas and Real Solutions*; Ziemba, E., Ed.; Springer: Cham, Switzerland, 2017; Volume 277, pp. 3–19. [CrossRef]
16. Kamali, A. IoT's Potential to Measure Performance of MHE in Warehousing. *Int. J. Biom. Bioinform.* **2019**, *11*, 93–99.
17. Borangiu, T.; Trentesaux, D.; Thomas, A.; Leitão, P.; Barata, J. Digital transformation of manufacturing through cloud services and resource virtualization. *Comput. Ind.* **2019**, *108*, 150–162. [CrossRef]
18. Want, R.; Schilit, B.N.; Jenson, S. Enabling the Internet of Things. *Computer* **2015**, *48*, 28–35. [CrossRef]
19. Maslarić, M.; Nikoličić, S.; Mirčetić, D. Logistics Response to the Industry 4.0: The Physical Internet. *Open Eng.* **2016**, *6*. [CrossRef]
20. Montreuil, B. Toward a Physical Internet: Meeting the global logistics sustainability grand challenge. *Logist. Res.* **2011**, *3*, 71–87. [CrossRef]
21. Prasse, C.; Nettstraeter, A.; Hompel, M.T. How IoT will change the design and operation of logistics systems. In Proceedings of the 2014 International Conference on the Internet of Things (IOT), Cambridge, MA, USA, 6–8 October 2014; pp. 55–60. [CrossRef]
22. Trab, S.; Bajic, E.; Zouinkhi, A.; Thomas, A.; Abdelkrim, M.N.; Chekir, H.; Ltaief, R.H. A communicating object's approach for smart logistics and safety issues in warehouses. *Concurr. Eng. Res. Appl.* **2016**, *25*, 53–67. [CrossRef]
23. Wan, J.; Yang, J.; Wang, Z.; Hua, Q. Artificial Intelligence for Cloud-Assisted Smart Factory. *IEEE Access* **2018**, *6*, 55419–55430. [CrossRef]
24. Pata, S.D.; Milici, D.L.; Poienar, M.; Cenusa, M. Management system for the control of the forklifts activity in a factory. In Proceedings of the 8th International Conference on Modern Power Systems (MPS), Cluj Napoca, Romania, 21–23 May 2019; pp. 1–4. [CrossRef]
25. Nissanka, S.A.; Senevirathna, M.A.J.R.; Dharmawardana, M. IoT based automatic storing and retrieval system. In Proceedings of the 2016 Manufacturing & Industrial Engineering Symposium (MIES), Colombo, Sri Lanka, 22 October 2016; pp. 1–5. [CrossRef]
26. Yan, H.; Hua, Q.; Wang, Y.; Wei, W.; Imran, M. Cloud robotics in Smart Manufacturing Environments: Challenges and countermeasures. *Comput. Electr. Eng.* **2017**, *63*, 56–65. [CrossRef]
27. Hussnain, A.; Ferrer, B.R.; Lastra, J.L.M. Towards the deployment of cloud robotics at factory shop floors: A prototype for smart material handling. In Proceedings of the 2018 IEEE Industrial Cyber-Physical Systems (ICPS), St. Petersburg, Russia, 15–18 May 2018; pp. 44–50. [CrossRef]
28. Gregor, T.; Krajčovič, M.; Więcek, D. Smart Connected Logistics. *Procedia Eng.* **2017**, *192*, 265–270. [CrossRef]
29. Agalianos, K.; Ponis, S.T.; Aretoulaki, E.; Plakas, G.; Efthymiou, O. Discrete Event Simulation and Digital Twins: Review and Challenges for Logistics. *Procedia Manuf* **2020**, in press.
30. Ahmad, S.; Badwelan, A.; Ghaleb, A.M.; Qamhan, A.; Sharaf, M.; Alatefi, M.; Moohialdin, A. Analyzing Critical Failures in a Production Process: Is Industrial IoT the Solution? *Wirel Commun. Mob. Comput.* **2018**, 1–12. [CrossRef]
31. Arnaiz, A.; Iung, B.; Adgar, A.; Naks, T.; Tohver, A.; Tommingas, T.; Levrat, E. Information and communication technologies within E-maintenance. In *E-Maintenance*; Holmberg, K., Adgar, A., Arnaiz, A., Jantunen, E., Mascolo, J., Mekid, S., Eds.; Springer: London, UK, 2010; pp. 39–60. [CrossRef]
32. Manyika, J.; Chui, M. By 2025, Internet of Things Applications Could Have $ 11 Trillion Impact. Available online: https://www.mckinsey.com/mgi/overview/in-the-news/by-2025-internet-of-things-applications-could-have-11-trillion-impact (accessed on 16 November 2019).
33. Roidl, M.; Emmerich, J.; Riesner, A.; Masoudinejad, M.; Kaulbars, D.; Ide, C.; Wietfeld, C.; Hompel, M.T. Performance availability evaluation of smart devices in materials handling systems. In Proceedings of the International Conference on Communications in China—Workshops (CIC/ICCC), Shanghai, China, 13 October 2014; pp. 6–10. [CrossRef]

34. Montreuil, B.; Rougès, J.-F.; Cimon, Y.; Poulin, D. The Physical Internet and Business Model Innovation. *Technol. Innov. Manag. Rev.* **2012**, *2*, 32–37. [CrossRef]
35. Fernandez-Carames, T.M.; Fraga-Lamas, P. A Review on Human-Centered IoT-Connected Smart Labels for the Industry 4.0. *IEEE Access* **2018**, *6*, 25939–25957. [CrossRef]

© 2020 by the authors. Licensee MDPI, Basel, Switzerland. This article is an open access article distributed under the terms and conditions of the Creative Commons Attribution (CC BY) license (http://creativecommons.org/licenses/by/4.0/).

Review

A Systematic Review on Technologies for Data-Driven Production Logistics: Their Role from a Holistic and Value Creation Perspective

Masoud Zafarzadeh [1,*], Magnus Wiktorsson [1] and Jannicke Baalsrud Hauge [1,2]

1. Department of Sustainable Production Development, KTH Royal Institute of Technology, 114 28 Stockholm, Sweden; magwik@kth.se
2. BIBA Institute, 28359 Bremen, Germany; jmbh@kth.se
* Correspondence: masoudz@kth.se; Tel.: +46-8-790-94-93

Citation: Zafarzadeh, M.; Wiktorsson, M.; Baalsrud Hauge, J. A Systematic Review on Technologies for Data-Driven Production Logistics: Their Role from a Holistic and Value Creation Perspective. *Logistics* 2021, 5, 24. https://doi.org/10.3390/logistics5020024

Academic Editor: Benjamin Nitsche

Received: 25 February 2021
Accepted: 23 March 2021
Published: 23 April 2021

Publisher's Note: MDPI stays neutral with regard to jurisdictional claims in published maps and institutional affiliations.

Copyright: © 2021 by the authors. Licensee MDPI, Basel, Switzerland. This article is an open access article distributed under the terms and conditions of the Creative Commons Attribution (CC BY) license (https://creativecommons.org/licenses/by/4.0/).

Abstract: A data-driven approach in production logistics is adopted as a response to challenges such as low visibility and system rigidity. One important step for such a transition is to identify the enabling technologies from a value-creating perspective. The existing corpus of literature has discussed the benefits and applications of smart technologies in overall manufacturing or logistics. However, there is limited discussion specifically on a production logistics level, from a systematic perspective. This paper addresses two issues in this respect by conducting a systematic literature review and analyzing 142 articles. First, it covers the gap in literature concerning mapping the application of these smart technologies to specific production logistic activities. Ten groups of technologies were identified and production logistics activities divided into three major categories. A quantitative share assessment of the technologies in production logistics activities was carried out. Second, the ultimate goal of implementing these technologies is to create business value. This is addressed in this research by presenting the "production logistics data lifecycle" and the importance of having a balanced holistic perspective in technology development. The result of this paper is beneficial to build a ground to transit towards a data-driven state by knowing the applications and use cases described in the literature for the identified technologies.

Keywords: data-driven; smart; process automation; production logistics; technology; transition; autonomous systems

1. Introduction

Recent developments in information and communication technologies (ICT) have the potential to create business value by supporting the transition towards data-driven manufacturing and autonomous supply chains [1,2]. These technologies enable seamless data flow and link information to moving goods and material. Implementation of these technologies is not only a prerequisite for data-driven manufacturing and autonomous supply chains [3,4], but also increases visibility in the internal logistics operations.

Within data-driven manufacturing, data is the backbone of the system, which embodies intelligence into manufacturing systems. Tao et al. [5] have conceptualized data-driven smart manufacturing and identified several characteristics. Data-driven manufacturing systems are self-regulated through exploiting real-time monitoring of manufacturing processes. Through exploiting multisource data from manufacturing processes, it will be possible to have rigorous control over the production process. By applying resource-related data, tasks and work instructions data, it will be possible to have smart planning and scheduling across the organization. Customer data such as demands, preferences, limitations and behaviors will be considered for overall system efficiency. Through exploiting historical and real-time data, it will be possible to perform quality control and preventative maintenance proactively [6]. These characteristics open up a new horizon for production logistics (PL), which is indispensable for any manufacturing system.

Even if it be claimed that data-driven smart manufacturing characteristics are valid for production logistics [5], current practices within production logistics is still perceived as a field tied up with non-value-adding activities and lacking high level of responsiveness. To understand the importance of streamlining the PL processes through digitalization, following statement is interesting to consider: "A typical manufacturing company dedicates 25% of its employees, 55% of its factory space, and 87% of its production time to material handling" (Horňáková et al. [7]; adopted from Davich [8]). To facilitate the transition towards data-driven production logistics, it is important to have a systematic perspective regarding the possibilities created by technologies. Several studies reviewed these enabling technologies on a high level in connection with concepts such as smart manufacturing [9], smart logistics [10] and Industry 4.0 [11]. On the other hand, there are studies that looked in to this domain in more details by investigating the application of data-driven technologies in one specific area such as tracing [12], route planning [13] or warehousing [14]. However, the literature has a gap in addressing the application of data-driven enabling technologies in production logistics from a systematic point of view, covering all the activities in a PL system. Thus, we are dealing with studies either conceptualizing data-driven related topics by discussing the possibilities that the technologies can create on enterprise level or reporting benefits on detailed level.

In addition to this existing gap, Klingenberg et al. [11] argue that the absence of a framework in the existing literature reviews with respect to data as the main building block of the data-driven technologies leads to a conceptual panacea. As a consequence of this issue, it is not clear how these technologies in cooperation with each other can contribute to create value for the production logistics systems.

This study intends to cover the described gap by a systematic literature review of reported applications of enabling technologies in production logistics activities, in order to clarify how technologies, in cooperation with each other, can create value for PL systems.

1.1. Related Works and Research Gaps

Perceived benefits is one of the major determinants in employing smart data-driven technologies and methods [15]. Thus, it is necessary to clarify what benefits can be gained through technologies implementation for companies. As mentioned, earlier studies either review the data-driven enabling technologies on the enterprise level, such as smart manufacturing, smart logistics and Industry 4.0, or discuss the subject on a detailed level focusing one specific application. For example, enabling technologies for Industry 4.0 with focus on state-of-the-art and future trends by Alcacer and Machado [16], presenting and discussing key technologies and their characteristics, and the concept of a smart factory. They describe the enabling technologies, but little attention has been paid to the use cases and especially internal logistics of manufacturing firms. Furthermore, innovative technologies adopted in logistics management is reviewed by Lagorio et al. [17], and implementation of Industry 4.0 related technologies within intralogistics is discussed by Saucedo and Jania [18]. In another study, 11 groups of smart manufacturing enabling technologies were identified and their association with smart manufacturing characteristics investigated by Mittal et al. [19], discussing the application of these technologies on a high level. Oztemel and Gursev [20] is another example reviewing the enabling technologies and some initiatives and projects related to Industry 4.0. One study that has discussed application examples of smart manufacturing, is done by Thoben et al. [21], who have mentioned internal logistics in a form of cyberphysical logistics systems. Some other studies have covered technologies applications and use cases targeting production logistics [22–24], but these research lack a systematic perspective to cover all the related PL activities. From a supply chain perspective, Chavez et al. [25] introduced a conceptual framework for data-driven supply chains. Still, the framework does not detail the connection to the enabling technologies and some specific areas of internal logistics such as material handling.

In conclusion, even though the mentioned reviews have analyzed applications related to internal logistics, the overall picture is fragmented and it is not possible to draw a conclusion on how these technologies can actually be useful for production logistics, from a system perspective. Either the existing reviews aim to determine the benefits of implementing enabling technologies on the enterprise level, or they study the application of a selected set of enabling technologies on a detailed level. For example, using RFID for items tracing [12], cloud robotics for route planning [13] or Internet-of-Thing for warehousing [14].

1.2. Research Purpose, Motivation and Article Structure

The purpose of this article is to review the data-driven enabling technologies and their relation with production logistics activities, from a comprehensive and system perspective. Building upon the identified gap presented in Section 1.1 above, there are three major reasons to perform a systematic literature review in this respect.

First, as technological advancements have created more opportunities to collect big amount of data from various data sources, the term data-driven appears in literature more often. Data-driven is widely discussed in relation to decision-making science. However, from the production logistics perspective and in conjunction with topics such as Industry 4.0 and smart manufacturing, this concept is still elusive with different interpretations, needing clarity. In a study by Rossit et al. [26], it is discussed as a scheduling approach in smart manufacturing and cyber-physical systems (CPS). Even though they have referred to frameworks developed for data-driven decision-making, the result of the work is limited to scheduling and other activities are not addresses. In another example, Woo et al. [27] introduced big data analytics platform in manufacturing. In their platform, data-driven models used a predictive planning tool to support decision-making. In some other studies, the term data-driven is used to describe the aim of the research but there is little effort to clarify the data-driven concept in the text, e.g., [12,28,29].

Second, as described in Section 1.1, PL can be perceived as a subsystem for either manufacturing or supply chain. The consequence of this duality is that it is not clear when to apply what technology, and for which production logistics activity. There are studies that have reviewed the data-driven and smart-manufacturing enabling technologies [11,16,19,27,28]. However, to the knowledge of the authors, there is no literature review dedicated to production logistics. In this research, production logistics refers to those activities that happen within production systems. In other words, the internal logistics activities that aim to support manufacturing or production in terms of planning, control and configuration of logistics flow, is considered as production logistics [30]. All the materials, tools and information flow that are necessary for a balanced and efficient production process, are components of production logistics [31].

Third, as ICT technologies are constantly evolving, there is a need to have an updated view on technologies that enable data-driven PL. In this research, data-driven production logistics refers to a closed loop PL system where all the activities are triggered by data and the outcome of activities are presented with data for further use. In this respect, data is collected from various sources by means of enabling technologies. Data analysis has a wide scope in order to have an accurate representation of physical objects and processes. Data need to be internalized through data integration, discovering meaningful information through extracting data features. The data time line has importance for the PL data-driven system, as some activities such as fleet control require real-time data in order to create value for the system.

The technologies discussed in the literature can be considered to be on three different levels [11]. The first is on the device or component level such as sensors or RFID (radio frequency identification), which usually are physical entities. The second is on the method level such as Wi-Fi. Connectivity protocols and software system development approaches such as SoA (service oriented architecture) are perceived as methods. The third is on the system level such as IoT (Internet-of-Things) and CPS (cyber-physical systems), which may consist of several devices and methods. As a result, in this article technology refers to devices, methods and systems, which are the result of scientific knowledge being used for practical purposes, in line with Collins dictionary [32].

In order to meet the purpose of this paper and cover the discussed gaps, it is first required to identify the enabling technologies and their application in PL. Secondly, it is necessary to understand how can the identified technologies create value from a system perspective. Two key research questions were posed in guiding the review:

1. What are the data-driven enabling technologies and their use cases in production logistics activities, as described in the literature?
2. How does the data-driven enabling technologies contribute to value creation in production logistics from a system perspective?

In the following section, the review methodology is outlined. In the result section, findings on the identified technologies key activities (RQ1) and the value creation discussion (RQ2) are presented. Based upon these findings, the discussion elaborates on the role of data life cycle in value creation for/within production logistics. In addition, the interconnection of the identified technologies was discussed. Finally, the article culminates with conclusions and future research possibilities.

2. Methodology

The method selected for reviewing the technologies enabling the data-driven smart production logistic was a systematic literature review (SLR). SLR was chosen as it helps to bring together relevant studies regardless of their location or even disciplinary background. Furthermore, an advantage of SLRs is that by keeping the research process transparent and unbiased, readers can have a clear conclusion and provide new opportunities for other researchers to have new experiments by knowing the exact details of the study performed according to SLR. In addition, properly managed, an SLR can shed light on a specific aspect of the reviewed studies [33]. In this case, this SLR highlights production logistics as one key manufacturing subsystem, which requires further studies. To the best of our knowledge, there is no literature review that has mapped the technologies and their relation to production logistics activities in the context of Industry 4.0 and smart manufacturing. This SLR is carried out in-line with the approach suggested by Tranfield, Denyer and Smart [34], using a three-stage process to perform a systematic literature review: (1) planning the review, (2) conducting the review and (3) reporting and dissemination.

2.1. Planning the Review

This first stage concerns planning the review of literature covering technologies enabling data-driven PL activities. To perform the review, several databases were examined and Scopus was chosen since it is the largest abstract and citation database of peer-reviewed literature. Compared to other examined databases, this database has rich material regarding production logistics, smart manufacturing, Industry 4.0 and data-driven enabling technologies. Scopus also integrates other databases such as the Web of Science, which makes it a reliable source for this study.

Initial Scoping

In order to define the initial scope, the authors defined three categories of search keywords/terms. Category 1 concerns keywords related to emerging concepts such as data-driven manufacturing/logistics, smart/intelligent manufacturing, smart/intelligent logistics, smart/digital factory, Industry 4.0, cyber-physical systems (CPS), digital twin, and Internet-of-Things (IoT). As the primary goal of this paper was to emphasize the role of data in PL systems, data-driven was chosen for the first category. Amongst the mentioned terms, Industry 4.0 is an elusive concept, vaguely defined and including a multitude of concepts [35], and already broadly discussed in the literature, hence excluded. The other terms such as CPS, IoT and digital twin have been mentioned in some of the literature as enabling technologies. Choosing any of these more specific terms could limit the search scope. Terms such as smart/digital factory are less common compared to smart/intelligent manufacturing. To choose between smart and intelligent, the number of hits in Google Scholar was compared. Consequently, beside data-driven, smart was chosen as the second keyword for the first category. Category 2 frames the context of the study. Authors dealt with several options such as manufacturing logistics, production logistics and internal logistics. As internal logistics applies to any possible sort of operation such as a healthcare system, hence is this term not appropriate for this research. As both the "manufacturing" and "logistics" terms have relevant material, it was decided to keep both of the terms for the second category. Category 3 defines the ultimate search items, which is the technologies. To make sure other related work would be captured, "solution" was also added to this category as the last keyword.

2.2. Conducting the Review

As a consequence of the initial scoping, the search query was defined as follows: (("data-driven" OR smart) AND (manufacturing OR logistic*) AND (technolog* OR solution*)).

A wildcard was used to maximize the search outcome. The results were limited from different angles: Time was limited from 2016-March 2020, language was limited to "English". In order to ensure the quality of the material, only those articles that are published in journals picked for further review and the type of sources was limited to "journals". Subject areas were limited to the following:

- Engineering;
- Computer Science;
- Business, Management and Accounting;
- Decision Sciences;
- Mathematics;
- Social Sciences;
- Economics, Econometrics and Finance;
- Environmental Science.

In addition, in order to make the search query even more precise, several keywords that were not relevant to this research, such as machining, cryptography, semiconductors, additive manufacturing, 3D printing and reference modeling were excluded from the search. This search query resulted in 717 hits. Figure 1 illustrates the number of articles per year from 2016 to mid-2020. It is clear that data-driven smart manufacturing and data-driven smart logistics are increasingly receiving attention by researchers.

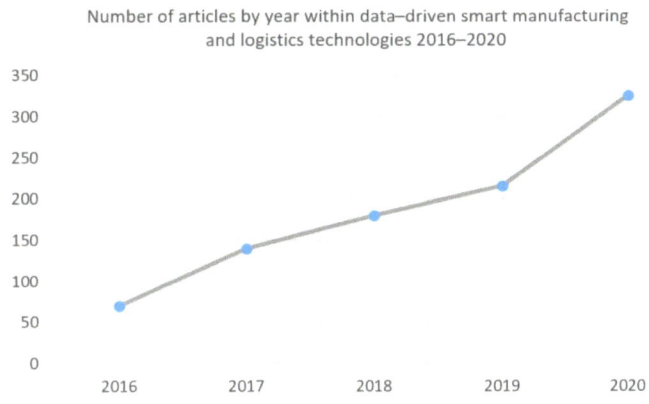

Figure 1. Number of articles by year within data-driven smart manufacturing and logistics technologies.

In the next step, based on the criteria shown in Table 1, all the abstracts of 717 articles were screened and 544 articles excluded from the list. It is worth mentioning that there were many articles related to city logistics, transportation and manufacturing that have keywords in common with production logistics, but perceived as irrelevant and off-topic, and thus removed. The remaining 173 papers were picked for full paper reading. After full paper screening, 57 other papers were excluded from the list, as they did not match the inclusion criteria listed in Table 1. During the full paper review, a backward snowball-search in the references of the relevant articles was carried out to search for further relevant articles; 26 new articles found in this step and added to the list. In total, 142 articles remained in the final list. Figure 2 illustrates the described steps.

Table 1. Inclusion and exclusion criteria.

	Inclusions	Exclusions
Production logistics	Any research related to internal logistics of production or manufacturing companies.	City logistics, cargos, road transportations, machining, assembly, product development, retailing, production planning, product design, maintenance, housing construction.
Enabling technologies	Any relevant technologies that might enable data collection, data processing, data storage, data streaming and data analysis or data visualization.	Automation technologies such as introduction of robots that are only focused on physical aspects of the flow.
Production logistics activities	Any relevant activities such as kitting, route planning, warehousing, packaging, material movement, which is associated with enabling technologies	Mathematical modeling optimization and data security.

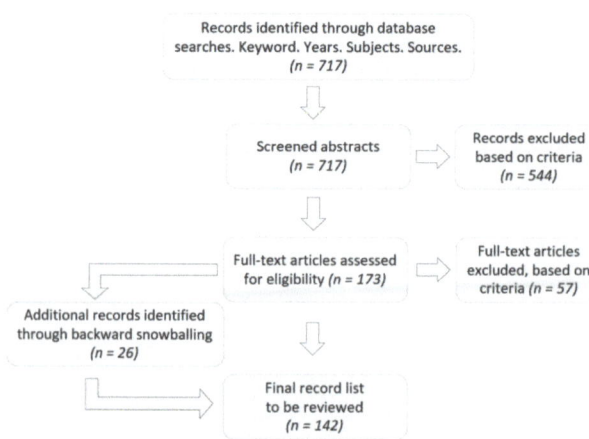

Figure 2. Systematic literature review steps in this research.

In order to minimize the risk of bias in the selection process, inclusion and exclusion criteria were developed, inspired by the PEO model (see [36]). Three main areas, including "production logistics", "enabling technologies" and "PL activities" were determined by the authors to examine inclusion and exclusion criteria. Table 1 shows these criteria.

In addition to the mentioned criteria, all the selected papers needed to be of high quality with respect to:
- Clarified aims and RQs;
- Clarity in study design and method;
- Contribution to the research field;
- Connection to the research field;
- Good theoretical alignment, and data quality.

Figure 3 depicts the journals and respective number of articles that were analyzed in this review. It should be noted that the figure only illustrates journals that had more than one hit.

Reviewed journals

Journal	Count
Int Journal of Production Research	12
Int Journal of Advanced Manufacturing Technology	12
Robotics and Computer-Integrated Manufacturing	9
Procedia Manufacturing	9
IFAC-PapersOnLine	8
Journal of Manufacturing Systems	5
Int Journal of Computer Integrated Manufacturing	5
IEEE Transactions on Industrial Informatics	5
Manufacturing Letters	4
Journal of Industrial Information Integration	4
Journal of Ambient Intelligence and Humanized Computing	4
Journal of Intelligent Manufacturing	3
Int Journal of Production Economics	3
IEEE Transactions on Systems, Man, and Cybernetics	3
IEEE Internet of Things Journal	3
Computers in Industry	3
Computers and Electrical Engineering	3
Wireless Networks	2
The Int Journal of Advanced Manufacturing Technology	2
Machines	2
Journal of the Chinese Institute of Engineers	2
Int Jrnl of Physical Distribution and Logistics Management	2
IEEE Transactions on Automation Science and Engineering	2
IEEE Communications Surveys and Tutorials	2
IEEE Communications Magazine	2
Enterprise Information Systems	2
Advances in Mechanical Engineering	2
Advanced Engineering Informatics	2

Figure 3. Reviewed journals with more than one article.

In total, 78 journals were included in the original 717 records in the SLR, whereof 50 of them had one article for further analysis. *International journal of advanced manufacturing* and *International journal of production research* have the highest number of articles in this review.

The next section is the third stage of the SLR, which is reporting and dissemination. Technologies and key activities (RQ1) identified in the full text screening and the discussion regarding value creation (RQ2) are presented in more details.

3. Identified Technologies and Related Production Logistics Activities

In the review of the 142 articles, 47 technologies were identified. These were divided into 10 groups based on their similarities and types. As explained in Section 1, each of the identified technologies belong to one of the three levels of technologies: device/component, methods or systems. For example, technologies for auto identification are devices, while embedded systems or IoT are perceived as system level technologies consisting of several technologies such as sensor networks, wireless connection and data analysis. Wireless communication protocols such as Wi-Fi, ZigBee or Bluetooth are methods, here also considered as technologies. Table 2 shows the identified technologies.

Table 2. Identified production logistics data-driven enabling technologies

Technology Group	Technologies
Auto Identification	RFID (Radio Frequency Identification) Barcode QR code FOT (Fingerprint of Things) and tag free traceability
Vision systems and image processing	Vision systems Point cloud
Mobile and industrial robots	Industrial robots Drones AGV and mobile robots
Internet-of-Things/ Internet-of-Services	IoT IoS RTLS (Real-Time Locating system) Node-RED
Smart devices	AR (Augmented Reality) VR (Virtual Reality) Pick by X (Voice or light) Smart glass Smart gloves Smart watches Tablet, mobile phone, etc.
Artificial intelligence and Big data	BD analytics AI Machine learning Apache Flume Apache Hadoop Apache Kafka MQTT
Wireless connection and communication networks	Cellular networks (2G/3G/4G/5G) Wireless connection Bluetooth Ultra sound Ultrawide band Wi-Fi ZigBee Industrial communication networks GPS (Global positioning system) Industrial wireless networks Sensor networks
Cloud and Fog/Edge computing	Cloud computing Fog/Edge computing
Cyber physical systems and simulation	CPS Digital twin Embedded systems Holonic manufacturing and Multi agent systems Simulation SoA (Service Oriented Architecture)
	Blockchain

Based on the goal of this paper, enabling technologies found in literature were reviewed with respect to their application in PL activities. All these activities are in line with inclusion and exclusion specifications presented in Table 1. The activities were categorized into three different groups as follows:

- Category 1: Shopfloor operational-related activities including activities that have a direct impact on material movement and material handling. The activities concern physical flow of material. In a PL system with a low level of automation and digitalization, usually these activities involve physical effort. From goods receiving until delivery to internal customers, all activates that involve direct contact with physical goods and material fall under this category.
- Category 2: Planning and scheduling-related activities are regarded as those logistics activities that are aimed to guide the overall operation, and make plans and schedules for an efficient production flow. While the first category concerns physical material flow, this category is about those activities that are known as planning and scheduling. Activities in this category are designed to assure PL system efficiency.
- Category 3: Control, track and trace-related activities are mainly focused on activities that monitor the behavior of logistics system elements such as resources, goods movement and inventory level. Activities in this category control the physical flow of material from items identification until conditions monitoring. This category is essential to increase efficiency of the activities in the two other categories.

For each of these categories, following sections and following tables depict production logistics activities and the data-driven enabling technologies identified in the reviewed literature.

3.1. Category 1: Shopfloor Operational-Related Activities

This category includes operational-related activities, including activities that have a direct impact on material movement and material handling. Usually these activities involve physical interaction with parts, raw material, machines, etc. For example, refilling material buffers, packaging, material-delivery to different working stations and kitting of material and parts for assembly. As presented in Table 3, each of the identified technologies are used for activities in one or several of the PL activities areas. Each of the identified technologies in the category "Described Technologies" in Table 3 belong to one of the three levels of technologies: device/component, methods and systems.

Table 3. Production logistics activities in Category 1 and association with the identified technologies in the literature.

	Production Logistics Activities	Described Technologies		References
Category 1. Shopfloor operational-related activities	Material ordering and buffer replenishment	• AGV and mobile robots • Big data and BD analytics • Cloud computing • Barcode • Vision system and image processing • Sensor networks • Embedded systems	• CPS • IoT • RFID • GPS • AI • Hadoop • QR code	[10,12,15,22,28,35,37–60]
	Goods receiving quality control and registration	• Cloud computing • Edge computing • Vision system and image processing • Industrial robot	• CPS • RFID • AR • Flume	[34,51,61–67]

Table 3. *Cont.*

Production Logistics Activities	Described Technologies		References
Kitting	• AR		[62]
Packaging	• Barcode • AGV and mobile robots • CPS	• RFID • AR • IoT	[10,14,36,62,68–70]
Palletization	• AR		[62]
Picking and Pick and place	• Vision systems and image processing • AGV and mobile robots • Industrial robot • Digital twin • Cloud computing • Sensor networks	• CPS • IoT • RFID • AR • Pick by X • Smart glass • Simulation	[10,14,62,65,69,71–82]
Material transportation and internal transportation optimization	• Vision systems and image processing • AGV and mobile robots • Digital twin • Edge computing • Cloud computing • Sensor networks • MAS and NEIMS	• CPS • IoT • RFID • Simulation • AR • Industrial robot	[12,13,15,34,40,62,71], [72,74,75,77,83–103]
Warehousing	• Vision systems and image processing • AGV and mobile robots • Industrial robot • Digital twin • Big data and BD analytics • Cloud computing • Edge computing • Sensor networks • MAS and NEIMS • Smart glass • Smart gloves • Smart watches • Tablet, smart phone, etc.	• Point cloud • Block chain • Drone • CPS • AI • IoT • RFID • QR code • AR • Pick by X • VR • Barcode	[10,14,27,28,43,45,46,49–53,58,62,63,68,71,73–75,79,91,98,103–121]

Some key examples from Table 3 of how technologies (device/component, methods or systems) were reported to be used in shopfloor operational related PL activities are described in the following.

Park et al. [37] designed and implemented a digital twin to address issues concerning dynamic situations of personalized production. One of the applications in their study was about the buffer handling process, which required constant monitoring of the buffer level. To meet the aim of the study, a CPS was designed and implemented and other technologies such as a collaborative robot. In a similar case, Thoben et al. [21] investigated a gear manufacturer working based on lean production, which is one of the first Industry 4.0 lighthouse projects in Germany. The CPS was established to increase the efficiency of the lean production. As a result, the buffer level was kept low despite high production variation. The delivery to production stations was based on demand-driven milk runs, which led to higher flexibility, a lower buffer level and dynamic scheduling. Load carriers were equipped with sensors that could monitor environmental parameters such as the temperature and acceleration. Operators had a PC to be able to communicate with the CPS to receive information regarding delivery or collection needs in real-time. Other IoT technologies such as auto-ID including RFID and QR codes can play a significant role to control buffer levels and WIP [12,37,38,107]. Trentesaux et al. [72] mentioned the possibility to solve issues such as inventory updates triggered by real-time events controlled in real-time based on service-orientated architecture (SOA) orchestration. In such a system, holons are used to act as an agent or a CPS to induce actions in the physical world.

Hohmann and Posselt [84] highlighted the effect of using CPS for goods registration in goods receiving as it can decrease the required time. To make sure that packages that arrive from suppliers have acceptable quality, vision inspection systems can be used to examine the dimension, shape, positioning and package orientation [61]. A ceiling camera can be used as a route-planning instrument to guide the AGV to transport different parts to different sections of the warehouse [74]. According to Egger and Masood [62], AR has the potential to be used for quality inspection by improving reaction speed and failure investigation. From a logistics perspective, parts may be investigated on the pallet as they arrive at goods receiving. Franceschini et al. [122] developed a prototype to do this task (Egger and Masood, 2020). Al-Jaroodi et al. [63] argued that edge computing can facilitate raw material quality control. Quality investigation data can be constantly communicated with other systems and provide an end-to-end integration amongst the existing systems. To make sure the right product has been received, vision systems can be used to monitor parameters such as dimensions, object ID, supplier ID, etc. [65,66].

To prepare kits for mixed-model assembly through order picking, Egger and Masood [62] mentioned that AR technology can be superior to conventional paper-based methods.

According to Sarupuri et al. [123], AR has the potential to help operators to have better performance in warehouses with high-rack storage [62]. Besides, according to experiments handled by the Fraunhofer Institute for Material Flow and Logistics in Dortmund, Germany, AR has the potential to be used in packaging and palletization [62], as the packaging speed and use of the space are improved [124].

By using 5G, it will be possible to have an efficient infrastructure for a smart storage system as it can accelerate the communication amongst system components [104].

Chen [46] argued that RFID can realize warehouse automation through electronic tags and stackers to manage warehouse scheduling and inventory highly intelligently. As an example, RFID technology can be used to register the incoming and outgoing flow of products into the warehouse environment [49] or to manage the expiration dates of products [51]. Chen et al. [98] highlighted the potential of CPS to support the idea of smart warehouses. According to Damiani et al. [105], AR and VR have the potential to be used to train warehouse operators to increase the quality of operators' interactions with their environment. Chung et al. [50] argued that a block chain has the potential to facilitate distributed, transparent, safe and scalable processes compared to centralized processes. For example, warehouse carry-in, warehouse load and warehouse carry-out processes can benefit from a block chain as the real-time trade transactions data can be analyzed to draw meaningful rules and have efficient decision-making. Culler and Long [74] introduced a smart warehouse project, where vision systems such as Kinect cameras were mounted on an AGV for obstacle avoidance. The main task for the AGV was to transport items within the warehouse environment. Semwal et al. [103] also introduced a CPS-based testbed warehouse where AGVs communicate with racks equipped with embedded boards with sensors. The communication amongst smart entities happens over Wi-Fi. Avventuroso [106] developed a digital twin system based on IoT to mimic warehouse operation. The results have proven that the decision-making process is more efficient. Bortolini et al. [52] argued that use of sensor networks in workstation storage helps to reduce the WIP inventory level as the system can adjust the replenishment request to the central warehouse according to the real-time data collected from the workstation storage. Within a CPS-based material handling system, data mining, predictive analytics and smart algorithms can be used in cloud or edge computing services for warehouse management and supply chain value [63]. Liao et al. [75] proposed a smart factory prototype where delivery orders from the cloud centre are sent to AGV to transport empty product containers from warehouses to production lines for further operation. Each of the product containers is equipped with an RFID tag, which retrieves data for that specific product from a cloud system through IoT. Zhong et al. [44] investigated a case study where RFID was used as a means to support warehouse management. As the warehouse manager finished with the logistics planning, raw materials were identified and prepared for delivery in the warehouse. In the next step, an operator got instructions over a mobile RFID reader to locate the required materials and transport them from the warehouse to machine buffers. The connections happened over an IoT-enabled network. Some other similar cases used RFID/QR codes in warehouse management mentioned in the table above. To manage warehouse operations including material movement, Zhang et al. [110] implemented a cloud-based smart system. Apart from other applications, operators were equipped with various types of handheld terminals such as tablets connected to a "warehouse management software database" through a web service in real-time. As a result, logistics activities were triggered automatically and the data was circulating constantly amongst the warehouse, WMS, managers and operators.

Gregor et al. [125], Lu et al. [89] and Liu et al. [86] highlighted the role of AGVs as they can receive orders and relevant data from the CPS to complete material movement tasks. Wang et al. [91] described a system where an AGV was equipped with an RFID reader to read and write data to the products' RFID tags. Researchers have mentioned the role of mobile robots supplied with real-time data to perform material movement and internal transportation of parts and materials [13,74,87,90,92–94,96,97,102]. Szafir et al. [102] did experiments with drones to locate misplaced boxes in a warehouse environment. Li et al. [60] described how industrial wireless networks along with cloud computing and big data can support smart manufacturing. Part of their work focused on material movement through a conveyor system connected to a cloud server and controlled in real-time for product transportation. Müller et al. [126] highlighted the role of sensor networks to collect real-time information from production, communicate with cyber systems and, after being analyzed by algorithms, transfer it back to physical equipment, in this case a conveyor system. To facilitate the connection with the operators responsible for material handling, devices such as tablets can be used. Tablets are connected to the CPS that collects data in real-time by means of RFID tags [94]. Beside, artificial intelligence application has been highlighted by Lee et al. [127]. Gröhn et al. [101] explored an automated system benefit of RIFD and sensor networks to control the conveyor system to transport materials across a production facility. CPS can be used to facilitate a highly flexible demand-driven material flow through simulation as data collection happens through technologies such as RFID tags and an electronic Kanban system [35]. Liao et al. [75] described a smart factory testbed built by Lego based on holonic manufacturing principles. Each holon has the possibility to make decisions and interact with other holons by having equivalent decision levels. One of the applications of the smart factory testbed in their experiment was autonomous decision-making regarding transportation of empty product containers between working stations.

Pick by vision can be used to indicate the picking location and picking quantities [62]. Smart glasses can be used to pick parts from a shelf as the glass can read the barcode and the operator has free hands to do the picking activities [71]. Costanzo et al. [73]

developed a point cloud environment where a collaborative robot could perform pick and place activities for in-store logistics scenarios with application in warehouses. Liao et al. [75] used a collaborative robot that received data from an IoT-based system equipped with a Raspberry Pi transmitting the destination place. The robot picked the object and placed it into the address received from the Raspberry Pi. In another similar case, Stark et al. [76] discussed the use of a digital twin for pick and place activities handled by robots. A Raspberry Pi was connected to sensors and actuators that communicated with the picking robot over Wi-Fi. Microcontrollers translated the commands for the picking robot. Lee et al. [14] tested a framework built upon an IoT-based WMS aiming to optimize order picking. Ramakrishnan et al. [128] used IoT beacons to manage shopfloor inventory leading to improved order picking. Wang et al. [78] analyzed an AR application in parts picking from storage. The operator received orders, locations and picking quantities through AR. In a case study by Meng et al. [69] in food manufacturing, RFID was used to form an IoT-based system, in which a robot picked raw materials from input crates and placed them inside empty food packages. In another case by Leung et al. [80], a cloud-based database was developed to support e-order consolidation and parts picking from storage. Kembro et al. [65] mentioned that vision systems and image processing can support picking activities by controlling whether the object is removed from its location or not.

3.2. Category 2: Planning and Scheduling-Related Activities

This category includes planning and scheduling-related activities, regarded as those logistics activities that are aimed to guide the overall operation, and make plans and schedules for an efficient production flow. Planning and scheduling of deliveries, layout planning and delivery route planning are some of the examples. As presented in Table 4, each of the technologies has an application in one or several of the PL activities areas. Each of the identified technologies belong to one of the three levels of technologies namely device or component, methods, and systems.

Table 4. Production logistics activities in Category 2 and association with the identified technologies in the literature.

	Production Logistics Activities	Described Technologies		References
Category 2. Planning and scheduling-related activities	Logistics resource planning	• Vision systems and image processing • Digital twin • Big data and BD analytics • Cloud computing • MAS and NEIMS	• CPS • Hadoop • IoT • RFID • Barcode	[10,22,44,48,50,53,55,67, 68,84,85,97,104,107,110, 113,129–131]

Table 4. *Cont.*

Production Logistics Activities	Described Technologies		References
Route planning	<ul><li>Vision systems and image processing</li><li>AGV and mobile robots</li><li>Big data and BD analytics</li><li>Holonic manufacturing</li><li>MAS and NEIMS</li><li>Cloud computing</li><li>Edge computing</li></ul>	<ul><li>CPS</li><li>AI</li><li>Barcode</li><li>IoT</li><li>RFID</li><li>Digital twin</li><li>Sensor networks</li></ul>	[10,12,13,49,61,67,74,83, 84,115,119,129,131–138]
Delivery planning and scheduling	<ul><li>AGV and mobile robots</li><li>Big data and BD analytics</li><li>Digital twin</li><li>Cloud computing</li><li>Tablet, smart phone</li><li>Edge computing</li><li>Holonic manufacturing</li><li>Sensor networks</li><li>MAS and NEIMS</li></ul>	<ul><li>Barcode</li><li>AI</li><li>CPS</li><li>IoS</li><li>IoT</li><li>RFID</li><li>RTLS</li><li>QR code</li><li>Pick by X</li></ul>	[10,15,38–40,44,45,48, 54,63,86,93,98,106,112, 113,115,116,129,132– 135,137,139,140]
Workflow analysis	<ul><li>Vision systems and image processing</li><li>Big data and BD analytics</li><li>Cloud computing</li><li>Machine learning</li><li>Big data and BD analytics</li></ul>	<ul><li>Hadoop</li><li>IoT</li><li>RFID</li><li>Flume</li></ul>	[40,44,53,65,83,85,119]
Modeling and simulation	<ul><li>AGV and mobile robots</li><li>Big data and BD analytics</li><li>Embedded systems</li><li>Digital twin</li></ul>	<ul><li>IoT</li><li>RFID</li><li>AR</li></ul>	[48,72,141]
Layout planning and optimization	<ul><li>Big data and BD analytics</li><li>Simulation</li></ul>	<ul><li>RFID</li><li>VR</li></ul>	[119,142]

Some key examples from Table 4 of how technologies (device/component, methods or systems) were reported to be used in planning and scheduling-related PL activities are described in the following.

Al-Jaroodi et al. [63] argued that by integrating the services of manufacturers, suppliers and transportation systems, it is possible to optimize raw material delivery scheduling. To realize the integration, forming a CPS-based system that collects data from the shopfloor in combination with data analytics techniques is necessary. Chen et al. [98] developed a CPS for circuit breaker production. In their case, multisource heterogeneous data was constantly collected from production lines. From a production logistics perspective, big data analytics can be used to do intelligent material assignment. In a similar case, Zhong et al. [44] proposed using RFID and wireless communication to support big data analytics aimed to have several managerial implications including logistics planning and scheduling. The role of big data analytics also highlighted for PL planning and scheduling has been highlighted within smart factory context [143,144]. Hopkins and Hawking [116] mentioned pick up and delivery window planning as one of the big data analytics applications. Mahroof [115] investigated AI adoption in warehouse management and highlighted the importance of managing flexible planning techniques supporting long-range planning through matching short-term and long-term goals. Ding et al. [48] proposed a digital twin-based CPS for smart manufacturing. Part of their job focused on resource scheduling including logistics. They used an RFID tag, an embedded system device and a travelling pallet that were configured to each part or each batch of parts. As the parts became intelligent, they had the ability to communicate with the surrounding area through connectivity means such as Wi-Fi, Bluetooth and Zigbee. To deal with synchronization of logistics and production caused by high fluctuating demands, Qu et al. [131], Zhang et al. [110] and Hwang et al. [145] used IoT and cloud. Yu [146] developed a system benefit from IoT and GIS and witnessed improvements in logistics planning (adopted from [10]). Zhang et al. [110] proposed a method to improve the synchronization between production and warehouses. The system was built upon IoT and RFID tags and QR tags were used to collect the constant flow of data. Warehouse operators were equipped with tablets as forklift drivers were constantly updated with location information through their tablets. Consequently, any change in the production plan was communicated to the warehouse through IoT. Some other authors such as Zhuang et al. [147], Semunab et al. [139], Qu et al. [134] and Qu et al. [131] also suggested using RFID as a representative of IoT for planning and scheduling related activities. Zhang et al. [133] developed an active sensing system of real-time and multisource manufacturing information. Part of the architecture of the system was dedicated to material delivery. In the system, RFID and sensor networks had a central role and communication benefitted from a wireless connection. Kamagaew et al. [148] discussed the role of MAS in delivery planning using 50 different unmanned vehicles in a research project. The vehicles autonomously sought for their tasks and moved in the research hall. The system capacity adjusted depending on seasonal fluctuations as agents were capable of communicating with each other and other systems that controlled the planning and scheduling (adopted from [135]). A similar case regarding a MAS application for planning and scheduling was highlighted by Leusin et al. [140]. Sicari et al. [54] did an IoT-based case study for smart transport logistics where smart vehicles in combination with RFID tags and RFID scanners were used to complete the material ordering process within a warehouse environment. Node-RED was used to manage the ordering data flow, warehouse data flow, RFID scanner data flow and smart vehicle data flow.

Regarding resource planning, according to Chung et al. [50], cognitive manufacturing requires IoT technology to collect data and technologies such as Hadoop to analyze big data collected from multiple sources. Accordingly, one of the main goals of such a system is to minimize the human resource utilization rate. Da Silva et al. [97] highlighted the role of big data in resource planning. In addition to other technologies mentioned in Table 3, Zhang et al. [129] and Trappey et al. [53] discussed cloud computing as one of the main enablers for effective resource planning as data is updated and available in real-time.

As described by Frank et al. [28] adopted from Gilchrist [149], AI in combination with an ERP system can be used to predict long-term production demands and transform them to daily production orders. As a result, the raw material order volume will be more precise.

Using auto-ID technologies such as RFID in production lines can help to have a more accurate demand assessment. Besides, Kanban bins might be equipped with sensors capable of tracking fill rates. This can form a CPS, which at the end helps to have an effective material ordering system [34,150]. Dai et al. [49] highlighted the role of big data in material ordering as a large amount of data collected from the shopfloor may be used to analyze the consumption rate and predict the order point.

According to Cui et al. [141] a digital twin can play a central role to simulate the logistical processes in order to provide real-time bidirectional management between a physical object and its digital twin. Ding et al. [48] mentioned that a digital twin can help to optimize resource allocation and relevant planning in manufacturing processes including PL.

Cao et al. [12] adopted from Kim et al., [151], Dai et al. [49] and Zhang et al. [96] proposed methods for route planning and navigation by employing RFID technology. Position data from the shopfloor was collected in real-time and facilitated route planning and traffic management in a shopfloor environment. To transport parts, materials and machines, different means such as automated driving technology were already in use in production areas. Zhang et al. [129] suggested the use of AGVs that navigate based on machine learning techniques. Similar to this, Wan et al. [13] and Qu et al. [134] highlighted the role of using intelligent AGVs for route planning and logistics navigation. According to Winkelhaus and Grosse [10], Yang et al. [152] developed an architecture of a cloud platform for intelligent logistics management including logistics navigation. Mahroof [115] investigated the role of AI in warehouse management and route planning within a warehouse environment by controlling the amount of travel time in the warehouse. Zhang et al. [96] described a system consisting of several AGVs communicating via RFID and a ZigBee network to perform route planning and collision avoidance.

According to Trappey et al. [153], IoT can have a significant role in logistics workflow analyses by employing related technologies such as RFID, WSN and cloud computing bases for data collected in real-time. Huang et al. [83] argued that deploying IoT technology increases visibility and traceability in production processes. Data collected from the shopfloor can be used to have precise bottleneck prediction and further helps to have proactive dispatching based on the future bottleneck. Zhong et al. [44] introduced big data analytics for physical internet-based logistics data from a smart shopfloor equipped with RFID tags and wireless communication networks. The logistics trajectory was visualized through big data analytics aiming to evaluate the efficiency of logistics operators and operations through the defined behaviors and KPIs. The evaluation results could be used as managerial guidance for efficient decision-making.

According to Huang et al. [83], by analyzing RFID logistics data through a big data approach, logistics trajectories can be discovered for shopfloor layout optimization. Turner et al. [142] reviewed the possibility of using discrete event simulation (DES) and virtual reality in industry. In this respect, one of the areas was layout optimization, which had the potential to be investigated further to benefit from DES and VR technology.

3.3. Category 3: Control, Track and Trace-Related Activities

This category includes control, track and trace-related activities, mainly focused on activities that monitor the behavior of logistics system elements such as resources, goods movement and inventory level. These activities control whether the operation is following the plans and schedules in a reactive manner and has the possibility to be done proactively to help the system to adjust its behavior in line with the latest changes. As presented in Table 5, each of the technologies has an application in one or several of the PL activities areas. Each of the identified technologies belong to one of the three levels of technologies namely the device or component, methods and systems.

Table 5. Production logistics activities in Category 3 and association with the identified technologies in the literature.

	Production Logistics Activities	Described Technologies		References
Category 3. Control, track and trace related activities	Items identification	• Vision system and image processing • AGV and mobile robots • Sensor networks • Big data and BD analytics • Cloud computing • Edge computing • Embedded system • FOT and tag-free traceability	• CPS • QR code • IoT RFID • Barcode • Digital twin	[12,14,15,19,27,37,43,46–49,52,54,58,65,67,69,75,84,90,91,98,104,107,109,119–121,131,132,140,154–161]
	Items positioning (localization)	• Vision system and image processing • AGV and mobile robots • Big data and BD analytics • Edge computing • Cloud computing • Cellular networks • Ultrasound • Ultra-wideband • Embedded systems • Sensor networks • Bluetooth	• Barcode • CPS • Digital twin • GPS • 5G • Wi-Fi • Zigbee • IoT • RFID • RTLS • QR code	[10,12,15,19,37,43,46,48,54,58,64,67,69,72,74,75,82–84,86,89,98,104,107,109,111,114,119,121,132,140,141,150,159,161–166]
	Items tracing (flow)	• Vision system and image processing • Block chain • AGV and mobile robots • Big data and BD analytics • Cloud computing • Edge computing • Networks and communication networks • Embedded systems • FOT and tag-free traceability • Sensor networks • Simulation • Cellular networks • Wireless connection	• Barcode • CPS • Digital twin • Hadoop • Wi-Fi • Zigbee • IoT • RFID • QR code • Pick by X • 5G • Bluetooth	[5,10,12,14,15,19,27,34,43,45,46,48,49,51,53,56,58,64,65,67–69,72,74,76,82,83,98,104,107,109,111,119–121,134,139–141,154–158,160,163,165–172]

Table 5. Cont.

Production Logistics Activities	Described Technologies		References
Inventory level controlling	<ul><li>Vision systems and image processing</li><li>Block chain</li><li>AGV and mobile robots</li><li>Big data and BD analytics</li><li>Cloud computing</li><li>Sensor networks</li><li>MAS and NEIMS</li><li>Simulation</li><li>Machine learning</li></ul>	<ul><li>Barcode</li><li>CPS</li><li>Digital twin</li><li>AI</li><li>IoT</li><li>RFID</li><li>SoA</li><li>Pick by X</li></ul>	[10,12,14,15,27,34,38,41, 49–52,54,56,57,59,67,72, 76,97–99,104,109,115, 116,119,121,139,141,155, 156,161,173–177]
Items condition monitoring	<ul><li>Vision system and image processing</li><li>Big data and BD analytics</li><li>Sensor networks</li></ul>	<ul><li>RFID</li><li>IoT</li></ul>	[53–55,67,70,121,170]

Some key examples from Table 5 of how technologies (device/component, methods or systems) were reported to be used in control, track and trace related activities PL activities are described in the following.

To monitor items' conditions such as temperature, humidity, vibration, etc., several technologies have been mentioned by researchers. According to Zhang et al. [70], RFID biosensor tags can be used for history checking, contamination warnings and status tracking. The biosensor tags monitor antigens–antibodies to detect bacteria. Similar cases to monitor environmental parameters by means of RFID sensors were reported by [54,67,121]. Tao and Qi [55] mentioned that by using smart chips, environmental data can be collected and uploaded to the cyber world. With big data, the cyber section can analyze any changes in product conditions. La Scalia et al. [170] proposed a system to use smart sensors to monitor the temperature, humidity, CO_2 and volatile organic compounds (VOCs). Apart from the sensors, cloud computing and GPS are other technologies that support real-time condition monitoring of perishable products. Trappey et al. [53] mentioned that WSN can be used in cold-chain logistics to monitor brightness, humidity, temperature, pressure and sound.

For items identification, items positioning and items tracing, one of the most cited technologies is RFID, as the references listed in Table 3. In some cases, RFID has been regarded as part of IoT and CPS technologies since it creates most of its value through connections with other logistics systems such as ERP, WMS, etc. [14,84,109,119]. Lai et al. [166] mentioned that many researchers have worked on finding accurate object location within an indoor environment with the help of different interfaces including Wi-Fi, Bluetooth, ZigBee, UWB, ultrasound, etc., and RFID as one of the main technologies. As mentioned by Zhang et al. [70], RFID can be a subsystem for technologies like block chains. Block chain implementation assists factories, distribution centers and retailers to trace their items from the very beginning until the final stages. Cui et al. [141] did a literature review and the results showed that almost 25% of big data applications concern monitoring. Cloud computing and sensor networks are two main technologies discussed by Mehmood et al. [58], as they can enable machine-to-machine communication amongst logistics equipment and machines. The communication amongst different machines and systems relies on cellular networks to facilitate mobility. Wigger et al. [157] investigated the possibility of tracing and identification of printed circuit boards (PCB) through fingerprint-of-things (FOT), in this case surface pattern photography. Fiducial markers would be soldered onto 115 PCBs by solder paste screen printing. Each soldered PCB would have unique identification. Using image processing technology, each of the PCBs would be uniquely tracked and identified. Similar cases have been reported for other materials such as paper, plastic, cork and metal [158]. Meroni et al. [155] designed an IoT-based monitoring platform to improve multipart business process monitoring. To meet the goal of their research, smart objects were used to share processed data in real-time. Objects equipped with smart sensors interacted via usual communication means such as Wi-Fi and 4G. The communication amongst smart objects followed the MQTT protocol suitable for a low bandwidth and resource constraint environment. Zhong et al. [107] used laser scanner and image processing technologies in addition to RFID. RFID tags helped to identify the objects and the laser scanner was used to observe the movement of resources in the production area. Kembro et al. [65] also highlighted the role of vision systems for object identification and visual goods tracking. In addition to the benefits of CPS to trace items, it is important to have reliable and near real-time communication technologies such as 5G. The reason is that current industrial standards have limited capacity to support constant streaming of large amounts of captured data such as videos [163,178]. Cannizzaro et al. [162] mentioned Wi-Fi and Bluetooth Low Energy (BLE) as technologies that facilitate indoor positioning. In line with their argument, implementing Wi-Fi requires effort in terms of topological distribution and the number of Wi-Fi access points, which increase costs and power consumption. On the other hand, BLE is suitable for short-range energy-efficient communication and compatible devices can transmit periodic messages. Chen et al. [98] proposed a CPS framework for smart manufacturing. The system benefits from AGVs, sensor networks and IoT technologies for production logistics activities. The AGV and RFID tags constantly update the digital twin with positioning and identification data. Data are transmitted over a cloud and shared with other subsystems in real-time.

4. Discussion

The identified technologies and their association with major PL activities are presented in Section 3. However, in order to further elaborate on RQ2, it is needed to determine on what level each of the technology groups are associated with PL activities categories. Besides, value creation as the main concern of any technological development need to be further analyzed. The following describes these concerns in more details.

4.1. Share Assessment of the Identified Technologies

Considering the technology grouping presented in Table 2, Figure 4 illustrates the share of each technology group within each PL activities category discussed in the literature. For instance, in 21% of the cases, "Auto Identification" technologies was mentioned as the data-driven enabling technology that has an application in production logistics.

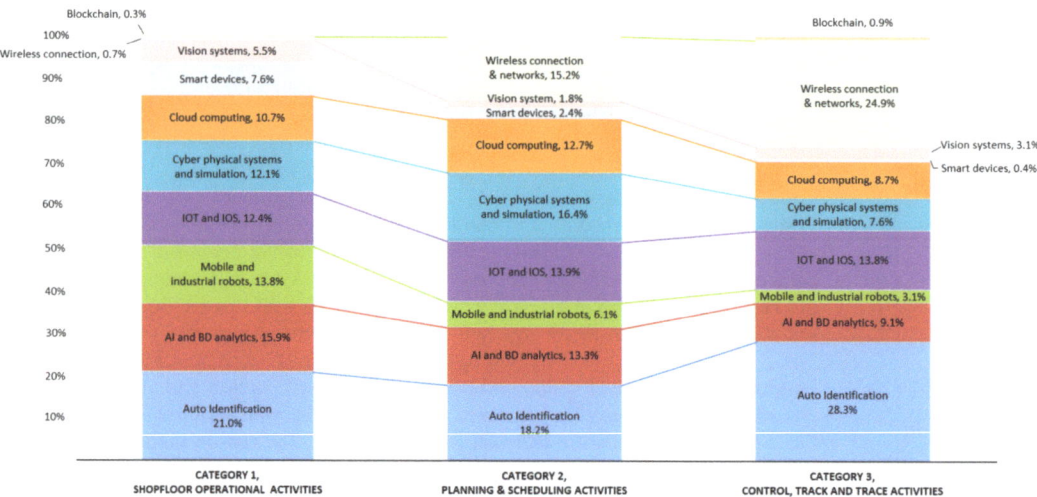

Figure 4. Share of the identified technologies supporting production logistics (PL) activities.

In the literature, autoidentification technologies have the highest share among the technologies for all three categories. Auto-id technologies have the most hits for category 3 in the literature, with 28% of articles on category 3 describing Auto-id solutions. In many cases auto identification technologies are mentioned alongside other types of technologies such as IoT or mobile robots in order to support a working process like material ordering. For category 2 and 3, much of the literature mentioned the importance of using technologies such as RFID as the preferred data collection method to perform activities such as real-time tracking, delivery planning and items historical condition monitoring. In some cases, auto-id technologies are part of a bigger technological system such as the block chain. Nevertheless, the literature review suggests that auto-id technologies can be applied either as a stand-alone technology or as a subsection of a bigger solution such as IoT or CPS. This explains why it was noticed so often in the literature.

Cyber-physical systems received more attention in the literature to perform planning and scheduling related activities (category 2) compared with the two other categories. For category 1, the share of CPS is 12% and one of the purposes of using this technology is to increase efficiency on the shopfloor as stated in Section 3. Even though the number of use cases for CPS in category 2 is less, there are evidences of creating value for PL systems through integrating CPS with other information systems such as ERP and WMS. In addition, CPS is mentioned as one of the main enabler of a smart factory concept including smart warehouse and smart material handling.

As tracking and tracing activities require constant monitoring of the moving items across production facilities, the role of wireless technologies become more obvious, as pointed out in Figure 4. The same argument is true for planning related activities in category 2. For category 1, the role of wireless connection technologies are less mentioned by the literature despite the fact that an effective connectivity has a fundamental role in a well-established data-driven system.

IoT and IoS (Internet of Services) related technologies appeared with almost the same frequency for all three categories. Dealing with the synchronization issue between manufacturing and internal logistics is one of the main use cases mentioned for IoT/IoS. In addition, in line with cases from Section 3, constant connectivity of PL instruments facilitates optimization of the material flow and work flow analysis.

For shopfloor operational activities, AI and big data (BD) analytics are mentioned more often compared with the two other categories. As stated in Section 3, cases related to decision-making have been reported for AI and data analytics in shopfloor activities. As a result, those activities that require real-time feedback from the cyber space can benefit from AI related techniques to address the issues in an optimal manner. For planning purposes such as warehouse management, AI and BD have shown great potential according to the literature stated in Section 3. One of the prerequisites of resource planning is to analyze data from multiple sources. According to the findings, BD analytics has the potential to address this issue. To complete the tracking activities in category 3, literature suggests using AI alongside vision systems or sensor networks.

Cloud computing is mentioned more often for planning and scheduling related activities compared with the two other categories. Cloud computing technologies are mentioned in the literature together with other technologies such as smart devices. This is mainly to assure constant data availability. Cloud computing support activities such as condition monitoring, internal navigation, resource planning and machine-to-machine communication.

To deal with the physical movement of items across the production facilities and dealing with stationary activities such as packaging and palletization, mobile robots and industrial robots are mentioned more in category 1. In fact, AGVs, industrial robots and drones are mentioned very few times in the two other categories.

Using smart devices in shopfloor operation has more hits in the literature as it involves physical material flow operation. In fact, the number of cases for controlling and tracking are few, with the exception of some described cases in planning related activities.

Vision systems and image processing has more appearance in shopfloor operational related activities as it can support activities such as quality control and navigation. It has even use cases for tracking items movement. Limited applications were mentioned for planning and scheduling by using smart cameras to inventory control.

Block chain technology is mentioned in the literature with a limited number mainly in conditions where several actors play a role across the supply chain. Tracking and tracing items and managing inventories are some examples.

4.2. The Role of Data Life Cycle in Value Creation

Each of the aforementioned technologies contribute to do one or several steps of acquiring, transferring, storing, analyzing or visualizing data [11]. Considering the data applications presented in Section 3, just collecting data from the shopfloor will not be enough to create value for the PL system. In order to create value for PL systems, it is important that the collected data from data sources, follow the data life cycle presented in Figure 5. As illustrated, the identified technologies support the value creation process by contributing to one or several steps of the presented data life cycle.

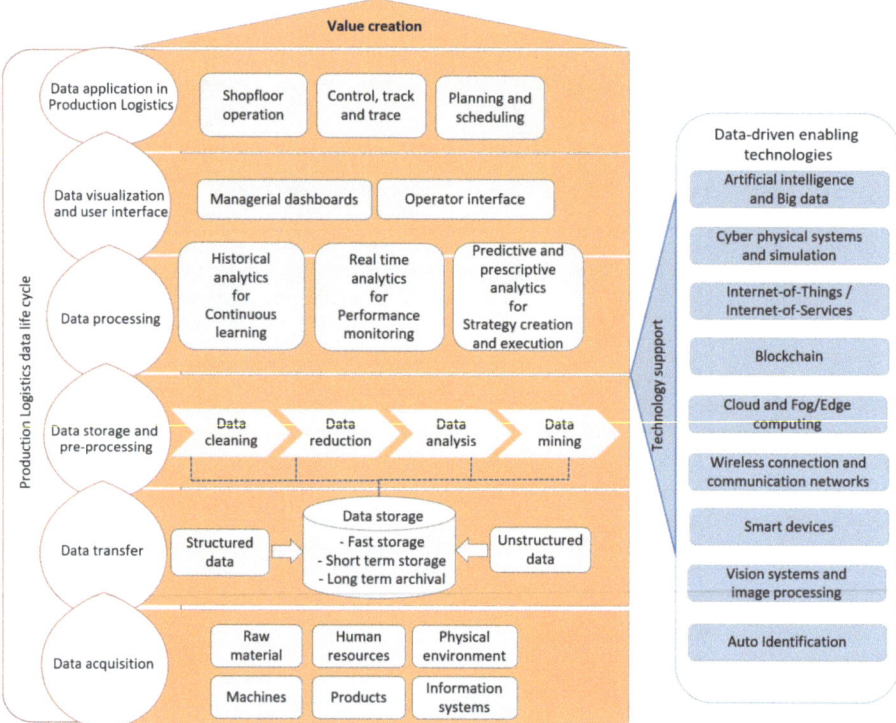

Figure 5. Data life cycle in production logistics adopted from [5,49,116].

There are several data sources such as raw material, products, machines, human resources, physical environment such as buildings and existing IT systems such as enterprise systems and information systems. Any technology such as auto-id, vision systems, robots and sensor networks can be used to collect data [65,91,118,170]. To transfer the collected data, cellular networks and wireless connections can be used [104]. As the volume of data is significantly large, data needs to be stored for further use. Before storing the data, it is necessary to process the collected data, as there might exist redundancy, duplications and noise, and generally raw data might be of low quality. Typically, the data preprocessing includes data cleaning, data integration and data compression [49].

For data storage, there are different possibilities including conventional database technologies and new approaches such as cloud services. Cloud services have the potential to provide a flexible, cost-efficient solution [110]. The data can be stored either as structured (digits, symbols and tables) or unstructured (video, audio, etc.) [5]. In order to use the value of the data, the massive amount of data needs to be reduced in to ordered, meaningful and simplified data [179]. Real-time analytics help to monitor the performance of the system in real-time and align the operation with strategic goals and targets. Predictive and prescriptive analytics support planning, forecasting and simulation for envisioning and execution of strategies [116]. The results support production logistics activities to create value for the production process.

The processed data will be visualized through managerial dashboards or operators' interface will be used for other systems such as enterprise resource planning (ERP) or warehouse management systems (WMS). The visualized data on managerial dashboards and operator interface can support decision-making processes or work instructions [94].

4.3. PL Activities Correlation Assessment for Value Creation

As presented in Section 3, there are three categories for PL activities. In order to complete the data life cycle and create value, all these three categories have to be linked to each other by means of data transferring technologies as shown in Figure 6. Three categories of PL activities are linked with their data-driven enabling technologies. In the centre of the picture, the connectivity technologies transfer the collected or analyzed data through the PL system. Cloud data center store data and solutions such as edge computing can be used to perform near device computations. Those data that require longer storage will be stored in the cloud data centre.

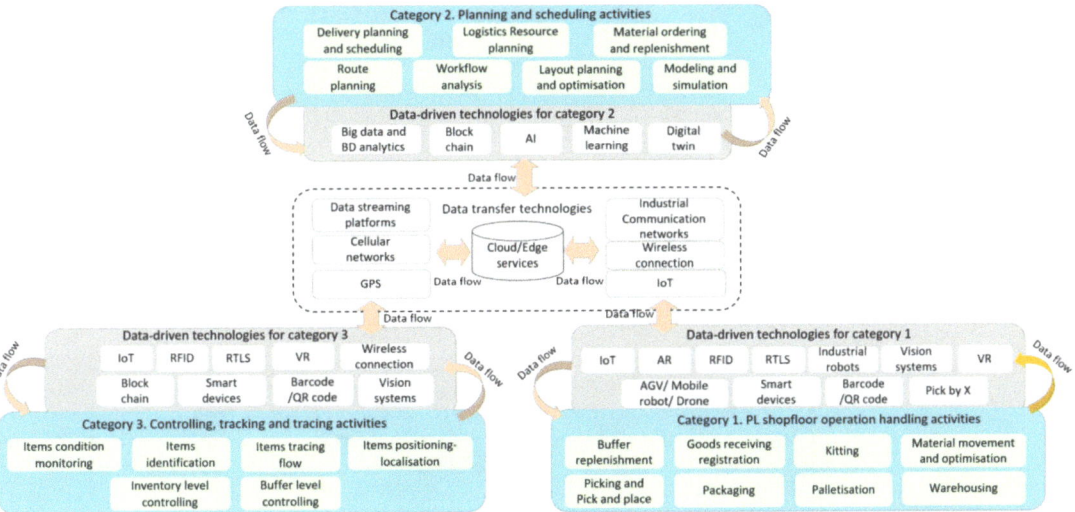

Figure 6. The correlation between three categories of PL activities and their respective data-driven technologies.

In the operational-related activities category, data acquisition and data visualization technologies support activities such as picking, packaging, warehousing, etc. Data is captured from these activities to follow the data life cycle steps and will come back to the shopfloor in the form of work instructions and decision-making support visualized by means of a human–machine interface (HMI) such as pick by vision. If the activities are automated, the machines or robots will receive instructions or decision-making support such as real-time coordinates for AGV navigation. As the operations move on, these activities need to be monitored to make sure they are in line with the operational targets. Technologies such as RFID, virtual reality (VR) and vision systems play an important role in monitoring. Tracing and tracking the operation is heavily dependent on data transferring technologies such as IoT, wireless networks and cellular networks.

The stability of networks is necessary to make sure data is produced and consumed at the right time. Otherwise, data will have less value for the operation. To have an efficient PL system, in addition to having a long-term plan and strategy, it is essential to have a dynamic planning system to be able to cope with the latest changes occurring on the shopfloor. This will not happen unless there are strong data analysis tools and techniques that can analyze historical and real-time data. Big data, block chain and AI are some examples of these technologies. Dynamic delivery planning, dynamic route planning and dynamic logistics resource planning are some examples of the activities that require real-time data. Layout planning, modeling and simulation, and workflow analysis are examples of activities that need historical information. The data produced by each of these three categories needs to be transferred through technologies such as industrial wireless networks, wireless connections, cellular networks and enterprise service bus (ESB). To store the data, cloud services can provide a flexible and cost-effective solution as the data will be available with no physical restrictions. The data is available to all other activities and all stakeholders can access the required data at any time.

In order to have a balanced data-driven PL system, it is imperative that each of the three PL categories receives consistent support from the enabling technologies. Data quality needs to be secured in all the data life cycle stages, from data acquisition to data visualization and user interface. It is reasonable to argue that data availability should be the main concern for a data-driven system.

As a result, all the means and technologies should have a high level of reliability, which indicates any technology introduction requires thorough consideration. The enabling technologies should be developed and implemented in a homogenous manner, aiming to create a balanced system supporting data flow across the system. Considering the importance of system reliability and data availability, partial investment in enabling technologies will not be sufficient. Consequently, regardless of the type of technology, a systematic approach towards PL development is a prerequisite to meeting data-driven manufacturing and autonomous supply chains. This result has importance for PL system owners, as they should pose clear requirements towards technology developers to deliver a reliable, robust and homogenous system. Besides, long-term targets should be favored over short-term outcomes in organizational strategies.

The number of industrial implementation for some of the technologies is few in comparison with older technologies such as RFID. For example, there is little empirical evidence from implementing technologies within data storage, data processing, and data visualization. Most of the work is in the preparatory or theoretical level.

The variety of technologies in data acquisition is relatively high compared to other data life cycle stages. High variation in data collection challenges other steps in the data life cycle as having so many data sources and data formats requires considerable effort to complete the life cycle and create value. In addition, the technologies maturity level is inhomogeneous. Technologies related to data acquisition and data transfer have a longer implementation history compared to technologies in data storage, data processing and data visualization. Companies who wish to invest on technologies should be aware of the fact that, those new technologies might suffer from immaturity. As an example, AI, Big Data analytics, block chain and machine learning are constantly evolving compare to some other technologies such as RFID and Barcode. This can cause compatibility issues as some of the older technologies might be obsolete and new technologies might have integration problems with legacy systems. As a result, having a long-term perspective in technology assessment is inevitable.

5. Conclusions and Future Research

In this paper, data-driven PL enabling technologies and their use cases were presented based on a SLR through reviewing 142 journal articles, and their association with PL activities were discussed. Production logistics activities were divided into three main categories including shopfloor activities, planning and scheduling activities, and controlling, tracking and tracing activities. The identified technologies were grouped in to 10 types and for each PL activity category, the share of technologies assessed accordingly. The result helps researchers and business owners to have a more precise picture on how technologies are mentioned in the literature for PL activities from a system perspective. This helps to build a ground to transit towards a data-driven state by knowing the applications and use cases described in the literature for the technologies.

In addition, it is discussed how the identified technologies can contribute to value creation from a holistic perspective. The production logistics data life cycle is presented and different steps within the life cycle is described. As discussed in Section 4, performing data collection, data transfer, data storage, data analysis and data visualization should happen as a chain in order to create business value for the production logistics system. Simply collecting or storing data does not lead to value creation.

It is argued that employing a data-driven approach in PL requires balanced long-term attention to technological enablers as the maturity level of existing technologies are inhomogeneous. Some of the technologies might become obsolete over time and some others are evolving and will have wider applications such as data analytics. This needs to be considered in technology assessment processes. In line with Figure 6, there are several technologies that are associated with PL activities categories. Even though data transfer technologies have no direct value-creation for PL, their stability is of great importance to have a sustainable data-driven system.

This research has contributed to both academia and industry in the following ways. Several activities within production logistics are presented with respect to those technologies that help to adopt a data-driven approach for manufacturing and autonomous supply chains. Categorizing the PL activities is also helping the researchers to have a more comprehensive perspective regarding technology assessment. This research has provided the opportunity to have a wider look onto the digitalization journey for companies by presenting the "big picture" while identifying technologies and their application in data-driven PL. From a value creation perspective, the importance of having a long-term perspective and balanced development are discussed. This will help decision makers for any future investments.

Following points are suggested for future research:

- This study did not investigate the impact of each technology on PL system performance. Thus, for future research, it is suggested to study and measure how system performance can be affected after the PL system is transited towards a data-driven state. The outcome of this paper is beneficial to suggest technologies enabling the transition towards a data-driven state. In particular and considering Figure 6, those technologies related to PL planning and scheduling have a shorter history of implementation compared to the two other categories. As a result, it is hard to judge the efficiency of the technologies in the planning and scheduling category within different industrial situations. It is therefore interesting for future research to examine the efficiency and implementation feasibility of technologies related to planning and scheduling from a production logistics perspective.
- Even though this study has discussed the supporting role of identified technologies to complete the data-life cycle and value creation, still, the corresponding role of each technology in each phase of data-life cycle needs further investigation. By performing such a study in future, it will be clear which areas need more attention from a technology developers' perspective.
- This study carried out a quantitative assessment on technology share for PL activity categories. Thus, it will be interesting to investigate which of these use cases has been already proven and are feasible for implementation and which technologies require further approval. This can be significant to recognize the challenges ahead of a digitalization transition.

Author Contributions: Conceptualization, M.W., J.B.H. and M.Z.; methodology, M.Z., M.W., J.B.H.; validation, M.W., J.B.H. and M.Z.; formal analysis, M.Z., M.W., J.B.H.; data curation, M.Z.; writing—original draft preparation, M.Z.; writing—review and editing, M.W., J.B.H.; visualization, M.Z.; supervision, M.W., J.B.H.; funding acquisition, M.W., J.B.H. All authors have read and agreed to the published version of the manuscript.

Funding: This research was funded by Vinnova and Produktion2030 for the project DigiLog—digital and physical testbed for logistic operations in production, reference number 2017-04778.

Institutional Review Board Statement: Not applicable.

Informed Consent Statement: Not applicable.

Data Availability Statement: The data presented in this study are already presented in this manuscript.

Acknowledgments: The authors would like to acknowledge the financial support of Vinnova and Produktion2030 for the project DigiLog—digital and physical testbed for logistic operations in production.

Conflicts of Interest: The authors declare no conflict of interest. The funders had no role in the design of the study; in the collection, analyses, or interpretation of data; in the writing of the manuscript, or in the decision to publish the results.

References

1. Cámara, S.B.; Fuentes, J.M.; Marín, J.M.M. Cloud computing, Web 2.0, and operational performance. *Mediat. Role Supply Chain Integr.* **2015**, *26*, 3.
2. Novais, L.; Marín, J.M.M.; Moyano-Fuentes, J. Lean Production implementation, Cloud-Supported Logistics and Supply Chain Integration: Interrelationships and effects on business performance. *Int. J. Logist. Manag.* **2020**, *31*, 629–663. [CrossRef]
3. Barreto, L.; Amaral, A.; Pereira, T. Industry 4.0 implications in logistics: An overview. *Procedia Manuf.* **2017**, *13*, 1245–1252. [CrossRef]
4. Treiblmaier, H.; Mirkovski, K.; Lowry, P.B.; Zacharia, Z.G. The physical internet as a new supply chain paradigm: A systematic literature review and a comprehensive framework. *Int. J. Logist. Manag.* **2020**, *31*, 239–287. [CrossRef]
5. Tao, F.; Qi, Q.; Liu, A.; Kusiak, A. Data-driven smart manufacturing. *J. Manuf. Syst.* **2018**, *48*, 157–169. [CrossRef]
6. Nitsche, B. Unravelling the Complexity of Supply Chain Volatility Management. *Logistics* **2018**, *2*, 14. [CrossRef]
7. Horňáková, N.; Jurík, L.; Chovanová, H.H.; Cagáňová, D.; Babčanová, D. AHP method application in selection of appropriate material handling equipment in selected industrial enterprise. *Wirel. Netw.* **2019**, 1–9. [CrossRef]
8. Davich, T. Material Handling Solutions: A Look into Automated Robotics. Resource Document. 2010. Available online: https://tctest.wiscweb.wisc.edu/wp-content/uploads/sites/142/2017/04/Davich2010.pdf (accessed on 6 April 2021).
9. Kang, H.S.; Lee, J.Y.; Choi, S.; Kim, H.; Park, J.H.; Son, J.Y.; Kim, B.H.; Noh, S.D. Smart manufacturing: Past research, present findings, and future directions. *Int. J. Precis. Eng. Manuf. Technol.* **2016**, *3*, 111–128. [CrossRef]
10. Winkelhaus, S.; Grosse, E.H. Logistics 4.0: A systematic review towards a new logistics system. *Int. J. Prod. Res.* **2020**, *58*, 18–43. [CrossRef]
11. Klingenberg, C.O.; Borges, M.A.V.; Antunes, J.A.V., Jr. Industry 4.0 as a data-driven paradigm: A systematic literature review on technologies. *J. Manuf. Technol. Manag.* **2019**. Ahead of Publication. [CrossRef]
12. Cao, W.; Jiang, P.; Lu, P.; Liu, B. Real-time data-driven monitoring in job-shop floor based on radio frequency identification. *Int. J. Adv. Manuf. Technol.* **2017**, *92*, 2120–2357. [CrossRef]
13. Wan, J.; Tang, S.; Hua, Q.; Li, D.; Liu, C.; Lloret, J. Context-Aware Cloud Robotics for Material Handling in Cognitive Industrial Internet of Things. *IEEE Internet Things J.* **2017**, *5*, 2272–2281. [CrossRef]
14. Lee, C.; Lv, Y.; Ng, K.; Ho, W.; Choy, K. Design and application of Internet of things-based warehouse management system for smart logistics. *Int. J. Prod. Res.* **2018**, *56*, 2753–2768. [CrossRef]
15. Ghobakhloo, M. Determinants of information and digital technology implementation for smart manufacturing. *Int. J. Prod. Res.* **2020**, *58*, 2384–2405. [CrossRef]
16. Alcácer, V.; Cruz-Machado, V. Scanning the Industry 4.0: A Literature Review on Technologies for Manufacturing Systems. *Eng. Sci. Technol. Int. J.* **2019**, *22*, 899–919. [CrossRef]
17. Lagorio, A.; Zenezini, G.; Mangano, G.; Pinto, R. A systematic literature review of innovative technologies adopted in logistics management in logistics management. *Int. J. Logist. Res. Appl.* **2020**. [CrossRef]
18. Martinez, S.; Astrid, J. Evaluation of the Feasibility of Implementing Industry 4.0 Technologies in the Intralogistic Processes of the Logistics Operators of the Department of the Atlantic, a Look Towards the Continuous Improvement of Organizational Efficiency. In *Data Analysis and Optimization for Engineering and Computing Problems*; Vasant, P., Litvinchev, I., Marmolejo-Saucedo, J.A., Rodriguez-Aguilar, R., Martinez-Rios, F., Eds.; Springer International Publishing: Berlin/Heidelberg, Germany, 2020.
19. Mittal, S.; Khan, M.A.; Romero, D.; Wuest, T. Smart manufacturing: Characteristics, technologies and enabling factors. *Proc. Inst. Mech. Eng. Part B J. Eng. Manuf.* **2019**, *233*, 1342–1361. [CrossRef]
20. Oztemel, E.; Gursev, S. Literature review of Industry 4.0 and related technologies. *J. Intell. Manuf.* **2020**, *31*, 127–182. [CrossRef]
21. Thoben, K.D.; Wiesner, S.A.; Wuest, T. 'Industrie 4.0' and smart manufacturing-a review of research issues and application examples. *Int. J. Autom. Technol.* **2017**, *11*, 4–16. [CrossRef]
22. Chien, C.-F.; Hong, T.-Y.; Guo, H.-Z. An empirical study for smart production for TFT-LCD to empower Industry 3.5. *J. Chin. Inst. Eng.* **2017**, *40*, 552–561. [CrossRef]
23. Lin, K.C.; Shyu, J.Z.; Ding, K. A Cross-Strait Comparison of Innovation Policy under Industry 4.0 and Sustainability Development Transition. *Sustainability* **2017**, *9*, 786. [CrossRef]
24. Chiarello, F.; Trivelli, L.; Bonaccorsi, A.; Fantoni, G. Extracting and mapping industry 4.0 technologies using wikipedia. *Comput. Ind.* **2018**, *100*, 244–257. [CrossRef]
25. Chavez, R.; Yu, W.; Jacobs, M.A.; Feng, M. Data-driven supply chains, manufacturing capability and customer satisfaction. *Prod. Plan. Control* **2017**, *28*, 906–918. [CrossRef]
26. Rossit, D.A.; Tohmé, F.; Frutos, M. A data-driven scheduling approach to smart manufacturing. *J. Ind. Inf. Integr.* **2019**, *15*, 69–79. [CrossRef]

27. Woo, J.; Shin, S.-J.; Seo, W.; Meilanitasari, P. Developing a big data analytics platform for manufacturing systems: Architecture, method, and implementation. *Int. J. Adv. Manuf. Technol.* **2018**, *99*, 2193–2217. [CrossRef]
28. Frank, A.G.; Dalenogare, L.S.; Ayala, N.F. Industry 4.0 technologies: Implementation patterns in manufacturing companies. *Int. J. Prod. Econ.* **2019**, *210*, 15–26. [CrossRef]
29. Ghobakhloo, M.; Ching, N.T. Adoption of digital technologies of smart manufacturing in SMEs. *J. Ind. Inf. Integr.* **2019**, *16*, 100107. [CrossRef]
30. Strandhagen, J.W.; Alfnes, E.; Vallandingham, L.R. The fit of Industry 4.0 applications in manufacturing logistics: A multiple case study. *Adv. Manuf.* **2017**, *5*, 344–358. [CrossRef]
31. Nagy, G.; Illés, B.; Bányai, Á. Impact of Industry 4.0 on production logistics. *IOP Conf. Series: Mater. Sci. Eng.* **2018**, *448*, 012013. [CrossRef]
32. Collins Dictionary. 2020. Available online: https://www.collinsdictionary.com/dictionary/english/technology#:~{}:text=Technologyreferstomethods%2Csystems (accessed on 1 June 2020).
33. Thorpe, R.; Holt, R.; Macpherson, A.; Pittaway, L. Using Knowledge within Small and Medium-sized Firms: A Systematic Review of the Evidence. *Int. J. Manag. Rev.* **2005**, *4*, 257–281. [CrossRef]
34. Tranfield, D.; Denyer, D.; Smart, P. Towards a Methodology for Developing Evidence-Informed Management Knowledge by Means of Systematic Review. *Br. J. Manag.* **2003**, *14*, 207–222. [CrossRef]
35. Hofmann, E.; Rüsch, M. Industry 4.0 and the current status as well as future prospects on logistics. *Comput. Ind.* **2017**, *89*, 23–34. [CrossRef]
36. Eklund, J.; Palm, K.; Bergman, A.; Rosenblad, C.; Aronsson, G. Work environment of the future—Trends, digitalization and employment forms: Three systematic reviews. Available online: https://sawee.se/publications/work-environment-of-the-future-trends-digitalization-and-employment-forms/ (accessed on 6 April 2021).
37. Park, K.T.; Nam, Y.W.; Lee, H.S.; Im, S.J.; Noh, S.D.; Son, J.Y.; Kim, H. Design and implementation of a digital twin application for a connected micro smart factory. *Int. J. Comput. Integr. Manuf.* **2019**, *32*, 596–614. [CrossRef]
38. Ren, S.; Zhao, X.; Huang, B.; Wang, Z.; Song, X. A framework for shopfloor material delivery based on real-time manufacturing big data. *J. Ambient. Intell. Humaniz. Comput.* **2018**, *10*, 1093–1108. [CrossRef]
39. Sanders, A.; Elangeswaran, C.; Wulfsberg, J. Industry 4.0 implies lean manufacturing: Research activities in industry 4.0 function as enablers for lean manufacturing. *J. Ind. Eng. Manag.* **2016**, *9*, 811–833. [CrossRef]
40. Wang, S.; Zhang, C.; Liu, C.; Li, D.; Tang, H. Cloud-assisted interaction and negotiation of industrial robots for the smart factory. *Comput. Electr. Eng.* **2017**, *63*, 66–78. [CrossRef]
41. Zhang, Y.; Qian, C.; Lv, J.; Liu, Y. Agent and Cyber-Physical System Based Self-Organizing and Self-Adaptive Intelligent Shopfloor. *IEEE Trans. Ind. Inform.* **2017**, *13*, 737–747. [CrossRef]
42. Zhang, Y.; Wang, W.; Wu, N.; Qian, C. IoT-Enabled Real-Time Production Performance Analysis and Exception Diagnosis Model. *IEEE Trans. Autom. Sci. Eng.* **2016**, *13*, 1318–1332. [CrossRef]
43. Zheng, M.; Ming, X. Construction of cyber-physical system–integrated smart manufacturing workshops: A case study in automobile industry. *Adv. Mech. Eng.* **2017**, *9*, 1–17. [CrossRef]
44. Zhong, R.Y.; Xu, C.; Chen, C.; Huang, G.Q. Big Data Analytics for Physical Internet-based intelligent manufacturing shop floors. *Int. J. Prod. Res.* **2017**, *55*, 2610–2621. [CrossRef]
45. Zhuang, C.; Liu, J.; Xiong, H. Digital twin-based smart production management and control framework for the complex product assembly shop-floor. *Int. J. Adv. Manuf. Technol.* **2018**, *96*, 1149–1163. [CrossRef]
46. Chen, W. Intelligent manufacturing production line data monitoring system for industrial internet of things. *Comput. Commun.* **2020**, *151*, 31–41. [CrossRef]
47. Qu, T.; Thürer, M.; Wang, J.; Wang, Z.; Fu, H.; Li, C.; Huang, G.Q. System dynamics analysis for an Internet-of-Things-enabled production logistics system. *Int. J. Prod. Res.* **2017**, *55*, 2622–2649. [CrossRef]
48. Ding, K.; Chan, F.T.; Zhang, X.; Zhou, G.; Zhang, F. Defining a Digital Twin-based Cyber-Physical Production System for autonomous manufacturing in smart shop floors. *Int. J. Prod. Res.* **2019**, *57*, 6315–6334. [CrossRef]
49. Dai, H.-N.; Wang, H.; Xu, G.; Wan, J.; Imran, M. Big data analytics for manufacturing internet of things: Opportunities, challenges and enabling technologies. *Enterp. Inf. Syst.* **2020**, *14*, 1279–1303. [CrossRef]
50. Chung, K.; Yoo, H.; Choe, D.; Jung, H. Blockchain Network Based Topic Mining Process for Cognitive Manufacturing. *Wirel. Pers. Commun.* **2019**, *105*, 583–597. [CrossRef]
51. Chang, H. Performance evaluation framework design for smart sensor business. *J. Supercomput.* **2017**, *74*, 4481–4496. [CrossRef]
52. Bortolini, M.; Ferrari, E.; Gamberi, M.; Pilati, F.; Faccio, M. Assembly system design in the Industry 4.0 era: A general framework. *IFAC-PapersOnLine* **2017**, *50*, 5700–5705. [CrossRef]
53. Trappey, A.J.C.; Trappey, C.V.; Fan, C.-Y.; Hsu, A.P.T.; Li, X.-K.; Lee, I.J.Y. IoT patent roadmap for smart logistic service provision in the context of Industry 4.0. *J. Chin. Inst. Eng.* **2017**, *40*, 593–602. [CrossRef]
54. Sicari, S.; Rizzardi, A.; Coen-Porisini, A. How to evaluate an Internet of Things system: Models, case studies, and real developments. *Software: Pract. Exp.* **2019**, *49*, 1663–1685. [CrossRef]
55. Tao, F.; Qi, Q. New IT Driven Service-Oriented Smart Manufacturing: Framework and Characteristics. *IEEE Trans. Syst. Man Cybern. Syst.* **2017**, *49*, 81–91. [CrossRef]

56. Lyu, Z.; Lin, P.; Guo, D.; Huang, G.Q. Towards Zero-Warehousing Smart Manufacturing from Zero-Inventory Just-In-Time production. *Robot. Comput. Manuf.* **2020**, *64*, 101932. [CrossRef]
57. De Sousa Jabbour, A.B.L.; Jabbour, C.J.C.; Godinho-Filho, M.; Roubaud, D. Industry 4.0 and the circular economy: A proposed research agenda and original roadmap for sustainable operations. *Ann. Oper. Res.* **2018**, *270*, 273–286. [CrossRef]
58. Mehmood, Y.; Marwat, S.N.K.; Kuladinithi, K.; Förster, A.; Zaki, Y.; Görg, C.; Timm-Giel, A. M2M Potentials in logistics and transportation industry. *Logist. Res.* **2016**, *9*, 15. [CrossRef]
59. Kolberg, D.; Knobloch, J.; Zühlke, D. Towards a lean automation interface for workstations. *Int. J. Prod. Res.* **2017**, *55*, 2845–2856. [CrossRef]
60. Li, X.; Li, D.; Wan, J.; Vasilakos, A.V.; Lai, C.-F.; Wang, S. A review of industrial wireless networks in the context of Industry 4.0. *Wirel. Netw.* **2017**, *23*, 23–41. [CrossRef]
61. Dotoli, M.; Fay, A.; Miśkowicz, M.; Seatzu, C. An overview of current technologies and emerging trends in factory automation. *Int. J. Prod. Res.* **2019**, *57*, 5047–5067. [CrossRef]
62. Egger, J.; Masood, T. Augmented reality in support of intelligent manufacturing—A systematic literature review. *Comput. Ind. Eng.* **2020**, *140*, 106195. [CrossRef]
63. Al-Jaroodi, J.; Mohamed, N.; Jawhar, I. A service-oriented middleware framework for manufacturing industry 4.0. *ACM SIGBED Rev.* **2018**, *15*, 29–36. [CrossRef]
64. Kovalenko, I.; Saez, M.; Barton, K.; Tilbury, D. SMART: A System-Level Manufacturing and Automation Research Testbed. *Smart Sustain. Manuf. Syst.* **2017**, *1*, 20170006. [CrossRef]
65. Kembro, J.H.; Danielsson, V.; Smajli, G. Network video technology: Exploring an innovative approach to improving warehouse operations. *Int. J. Phys. Distrib. Logist. Manag.* **2017**, *47*, 623–645. [CrossRef]
66. Tu, M.; Lim, M.K.; Yang, M.F. IoT-based production logistics and supply chain system—Part 2 IoT-based cyber-physical system: A framework and evaluation. *Ind. Manag. Data Syst.* **2018**, *118*, 96–125. [CrossRef]
67. Mahmud, B. Internet of things (IoT) for manufacturing logistics on SAP ERP applications. *J. Telecommun. Electron. Comput. Eng.* **2017**, *9*, 43–47.
68. Kant, K.; Pal, A. Internet of Perishable Logistics. *IEEE Internet Comput.* **2017**, *21*, 22–31. [CrossRef]
69. Meng, Z.; Wu, Z.; Gray, J. RFID-Based Object-Centric Data Management Framework for Smart Manufacturing Applications. *IEEE Internet Things J.* **2019**, *6*, 2706–2716. [CrossRef]
70. Zhang, Y.; Xu, X.; Liu, A.; Lu, Q.; Xu, L.; Tao, F. Blockchain-Based Trust Mechanism for IoT-Based Smart Manufacturing System. *IEEE Trans. Comput. Soc. Syst.* **2019**, *6*, 1386–1394. [CrossRef]
71. Hao, Y.; Helo, P. The role of wearable devices in meeting the needs of cloud manufacturing: A case study. *Robot. Comput. Manuf.* **2017**, *45*, 168–179. [CrossRef]
72. Trentesaux, D.; Borangiu, T.; Thomas, A. Emerging ICT concepts for smart, safe and sustainable industrial systems. *Comput. Ind.* **2016**, *81*, 1–10. [CrossRef]
73. Costanzo, M.; De Maria, G.; Lettera, G.; Natale, C.; Pirozzi, S. Motion Planning and Reactive Control Algorithms for Object Manipulation in Uncertain Conditions. *Robotics* **2018**, *7*, 76. [CrossRef]
74. Culler, D.; Long, J. A Prototype Smart Materials Warehouse Application Implemented Using Custom Mobile Robots and Open Source Vision Technology Developed Using EmguCV. *Procedia Manuf.* **2016**, *5*, 1092–1106. [CrossRef]
75. Liao, Y.; Panetto, H.; Stadzisz, P.C.; Simão, J.M. A notification-oriented solution for data-intensive enterprise information systems—A cloud manufacturing case. *Enterp. Inf. Syst.* **2018**, *12*, 942–959. [CrossRef]
76. Stark, R.; Fresemann, C.; Lindow, K. Development and operation of Digital Twins for technical systems and services. *CIRP Ann.* **2019**, *68*, 129–132. [CrossRef]
77. Mueller, E.; Chen, X.-L.; Riedel, R. Challenges and Requirements for the Application of Industry 4.0: A Special Insight with the Usage of Cyber-Physical System. *Chin. J. Mech. Eng.* **2017**, *30*, 1050–1057. [CrossRef]
78. Wang, X.; Yew, A.; Ong, S.; Nee, A. Enhancing smart shop floor management with ubiquitous augmented reality. *Int. J. Prod. Res.* **2019**, *58*, 2352–2367. [CrossRef]
79. Masood, T.; Egger, J. Augmented reality in support of Industry 4.0—Implementation challenges and success factors. *Robot. Comput. Manuf.* **2019**, *58*, 181–195. [CrossRef]
80. Leung, K.; Choy, K.; Siu, P.K.; Ho, G.; Lam, H.; Lee, C.K. A B2C e-commerce intelligent system for re-engineering the e-order fulfilment process. *Expert Syst. Appl.* **2018**, *91*, 386–401. [CrossRef]
81. Wahrmann, D.; Hildebrandt, A.-C.; Schuetz, C.; Wittmann, R.; Rixen, D. An Autonomous and Flexible Robotic Framework for Logistics Applications. *J. Intell. Robot. Syst.* **2017**, *93*, 419–431. [CrossRef]
82. Schuhmacher, J.; Baumung, W.; Hummel, V. An Intelligent Bin System for Decentrally Controlled Intralogistic Systems in Context of Industrie 4.0. *Procedia Manuf.* **2017**, *9*, 135–142. [CrossRef]
83. Huang, B.; Wang, W.; Ren, S.; Zhong, R.Y.; Jiang, J. A proactive task dispatching method based on future bottleneck prediction for the smart factory. *Int. J. Comput. Integr. Manuf.* **2019**, *32*, 278–293. [CrossRef]
84. Hohmann, C.; Posselt, T. Design challenges for CPS-based service systems in industrial production and logistics. *Int. J. Comput. Integr. Manuf.* **2018**, *32*, 329–339. [CrossRef]
85. Leng, J.; Zhang, H.; Yan, D.; Liu, Q.; Chen, X.; Zhang, D. Digital twin-driven manufacturing cyber-physical system for parallel controlling of smart workshop. *J. Ambient. Intell. Humaniz. Comput.* **2019**, *10*, 1155–1166. [CrossRef]

86. Liu, B.; Zhang, Y.; Zhang, G.; Zheng, P. Edge-cloud orchestration driven industrial smart product-service systems solution design based on CPS and IIoT. *Adv. Eng. Inform.* **2019**, *42*, 100984. [CrossRef]
87. Li, G.; Zeng, B.; Liao, W.; Li, X.; Gao, L. A new AGV scheduling algorithm based on harmony search for material transfer in a real-world manufacturing system. *Adv. Mech. Eng.* **2018**, *10*. [CrossRef]
88. Küsters, D.; Praß, N.; Gloy, Y.-S. Textile Learning Factory 4.0—Preparing Germany's Textile Industry for the Digital Future. *Procedia Manuf.* **2017**, *9*, 214–221. [CrossRef]
89. Lu, S.; Xu, C.; Zhong, R.Y.; Wang, L. A RFID-enabled positioning system in automated guided vehicle for smart factories. *J. Manuf. Syst.* **2017**, *44*, 179–190. [CrossRef]
90. Madsen, O.; Møller, C. The AAU Smart Production Laboratory for Teaching and Research in Emerging Digital Manufacturing Technologies. *Procedia Manuf.* **2017**, *9*, 106–112. [CrossRef]
91. Wang, S.; Wan, J.; Li, D.; Zhang, C. Implementing Smart Factory of Industrie 4.0: An Outlook. *Int. J. Distrib. Sens. Netw.* **2016**, *12*. [CrossRef]
92. Wan, J.; Chen, B.; Imran, M.; Tao, F.; Li, D.; Liu, C.; Ahmad, S. Toward dynamic resources management for IoT-based manufacturing. *IEEE Commun. Mag.* **2018**, *56*, 52–59. [CrossRef]
93. Tang, D.; Zheng, K.; Zhang, H.; Zhang, Z.; Sang, Z.; Zhang, T.; Espinosa-Oviedo, J.-A.; Vargas-Solar, G. Using autonomous intelligence to build a smart shop floor. *Int. J. Adv. Manuf. Technol.* **2017**, *94*, 1597–1606. [CrossRef]
94. Rojko, A. Industry 4.0 Concept: Background and Overview. *Int. J. Interact. Mob. Technol.* **2017**, *11*, 77–90. [CrossRef]
95. Yan, H.; Hua, Q.; Wang, Y.; Wei, W.; Imran, M. Cloud robotics in Smart Manufacturing Environments: Challenges and countermeasures. *Comput. Electr. Eng.* **2017**, *63*, 56–65. [CrossRef]
96. Zhang, Y.; Zhu, Z.; Lv, J. CPS-Based Smart Control Model for Shopfloor Material Handling. *IEEE Trans. Ind. Inform.* **2018**, *14*, 1764–1775. [CrossRef]
97. Da Silva, V.L.; Kovaleski, J.L.; Pagani, R.N. Technology transfer in the supply chain oriented to industry 4.0: A literature review. *Technol. Anal. Strat. Manag.* **2018**, *31*, 546–562. [CrossRef]
98. Chen, G.; Wang, P.; Feng, B.; Li, Y.; Liu, D. The framework design of smart factory in discrete manufacturing industry based on cyber-physical system. *Int. J. Comput. Integr. Manuf.* **2019**, *33*, 79–101. [CrossRef]
99. Cadavid, J.P.U.; Lamouri, S.; Grabot, B.; Pellerin, R.; Fortin, A. Machine learning applied in production planning and control: A state-of-the-art in the era of industry 4.0. *J. Intell. Manuf.* **2020**, *31*, 1531–1558. [CrossRef]
100. Suginouchi, S.; Kokuryo, D.; Kaihara, T. Value Co-creative Manufacturing System for Mass Customization: Concept of Smart Factory and Operation Method Using Autonomous Negotiation Mechanism. *Procedia CIRP* **2017**, *63*, 727–732. [CrossRef]
101. Gröhn, L.; Metsälä, S.; Nyholm, M.; Saikko, L.; Väänänen, E.; Gulzar, K.; Vyatkin, V. Manufacturing System Upgrade with Wireless and Distributed Automation. *Procedia Manuf.* **2017**, *11*, 1012–1018. [CrossRef]
102. Szafir, D.; Mutlu, B.; Fong, T. Designing planning and control interfaces to support user collaboration with flying robots. *Int. J. Robot. Res.* **2017**, *36*, 514–542. [CrossRef]
103. Semwal, T.; Jha, S.S.; Nair, S.B. On Ordering Multi-Robot Task Executions within a Cyber Physical System. *ACM Trans. Auton. Adapt. Syst.* **2018**, *12*, 1–27. [CrossRef]
104. Cheng, J.; Chen, W.; Tao, F.; Lin, C.-L. Industrial IoT in 5G environment towards smart manufacturing. *J. Ind. Inf. Integr.* **2018**, *10*, 10–19. [CrossRef]
105. Damiani, L.; Demartini, M.; Guizzi, G.; Revetria, R.; Tonelli, F. Augmented and virtual reality applications in industrial systems: A qualitative review towards the industry 4.0 era. *IFAC PapersOnLine* **2018**, *51*, 624–630. [CrossRef]
106. Avventuroso, G.; Silvestri, M.; Pedrazzoli, P. A Networked Production System to Implement Virtual Enterprise and Product Lifecycle Information Loops. *IFAC-PapersOnLine* **2017**, *50*, 7964–7969. [CrossRef]
107. Zhong, X.; Xu, R.Y.; Wang, L. IoT-enabled Smart Factory Visibility and Traceability Using Laser-scanners. *Procedia Manuf.* **2017**, *10*, 1–14. [CrossRef]
108. Závadská, Z.; Závadský, J. Quality managers and their future technological expectations related to Industry 4.0. *Total. Qual. Manag. Bus. Excel.* **2018**, *31*, 717–741. [CrossRef]
109. Guo, D.; Zhong, R.Y.; Lin, P.; Lyu, Z.; Rong, Y.; Huang, G.Q. Digital twin-enabled Graduation Intelligent Manufacturing System for fixed-position assembly islands. *Robot. Comput. Manuf.* **2020**, *63*, 101917. [CrossRef]
110. Zhang, K.; Wan, M.; Qu, T.; Jiang, H.; Li, P.; Chen, Z.; Xiang, J.; He, X.; Li, C.; Huang, G.Q. Production service system enabled by cloud-based smart resource hierarchy for a highly dynamic synchronized production process. *Adv. Eng. Inform.* **2019**, *42*, 100995. [CrossRef]
111. Zheng, P.; Lin, Y.; Chen, C.-H.; Xu, X. Smart, connected open architecture product: An IT-driven co-creation paradigm with lifecycle personalization concerns. *Int. J. Prod. Res.* **2018**, *57*, 2571–2584. [CrossRef]
112. Zhang, K.; Qu, T.; Zhou, D.; Thürer, M.; Liu, Y.; Nie, D.; Li, C.; Huang, G.Q. IoT-enabled dynamic lean control mechanism for typical production systems. *J. Ambient Intell. Humaniz. Comput.* **2019**, *10*, 1009–1023. [CrossRef]
113. Yang, H.; Kumara, S.; Bukkapatnam, S.T.; Tsung, F. The internet of things for smart manufacturing: A review. *IISE Trans.* **2019**, *51*, 1190–1216. [CrossRef]
114. Priya, B.; Malhotra, J. 5GAuNetS: An autonomous 5G network selection framework for Industry 4.0. *Soft Comput.* **2020**, *24*, 9507–9523. [CrossRef]

115. Mahroof, K. A human-centric perspective exploring the readiness towards smart warehousing: The case of a large retail distribution warehouse. *Int. J. Inf. Manag.* **2019**, *45*, 176–190. [CrossRef]
116. Hopkins, J.; Hawking, P. Big Data Analytics and IoT in logistics: A case study. *Int. J. Logist. Manag.* **2018**, *29*, 575–591. [CrossRef]
117. Li, J.-Q.; Yu, F.R.; Deng, G.; Luo, C.; Ming, Z.; Yan, Q. Industrial Internet: A Survey on the Enabling Technologies, Applications, and Challenges. *IEEE Commun. Surv. Tutorials* **2017**, *19*, 1504–1526. [CrossRef]
118. Feng, J.; Li, F.; Xu, C.; Zhong, R.Y. Data-Driven Analysis for RFID-Enabled Smart Factory: A Case Study. *IEEE Trans. Syst. Man, Cybern. Syst.* **2018**, *50*, 81–88. [CrossRef]
119. Ding, K.; Jiang, P. RFID-based production data analysis in an IoT-enabled smart job-shop. *IEEE/CAA J. Autom. Sin.* **2018**, *5*, 128–138. [CrossRef]
120. Zhou, W.; Piramuthu, S.; Chu, F.; Chu, C. RFID-enabled flexible warehousing. *Decis. Support Syst.* **2017**, *98*, 99–112. [CrossRef]
121. Kim, J.-Y.; Park, D.-J. Internet-of-Things Based Approach for Warehouse Management System. *Int. J. Multimedia Ubiquitous Eng.* **2016**, *11*, 159–166. [CrossRef]
122. Franceschini, F.; Galetto, M.; Maisano, L.; Mastrogiacomo, D. Towards the use 20 of augmented reality techniques for assisted acceptance sampling. *Proc. Inst. Mech. Eng. Part B J. Eng. Manuf.* **2016**, *230*, 1870–1884. [CrossRef]
123. Sarupuri, B.; Lee, G.A.; Billinghurst, M. Using augmented reality to assist forklift operation. In Proceedings of the 28th Australian Conference on Computer-Human Interaction—OzCHI '16, Launceston, Tasmania, 29 November–2 December 2016; pp. 16–24.
124. Mättig, B.; Lorimer, I.; Kirks, T.; Jost, J. Analysis of the application of Augmented Reality in the packaging process considering specific requirements on the visualization of information as well as the ergonomic integration of humans into the process. *Logist. J. Proc.* **2016**, *2016*.
125. Gregor, M.; Medvecky, S.; Grznar, P.; Gregor, T. Smart Industry Requires Fast Response from Research to Innovation. *Commun. Sci. Lett. Univ. Zilina* **2017**, *19*, 68–73.
126. Mueller, R.; Vette, M.; Hoerauf, L.; Speicher, C.; Burkhard, D. Lean information and communication tool to connect shop and top floor in small and medium-sized enterprises. In Proceedings of the 27th International Conference on Flexible Automation and Intelligent Manufacturing, Modena, Italy, 27–30 June 2017; Volume 11, pp. 1043–1052.
127. Lee, J.; Davari, H.; Singh, J.; Pandhare, V. Industrial Artificial Intelligence for industry 4.0-based manufacturing systems. *Manuf. Lett.* **2018**, *18*, 20–23. [CrossRef]
128. Ramakrishnan, R.; Gaur, L.; Singh, G. Feasibility and Efficacy of BLE Beacon IoT Devices in Inventory Management at the Shop Floor. *Int. J. Electr. Comput. Eng. (IJECE)* **2016**, *6*, 2362. [CrossRef]
129. Zhang, J.; Ding, G.; Zou, Y.; Qin, S.; Fu, J. Review of job shop scheduling research and its new perspectives under Industry 4.0. *J. Intell. Manuf.* **2019**, *30*, 1809–1830. [CrossRef]
130. Tao, F.; Zhang, H.; Liu, A.; Nee, A.Y.C. Digital Twin in Industry: State-of-the-Art. *IEEE Trans. Ind. Inform.* **2019**, *15*, 2405–2415. [CrossRef]
131. Qu, T.; Lei, S.P.; Wang, Z.Z.; Nie, D.X.; Chen, X.; Huang, G.Q. IoT-based real-time production logistics synchronization system under smart cloud manufacturing. *Int. J. Adv. Manuf. Technol.* **2016**, *84*, 147–164. [CrossRef]
132. Zhang, Y.; Liu, S.; Liu, Y.; Li, R. Smart box-enabled product–service system for cloud logistics. *Int. J. Prod. Res.* **2016**, *54*, 6693–6706. [CrossRef]
133. Zhang, Y.; Wang, W.; Du, W.; Qian, C.; Yang, H. Coloured Petri net-based active sensing system of real-time and multi-source manufacturing information for smart factory. *Int. J. Adv. Manuf. Technol.* **2017**, *94*, 3427–3439. [CrossRef]
134. Qu, Y.J.; Ming, X.G.; Liu, Z.W.; Zhang, X.Y.; Hou, Z.T. Smart manufacturing systems: State of the art and future trends. *Int. J. Adv. Manuf. Technol.* **2019**, *103*, 3751–3768. [CrossRef]
135. Wilkesmann, M.; Wilkesmann, U. Industry 4.0—Organizing routines or innovations? *VINE J. Inf. Knowl. Manag. Syst.* **2018**, *48*, 238–254. [CrossRef]
136. Ding, K.; Lei, J.; Chan, F.T.; Hui, J.; Zhang, F.; Wang, Y. Hidden Markov model-based autonomous manufacturing task orchestration in smart shop floors. *Robot. Comput. Manuf.* **2020**, *61*, 101845. [CrossRef]
137. Pujo, P.; Ounnar, F.; Power, D.; Khader, S. Wireless Holon Network for job shop isoarchic control. *Comput. Ind.* **2016**, *83*, 12–27. [CrossRef]
138. Lin, C.-C.; Yang, J.-W. Cost-Efficient Deployment of Fog Computing Systems at Logistics Centers in Industry 4.0. *IEEE Trans. Ind. Inform.* **2018**, *14*, 4603–4611. [CrossRef]
139. Zulkifli, C.Z.; Semunab, S.N.; Ibrahim, A.B.; Noor, N.M. Implementation of Wireless Mobile Rfid Reader in Real World Industry Environment. *J. Teknol.* **2016**, *78*, 74–82. [CrossRef]
140. Leusin, M.E.; Kück, M.; Frazzon, E.M.; Maldonado, M.U.; Freitag, M. Potential of a Multi-Agent System Approach for Production Control in Smart Factories. *IFAC-PapersOnLine* **2018**, *51*, 1459–1464. [CrossRef]
141. Cui, Y.; Kara, S.; Chan, K.C. Manufacturing big data ecosystem: A systematic literature review. *Robot. Comput. Manuf.* **2020**, *62*, 101861. [CrossRef]
142. Turner, C.J.; Hutabarat, W.; Oyekan, J.; Tiwari, A. Discrete Event Simulation and Virtual Reality Use in Industry: New Opportunities and Future Trends. *IEEE Trans. Human-Machine Syst.* **2016**, *46*, 882–894. [CrossRef]
143. Ren, S.; Zhang, Y.; Liu, Y.; Sakao, T.; Huisingh, D.; Almeida, C.M.V.B. A comprehensive review of big data analytics throughout product lifecycle to support sustainable smart manufacturing: A framework, challenges and future research directions. *J. Clean. Prod.* **2019**, *210*, 1343–1365. [CrossRef]

144. Hwang, G.; Lee, J.; Park, J.; Chang, T.-W. Developing performance measurement system for Internet of Things and smart factory environment. *Int. J. Prod. Res.* **2017**, *55*, 2590–2602. [CrossRef]
145. Hwang, S. A network clock model for time awareness in the Internet of things and artificial intelligence applications. *J. Supercomput.* **2019**, *75*, 4309–4328. [CrossRef]
146. Yu, Q. Design of Logistics Tracking and Monitoring System Based on Internet of Things. *J. Residuals Sci. Technol.* **2016**, *13*, 43.1–43.4.
147. Yi, Y.; Yan, Y.; Liu, X.; Ni, Z.; Feng, J.; Liu, J. Digital twin-based smart assembly process design and application framework for complex products and its case study. *J. Manuf. Syst.* **2021**, *58*, 94–107. [CrossRef]
148. Kamagaew, A.; Stenzel, J.; Nettstrater, A.; Hompel, M.T. Concept of Cellular Transport Systems in facility logistics. In Proceedings of the The 5th International Conference on Automation, Robotics and Applications, Wellington, New Zealand, 6–8 December 2011; pp. 40–45.
149. Gilchrist, A. *Industry 4.0*, 1st ed.; O'Reilly Safari Learning Platform: Academic Edition; Apress: New York, NY, USA, 2016.
150. Cheng, Y.; Zhang, Y.; Ji, P.; Xu, W.; Zhou, Z.; Tao, F. Cyber-physical integration for moving digital factories forward towards smart manufacturing: A survey. *Int. J. Adv. Manuf. Technol.* **2018**, *97*, 1209–1221. [CrossRef]
151. Kim, J.; Tang, K.; Kumara, S.; Yee, S.T.; Tew, J. Value analysis of location-enabled radio-frequency identification information on delivery chain performance. *Int. J. Prod. Econ.* **2008**, *112*, 403–415. [CrossRef]
152. Yang, M.; Mahmood, M.; Zhou, X.; Shafaq, S.; Zahid, L. Design and Implementation of Cloud Platform for Intelligent Logistics in the Trend of Intellectualization. *China Commun.* **2017**, *14*, 180–191. [CrossRef]
153. Trappey, A.J.; Trappey, C.V.; Wu, J.-L.; Wang, J.W. Intelligent compilation of patent summaries using machine learning and natural language processing techniques. *Adv. Eng. Inform.* **2020**, *43*, 101027. [CrossRef]
154. Liu, Y.; Tong, K.; Mao, F.; Yang, J. Research on digital production technology for traditional manufacturing enterprises based on industrial Internet of Things in 5G era. *Int. J. Adv. Manuf. Technol.* **2020**, *107*, 1101–1114. [CrossRef]
155. Meroni, G.; Baresi, L.; Montali, M.; Plebani, P. Multi-party business process compliance monitoring through IoT-enabled artifacts. *Inf. Syst.* **2018**, *73*, 61–78. [CrossRef]
156. Westerkamp, M.; Victor, F.; Küpper, A. Tracing manufacturing processes using blockchain-based token compositions. *Digit. Commun. Netw.* **2020**, *6*, 167–176. [CrossRef]
157. Wigger, B.; Meissner, T.; Winkler, M.; Foerste, A.; Jetter, V.; Buchholz, A.; Zimmermann, A. Label-/tag-free traceability of electronic PCB in SMD assembly based on individual inherent surface patterns. *Int. J. Adv. Manuf. Technol.* **2018**, *98*, 3081–3090. [CrossRef]
158. Wigger, B.; Koinzer, I.; Meissner, T.; Barth, M.; Zimmermann, A. Robust and fast part traceability in a production chain exploiting inherent, individual surface patterns. *Robot. Comput. Manuf.* **2020**, *63*, 101925. [CrossRef]
159. Rajagopalan, A.K.; Shyamala, C. A lightweight inter-zonal authentication protocol for moving objects in low powered RF systems. *J. Intell. Fuzzy Syst.* **2019**, *36*, 2345–2354. [CrossRef]
160. Tu, M.; Lim, M.K.; Yang, M.F. IoT-based production logistics and supply chain system—Part 1 modeling IoT-based manufacturing IoT supply chain. *Ind. Manag. Data Syst.* **2018**, *118*, 65–95. [CrossRef]
161. Li, S.; Da Xu, L.; Zhao, S. The internet of things: A survey. *Inf. Syst. Front.* **2015**, *17*, 243–259. [CrossRef]
162. Cannizzaro, D.; Zafiri, M.; Pagliari, D.J.; Patti, E.; Macii, E.; Poncino, M.; Acquaviva, A. A Comparison Analysis of BLE-Based Algorithms for Localization in Industrial Environments. *Electronics* **2019**, *9*, 44. [CrossRef]
163. Cheffena, M. Industrial wireless communications over the millimeter wave spectrum: Opportunities and challenges. *IEEE Commun. Mag.* **2016**, *54*, 66–72. [CrossRef]
164. Lu, Y.; Liu, C.; Wang, K.I.-K.; Huang, H.; Xu, X. Digital Twin-driven smart manufacturing: Connotation, reference model, applications and research issues. *Robot. Comput. Manuf.* **2020**, *61*, 101837. [CrossRef]
165. Kurniadi, K.A.; Ryu, K. Development of IOT-based Reconfigurable Manufacturing System to solve Reconfiguration Planning Problem. *Procedia Manuf.* **2017**, *11*, 965–972. [CrossRef]
166. Lai, J.; Luo, C.; Wu, J.; Li, J.; Wang, J.; Chen, J.; Feng, G.; Song, H. TagSort: Accurate Relative Localization Exploring RFID Phase Spectrum Matching for Internet of Things. *IEEE Internet Things J.* **2020**, *7*, 389–399. [CrossRef]
167. Gurtu, A.; Johny, J. Potential of blockchain technology in supply chain management: A literature review. *Int. J. Phys. Distrib. Logist. Manag.* **2019**, *49*, 881–900. [CrossRef]
168. Krishnamurthy, R.; Cecil, J. A next-generation IoT-based collaborative framework for electronics assembly. *Int. J. Adv. Manuf. Technol.* **2018**, *96*, 39–52. [CrossRef]
169. Tao, F.; Cheng, J.; Qi, Q. IIHub: An Industrial Internet-of-Things Hub toward Smart Manufacturing Based on Cyber-Physical System. *IEEE Trans. Ind. Inform.* **2018**, *14*, 2271–2280. [CrossRef]
170. La Scalia, G.; Settanni, L.; Micale, R.; Enea, M. Predictive shelf life model based on RF technology for improving the management of food supply chain: A case study. *Int. J. RF Technol. Res. Appl.* **2016**, *7*, 31–42. [CrossRef]
171. Crnjac, M.; Veža, I.; Banduka, N. From concept to the introduction of industry 4.0. *Int. J. Ind. Eng. Manag.* **2017**, *8*, 21–30.
172. Goudos, S.K.; Dallas, P.I.; Chatziefthymiou, S.; Kyriazakos, S.A. A Survey of IoT Key Enabling and Future Technologies: 5G, Mobile IoT, Sematic Web and Applications. *Wirel. Pers. Commun.* **2017**, *97*, 1645–1675. [CrossRef]
173. De Felice, F.; Petrillo, A.; Zomparelli, F. Prospective design of smart manufacturing: An Italian pilot case study. *Manuf. Lett.* **2018**, *15*, 81–85. [CrossRef]

174. Georgakopoulos, D.; Jayaraman, P.P. Internet of things: From internet scale sensing to smart services. *Comput.* **2016**, *98*, 1041–1058. [CrossRef]
175. Diez-Olivan, A.; Del Ser, J.; Galar, D.; Sierra, B. Data fusion and machine learning for industrial prognosis: Trends and perspectives towards Industry 4.0. *Inf. Fusion* **2019**, *50*, 92–111. [CrossRef]
176. Qiu, T.; Chen, N.; Li, K.; Atiquzzaman, M.; Zhao, W. How Can Heterogeneous Internet of Things Build Our Future: A Survey. *IEEE Commun. Surv. Tutorials* **2018**, *20*, 2011–2027. [CrossRef]
177. Kousi, N.; Koukas, S.; Michalos, G.; Makris, S. Scheduling of smart intra—Factory material supply operations using mobile robots. *Int. J. Prod. Res.* **2018**, *57*, 801–814. [CrossRef]
178. Cheng, Y.; Chen, K.; Sun, H.; Zhang, Y.; Tao, F. Data and knowledge mining with big data towards smart production. *J. Ind. Inf. Integr.* **2018**, *9*, 1–13. [CrossRef]
179. Jeble, S.; Dubey, R.; Childe, S.J.; Papadopoulos, T.; Roubaud, D.; Prakash, A. Impact of big data and predictive analytics capability on supply chain sustainability. *Int. J. Logist. Manag.* **2018**, *29*, 513–538. [CrossRef]

Article

Towards Digital Twins of Multimodal Supply Chains

Anselm Busse *, Benno Gerlach, Joel Cedric Lengeling, Peter Poschmann, Johannes Werner and Simon Zarnitz

Competence Center for Logistic & IT-Systems (LogIT), Technische Universität Berlin, 10623 Berlin, Germany; gerlach@tu-berlin.de (B.G.); lengeling@logistik.tu-berlin.de (J.C.L.); poschmann@tu-berlin.de (P.P.); johannes.werner@tu-berlin.de (J.W.); simon.zarnitz@tu-berlin.de (S.Z.)
* Correspondence: anselm.busse@tu-berlin.de or info@logit.tu-berlin.de

Abstract: Both modern multi- and intermodal supply chains pose a significant challenge to control and maintain while offering numerous optimization potential. Digital Twins have been proposed to improve supply chains. However, as of today, they are only used for certain parts of the entire supply chain. This paper presents an initial framework for a holistic Digital Supply Chain Twin (DSCT) capable of including an entire multimodal supply chain. Such a DSCT promises to enable several improvements all across the supply chain while also be capable of simulating and evaluate several different scenarios for the supply chain. Therefore, the DSCT will not only be able to optimize multi- and intermodal supply chains but also makes them potentially more robust by identifying possible issues early on. This paper discusses the major requirements that such a DSCT must fulfil to be useful and how several information technologies that matured in recent years or are about the mature are the key enablers to fulfil these requirements. Finally, a suggested high-level architecture for such a DSCT is presented as a first step towards the realization of a DSCT, as presented in this work

Keywords: digital twin; supply chain; multimodal; intermodal; hinterland

Citation: Busse, A.; Gerlach, B.; Lengeling, J.C.; Poschmann, P.; Werner, J.; Zarnitz, S. Towards Digital Twins of Multimodal Supply Chains. *Logistics* **2021**, *5*, 25. https://doi.org/10.3390/logistics5020025

Academic Editor: Robert Handfield

Received: 28 February 2021
Accepted: 19 March 2021
Published: 26 April 2021

Publisher's Note: MDPI stays neutral with regard to jurisdictional claims in published maps and institutional affiliations.

Copyright: © 2021 by the authors. Licensee MDPI, Basel, Switzerland. This article is an open access article distributed under the terms and conditions of the Creative Commons Attribution (CC BY) license (https://creativecommons.org/licenses/by/4.0/).

1. Introduction

Globalization, the cross-border economic integration of companies, and changing customer behavior lead to the increasing complexity of supply chains and poses major challenges for companies ([1], p. 5, [2]). Functioning and efficient supply chains are crucial to modern society as it is the central factor to ensure the supply of goods matching the demand. Thus, they need to be repositioned to react flexibly and fast to these challenges to stay competitive in the long-term. As an interdisciplinary cross-sectional function for the planning, implementation, and control of all material and information flows, logistics plays a key role in meeting these challenges ([3], p. 5). For example, modern production and sales nowadays often follow just-in-time principles and try to reduce the necessity to store goods and raw materials. At the same time, companies increased their service orientation, mainly through a shift from a seller's to a buyer's market ([3], p. 5), which leads to an increase in the diversity of goods and customization of individual goods. On the one hand, they are highly complex and, on the other hand, they require the highest degree of flexibility [4] and efficient responsiveness to volatile markets [5] at very low costs.

Technological advances have allowed us to improve and manage such complex supply chains, for example, Transport Management Systems (TMS), Customer Relationship Management Systems (CMS), or Enterprise Resource Planning (ERP) Systems. However, the management and optimizations often happen only locally. In particular, in multimodal transport chains with many actors as crucial parts of supply chains, a considerable optimization potential might exist but cannot be leveraged. That is for two reasons—on the one hand, it is difficult to determine what actions in such a complex system can yield what results, and on the other hand, data is often not shared among different participants. As mentioned, logistics uses different technologies to address these challenges. However, the Digital Supply Chain Twin (DSCT) is discussed as a promising solution to develop a holistic and agile logistics network, at the latest after the DSCT was entered in Gartner's Hype Cycle 2017 as one of the most disruptive technologies in the supply chain. A DSCT is a dynamic simulation model [2,6,7] that aggregates the available data in a structured way and allows simulations on the supply chain, including transport chains that are close to reality. In this context, it is essential to differentiate between asset-focused twins (e.g., digital twins of individual machines) and digital supply chain twins. Asset-focused twins do not sufficiently represent the wide range of applications and the diverse areas of application and possibilities of implementing the whole concept. This allows for an evaluation of different scenarios and their outcome and allows the selection of the most beneficial setup. Because of its digital nature and easy accessibility, the DSCT will also allow the evaluation of unlikely scenarios and allow preparation for them, as was observed during the SARS-CoV-2 pandemic in 2020 and 2021. Furthermore, the DSCT would not only allow considering pure economic and reliability aspects but could also take into account ecological aspects and, therefore, could allow increasing ecological sustainability. Even though not presenting a final design, but only initial steps for a DSCT for multimodal supply chains, it outlines the potential and benefits and discusses its feasibility substantiated through a possible framework.

As a methodology for this paper, Design Science Research (DSR) is used. In DSR, an artifact is created to address an unsolved and vital problem. Thereby, the artifact should offer a solution for the defined problem and be drawn from existing knowledge (cf. [8]). In particular, for this research, we adopt the DSR process of Pfeffers [9]. We applied a Problem-Centered approach due to the reason the shortcomings in current transport networks were the entry point of our research. This is done on the maritime transport chain example, which represents an important element in international supply chains. Based on these shortcomings, the objectives of a solution are presented. Then, a vision for a DSCT made possible by using new technologies is presented and how exactly a DSCT can help overcome the existing shortcomings in transport networks and supply chains is highlighted. The evaluation of the artefact is performed theoretically, based on the outlined shortcomings. Therefore, no further iteration of the DSR process was conducted.

The remainder of the paper is structured as follows—Section 2 describes the current situation with multimodal supply chains and the intended goal. In Section 3, we list and describe the technologies that will enable DSCTs to reach the goals summarized in Section 2. The subsequent Section 4 describes and discusses the envisioned holistic digital supply chain twin. The final section concludes this paper.

2. Current and Target State of Multimodal Supply Chains

The coordination of today's supply chains is becoming an increasing challenge for logistics and industrial companies. On the one hand, the networks are showing increasing complexity due to a rising number of actors as well as global dimensions, while their vulnerability to disruptions is growing as a result of outsourcing, single-sourcing strategies, and the reduction of risk buffers through Just-in-time strategies. On the other hand, logistics and industrial companies are faced with increasing requirements regarding reliability, efficiency, and sustainability (cf. [10], p. 12f) (cf. [11]). Optimal control of such complex systems requires the highest possible transparency across the entire network. Nevertheless, transparency across the entire system is usually not available. At most, a stakeholder may have transparency over the part of the network the stakeholder operates in. But even this local transparency is often not available. The maritime transport chain is well suited to demonstrate the need for transparency.

More than 90% of the world's trade goods and about a quarter of Germany's foreign trade volume are transported by sea ([12], p. 8), multimodal transport chains such as the maritime transport chain are a central component of global logistics networks. The coordination of transport chains requires the synchronization of numerous consecutive transport and transshipment processes (see Figure 1). These are each carried out by a large number of different logistics actors, for example, freight forwarders, CT (Container Terminal) operators, shipping companies, rail companies, seaport terminal operators, to name only a few (cf. [13], pp. 208–211). Despite the significant need for cross-actor coordination, the information transparency between these actors is currently very low, so that no actor can trace the overall progress of transports in detail. One reason for this is that process tracking is only partially implemented so that no continuous status information is available for the whole chain. Another reason is that existing information is not systematically transmitted to other actors as a consequence of a low level of digitization of communication processes, missing compatibility of IT systems, and confidentiality requirements (cf. [14]).

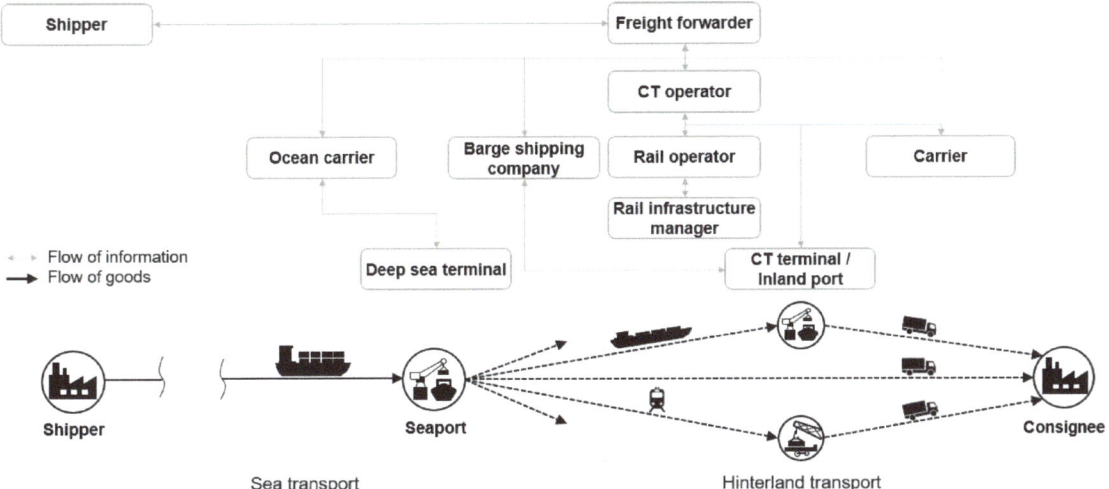

Figure 1. Exemplary flow of goods and information within a maritime transport chain.

Consequently, the planning and control of the transport chain follows a very static and less flexible top-down-process and does not take place in the sense of an overall optimum, but rather each actor carries out an isolated optimization for its area of responsibility. Hence, available capacities of transport modes and resources are not used optimally, and road transport is prioritized over more sustainable rail and water transport modes due to its flexibility. Furthermore, the uncertainty caused by a lack of information causes high-risk buffers within the chain and, as a result, long transport times. Another result of this situation is the less than optimal handling of disruptions, as the low level of transparency makes both early detection and cross-stakeholder coordination of measures more difficult (cf. [14]).

To meet the requirements named above, optimized and synchromodal transport planning and control procedures are required, which provides the following capabilities:

- *Visibility*: Real-time transparency across the entire transport network, including available capacities, disruptions, and process status information
- *Data Analysis*: Predictions on future states of the system, for example, upcoming disruptions and lacks of capacity
- *Extensive Decision Support*: Process optimization by providing decision support for both transport planning as well as handling of disruptions

Those capabilities would allow further management of the previously explored challenges. *Visibility* and *data analysis* improve resilience towards complexity and disruptions. Additionally, *visibility* and *data analysis* provide the opportunity to improve reliability and sustainability, while especially *extensive decision support* provides the opportunity to improve efficiency.

3. Enabler

To reach the goals discussed above, several technologies were identified that have only matured in in recent years or mature in the near future. This will allow the combining and adaptation of these technologies to reach the intended goal. Before going into more detail about how those technologies are used, they will be briefly introduced:

3.1. The Internet of Things

The Internet of Things (IoT) is a concept that allows things or objects to communicate with each other through a unique addressing scheme similar to computers that can communicate with each other over the internet [15]. This communication and addressing allow physical objects to interact with each other without mandatory human intervention. This is limited to communicating information about an object or thing like, for example, location or temperature and actions through actuators. Even though the first concepts were discussed in the 1980s and the term IoT was coined in 1999, real-world applications are only emerging in recent years as devices became substantially smaller and cheaper with more capabilities, especially regarding communication.

3.2. 5G

5G is the fifth generation standard for broadband cellular networks. Compared to its predecessor, 5G offers an increased performance regarding throughput and latency [16]. It also allows the deployment of private campus networks. In summary, this will allow a degree of ubiquitous connectivity that was unknown before. The introduction of 5G from 2016 promises new and innovative applications, particularly in the context of IoT.

3.3. Cloud Computing

Cloud Computing describes IT services such as computing power, storage, or applications, which can be used via the internet. According to NIST, cloud computing characteristics are on-demand self-service, Broad network access, Resource pooling, Rapid elasticity, and Measured service [17]. Thereby, realizable advantages of cloud computing can be financial, operational, or strategic. Possible financial advantages include lower investment, lower operating, and lower maintenance costs in IT. As the most significant operational advantages, elasticity and scalability of IT resources are seen, and a reduction of complexity can result in reduced administration and maintenance efforts. Strategic advantages can include better access to technologies, the development of new business areas, reduced barriers to market entry, or increased data security through better availability of IT systems [18].

3.4. Artificial Intelligence

Artificial Intelligence (AI) refers to the ability of an IT system to show human-like intelligent behaviors [19], which includes independent learning and thereby finding solutions independently [20]. Machine Learning is often used as a method in the field of AI and thus is an elementary component of AI procedures. It describes computer algorithms, which learn from data, such as recognizing patterns or showing desired behaviors. The characteristics for these algorithms are independent learning and improvement, and they can be categorized based on their approach to learning into Supervised Learning, Unsupervised Learning, and Reinforcement-Learning. Different application areas of AI are, for example, Natural Language Processing, Natural Image Processing, Expert systems, and Robotics [20].

3.5. Data Availability

The quantity of data generated is continuously increasing, which also applies to data in companies. An increase of up to 530% of globally generated data is forecast, from 33 ZB (zettabytes) in 2018 to 175 ZB in 2025 [21]. One reason for this increase can be the use of new technologies and concepts, such as sensors, Machine to Machine Communication, IoT, RFID, and so forth, [22]. Additionally, methods for using the data have also improved, for example, by using AI methods for the analysis of the data or cloud computing for the technical infrastructure.

3.6. Blockchain

Blockchain technology was conceptualized in the early 1980s but became available only in the 2000s. First, only as a digital currency, it has since evolved to a technology that allowed the immutable storage of data and ensured process execution. Through its distributed nature and consensus mechanism, it requires no trusted third party to establish trust [23]. The introduction of Smart Contracts [24] allows a very generalized use of blockchain technologies for applications that require a certain degree of trust regarding the integrity both of the data itself and the processing of the data.

3.7. Privacy-Preserving Computation

Combining information from different parties is often necessary to achieve a goal or perform optimization. However, sharing data is often not desired by the stakeholders for privacy or confidentiality reasons. Several technologies were developed that allow the usage of data or computation on data without revealing its content with varying restrictions, for example, Secure Multi-Party Computation, Homomorphic Encryption, Differential Privacy, Zero-Knowledge Proofs, or Trusted Execution Environments [25]. Even though initial research for some of these technologies started in the 1970s, most of them became usable only in recent years or are still in early stages of development.

4. Holistic Digital Supply Chain Twin

The current problems in intermodal transport networks call for a modern and digital solution. Several technological advances that were made in the past act as enablers in that regard, as previously described. This section outlines a possible solution that both tackles the identified problems and benefits greatly from the mentioned enablers: the Digital Supply Chain Twin.

A Digital Supply Chain Twin (DSCT) is a digital simulation model of a real logistics system, which features a long-term, bidirectional and timely data-link to that system. Through observing the digital model it is possible to acquire information about the real logistics system to conclude, make decisions and carry out actions in the real world [26]. The DSCT maps data, state, relations, and behavior of the logistics system in a digital simulation model and stores them permanently in a database (cf. Figure 2). Optimally, any relevant information obtained by observing the logistics system can (also) be obtained by observing the digital model. Three attributes characterize the data exchange between the logistics system and its DSCT:

- *Bidirectional*: Data is exchanged in both directions. Therefore, changes in the state of the logistics system lead to changes in the state of the digital model. Similarly, the knowledge gained from the digital model leads to actions or decision-making in the logistics system. A certain degree of automation of the data exchange is explicitly not a prerequisite for a DSCT.
- *Timely*: Data exchange takes place in a timely manner. The use case determines the specific frequency. Continuous updates in real-time are explicitly not a prerequisite for a DSCT unless the use case requires this.
- *Long-term*: The data exchange and thus the lifetime of the DSCT are designed for continuous, long-term use. Digital simulation models created as part of project activities or for one-time use are explicitly not considered DSCTs.

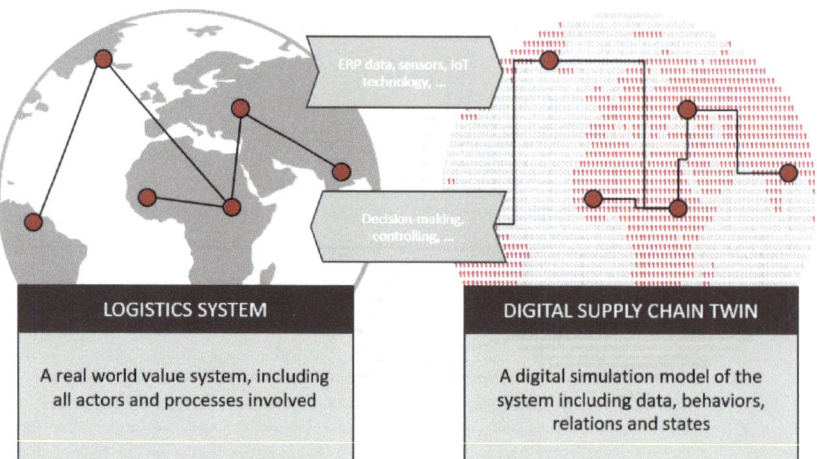

Figure 2. Concept of a Digital Supply Chain Twin (DSCT) (cf. [26]).

Gerlach and Zarnitz [26] propose four levels for the use of Digital Twins in Logistics and Supply Chain Management (LSCM), three of whom are to be considered Digital Supply Chain Twins (cf. Figure 3):

- Macro Level: DSCT of a multi stakeholder value network
- Macro Level: DSCT of an internal supply chain
- Site Level: DSCT of a logistics site (e.g., warehouses, production facilities, etc.)
- Asset Level: DT of a logistics asset (e.g., trucks, forklifts, etc.)

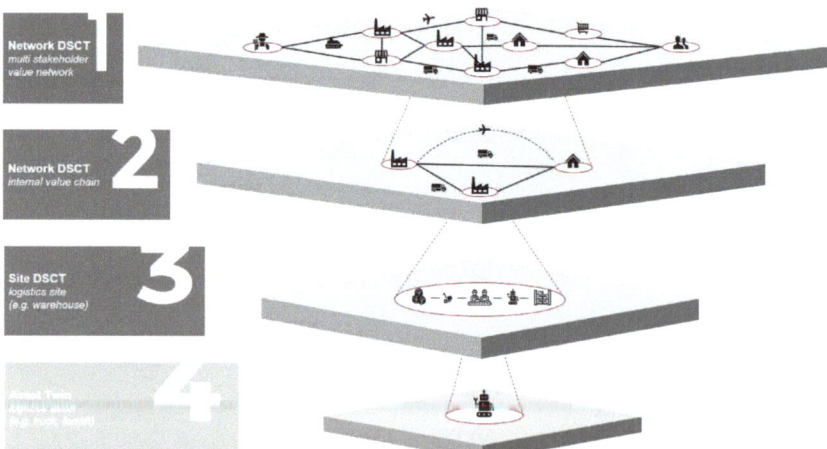

Figure 3. Relation of DSCTs and granularity of the supply chain (cf. [26]).

In the scientific literature, a DSCT is described in many ways. It can function as a means for providing enhanced visibility, traceability, and authentication (cf. [27]), as a decision-support system for disruption risk management (cf. [28]), or as a tool for resilient supply chain controlling (cf. [29]), just to mention a few. However, before going into more detail about the DSCT, a distinction from other similar systems should be made, currently being used in Logistics and Supply Chain Management.

4.1. Distinction from Other Digital Solutions

There are several digital solutions currently being used in LSCM. Firstly, there are Online Freight Exchange Platforms. An online freight exchange, also known as freight exchange, is an online service that connects haulage, logistics, and freight forwarding companies on the web. It allows the companies to go through a database for available freight and market their available vehicle capacity. However, most such platforms lack holistic optimization capabilities. Also, the level of detail regarding freight and order information is not sufficient for sophisticated analyses (cf. [30]).

Other commonly used digital systems for organizing freight orders include Advanced Planning and Scheduling Systems (APS-Systems), Transport Management Systems (TMS), and Supply Chain Management Systems (SCM-Systems). These systems might or might not be integrated with a companies ERP system (cf. Chapter 4.1 [31]). In simplified terms, an SCM system represents an ERP system extended to include the cross-company view. Due to the plurality of existing supply chain management systems, it is not always easy to clearly distinguish them from other software packages, such as ERP/APS systems or TMS. Precisely because modern ERP solutions also integrate the interface to external partners as an architectural concept, functional as well as business process-related overlaps of the system solutions sometimes inevitably arise (cf. Chapter 4.7 [31]). However, regardless of the specific definition, all these solutions show clear disadvantages compared to the DSCT:

1. Update Frequency: Most of the currently used systems do not support real-time data exchange. While this is not a requirement for every single use case, it is crucial for time-sensitive tasks like acute risk management functionalities (cf. [28]).
2. Advanced Analytical Capabilities: The classic ERP system was static and focused on information retrieval only. Modern ERP systems are more user-oriented and offer some functions to analyze data. Still, in most cases, these functions are not sufficient for a holistic optimization approach toward an improved logistics performance (cf. Chapter 4.7 [31]).
3. Simulation Capabilities: Ultimately, there exist virtually no solutions today that feature simulation capabilities regarding the Supply Chain level (cf. Chapter 2.7 [32]). These are, however, indispensable for the assessment of probable future scenarios. Without the ability to run these what-if-scenarios, there are serious limitations to a systems decision-making capabilities (cf. [33]).

The DSCT promises to be an improvement in these regards. This paper, therefore, aims to define a theoretical framework for a DSCT in the context of intermodal transport chains. To achieve this, a set of requirements is first derived from the desired target state as well as the flaws of the currently used systems. Later it will be discussed to what extent the presented solution meets these requirements to ensure its effectiveness.

4.2. Requirements and Framework for a Digital Supply Chain Twin in Intermodal Transport Networks

Table 1 summarizes the chosen requirements necessary for implementing a DSCT in a supply chain. The Digital Supply Chain Twin can first and foremost create visibility and transparency along the entire supply chain, if the partners of the network are able and willing to share their data and thus form a collaborative environment. A digital, simulation-capable model is created based on the required data, which should be continuously updated to reflect the real, cross-system state. Depending on the use case, internal data from the systems of the actors, but also external data sources (e.g., weather, traffic, prices of competitors) can be combined. This forms the foundation for the DSCT to create a realistic model that is as precise as possible to carry out analyses/simulations based on this high data quality. In summary, data quality, quantity, and combination, and smart evaluation are the basic prerequisites for efficient use of the DSCT.

Table 1. Criteria for a solution.

Criteria	Reasoning
visibility and transparency	across the entire network, including...
update frequency	e.g., real time in some use cases
data collection	e.g., + external data + IoT-Data in some cases
data analysis	advanced predictive analytics + holistic optimization
simulation capabiltiies	enabling what-if-scenarios
decision support capabilities	for both transport planning as well as handling of disruptions

Figure 4 depicts an exemplary model of a Digital Supply Chain Twin. The Digital Supply Chain Twin digitally mirrors the physical supply chain by being fed by various information flows to simulate different scenarios. The information flows are bidirectional, generating information from the system's behavior, which can be converted into recommendations for action.

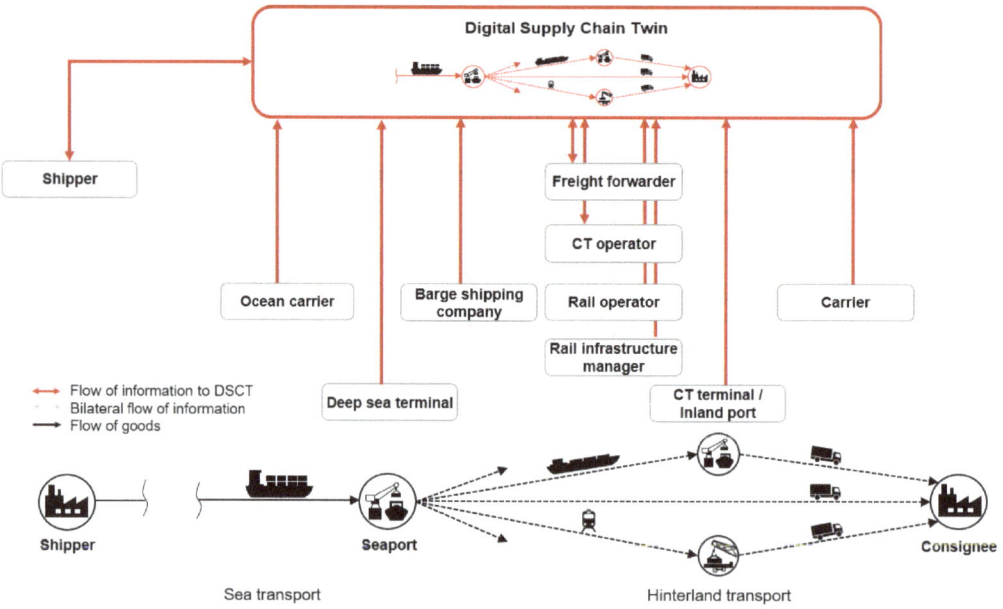

Figure 4. Exemplary flow of goods and information within a maritime transport chain with an additional DSCT.

Based on this, a high level architecture for the DSCT is proposed as depicted in Figure 5 that is discussed below regarding the design decisions as well as regarding the benefits that can potentially be gained from this approach. A more detailed architecture with an in-depth discussion of every component is beyond the scope of this paper. The framework describes a DSCT consisting out of five distinct modules. At the core of this framework is the *Supply Chain Model* module. This module models the physical supply chain and describes all its properties and interdependencies. It can be parametrized through data of the real world to give description states of the real-world supply chain inside the DSCT. The model could be realized through classical algorithms or could use AI technology as described in Section 3.4. To parameterize the Model, an *Interface* module is necessary. The *Interface* module has to fulfill several requirements. Most importantly, this module needs to translate data from multiple different data sources of the physical supply chain into processable data used as input for the Model module. Besides collecting, storing, and preprocessing data that could be enabled through IoT (cf. Section 3.1), 5G (cf. Section 3.2), data availability (cf. Section 3.5), and cloud computing (cf. Section 3.3) respectively, AI technology might be used to process unstructured data towards a structure usable in the Model module. Operations from the privacy-preserving computation domain as briefly discussed in Section 3.7 may be incorporated into this part of the DSCT to fulfill possible privacy and/or confidentiality requirements. If data integrity and trustworthiness is are further requirements for the use of the DSCT, they could be guaranteed through the use of blockchain technology as discussed in Section 3.6. The *Simulation* module that is enabled through the computing capacities provided through Cloud Computing can determine potential future states of the real-world supply chain through applying alternative parameters to the model of the DSCT. This allows to improve decision-making in the supply chain as the results and impact of one or several possible decisions can be determined without actually influencing the real supply chain. Furthermore, stratic planning processes like, for example, scenario planning [34] could use the DSCT to evaluate possible scenarios and outcomes in the longer term. The *Optimization* module utilizes both the *Supply Chain Model* module and the *Simulation* module in order to optimize the supply chain represented through the DSCT. Again, AI techniques are the most promising technology to realize this functionality. This module potentially allows a wide range of improvements in the supply chain like more efficient route planning, the maximization of carrier utilization, additional flexibility in order planning, optimized modal split planning, or the reduction of lead times. The *Reporting* module, finally, prepares the results from the *Optimization* module and the *Supply Chain Model* module individually for each stakeholder and provides them with a structured presentation of all the information and recommendations available through the DSCT.

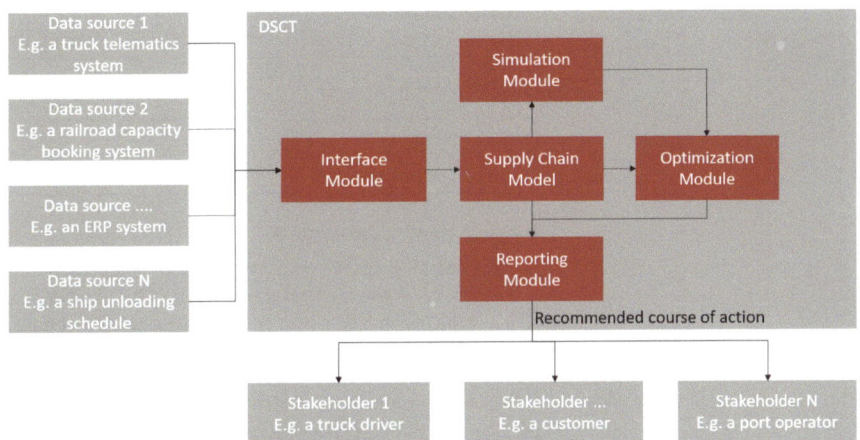

Figure 5. Proposed DSCT Framework.

4.3. Validation of the DSCT Framework

In this section, we validate the DSCT using the criteria mentioned above. For this purpose, we also consider how these criteria were met, for example, by using technologies and concepts that enable fulfillment. An overview of the results is given in Table 2.

For the collection of data, the *Interface* module of the DSCT is used, which allows a wide variety of data sources, for example, external data sources like environmental data for temperature forecasts. The amount of data available for this purpose has increased due to the greater availability of data. Also, actual data can be integrated using IoT-Technology. To consider the specifics of different stakeholders, which can be competitors, concepts of privacy-preserving computation are useful. These data can be stored using the scalability storage capacities of cloud computing. Besides that, the update frequency of the data can be increased using IoT-Technology capabilities (e.g., smaller and cheaper devices) in combination with the communication advantages of 5G. For example, this enables IoT sensors to be used more frequently. The next criterion fulfilled is the capabilities for data analysis based on the *Supply Chain Model* module as the core of the DSCT and can use advantages of cloud computing (e.g., scalability of computation power). Additionally, methods of AI can be used for automation and to generate new insights.

In contrast to this, for the simulation capabilities, no new technologies must be adopted. Since the DSCT, whose model is represented by the *Supply Chain Model* module, provides the foundation for the supply chain's dynamic simulation model. The same applies to decision support capabilities based on other parts of the DSCT, namely on the *Supply Chain Model* and *Simulation* modules. The DSCT itself also fulfills the visibility and transparency requirements as one of the main criteria, and it is provided to the stakeholders by the *Reporting* module. It depends mainly on the dynamic simulations of the optimization and the *Supply Chain Model* Module. For this purpose, technologies can be used, such as cloud computing and advances in connectivity.

Table 2. Validation of DSCT.

Criteria	Enabled by
visibility and transparency	cloud computing connectivity(5G)
update frequency	IoT-technology connectivity (5G)
data collection	IoT-technology cloud computing (storage) privacy-preserving computation
data analysis	cloud computing (computation) artificial intelligence
simulation capabilities	model module (DSCT)
decision support capabilities	reporting module (DSCT)

5. Discussion and Conclusions

In this paper, we have presented the idea of a DSCT for an entire multimodal supply chain. Contrary to the current state where DSCT only covers a small part of the supply chain, we aim for larger parts of the entire supply chain. We have discussed possible benefits resulting from a DSCT and which technologies can enable it. In particular, we have briefly outlined how the latest advances in IT play a major role.

For a complex supply chain like the maritime one discussed in this paper, with a complex hinterland transportation structure, a DSCT can have many benefits. For example, the prediction of delivery times could be improved through the DSCT by taking the various individual factors of the different transportation modes into account. The prediction could be further improved through machine learning of the DSCT to learn from previous transportations of goods through the supply chain. Another central capability of DSCT is a simulation that would allow gaining insides about the existing transport network. For example, it would be easy to determine the limits and bottlenecks of the supply chain that could arise when the number of ships that have to be unloaded increases. The DSCT could also be used to determine the most cost efficient measures to resolve those issues.

However, this work is only the first step towards a DSCT as many questions, especially regarding details, are still open. For example, even though several technologies exist that allow the shared use of data while maintaining the data's confidentiality, how such technologies can be integrated into the DSCT have to be considered in future work. Also, questions about the actual low-level architecture of DSCT have to be researched. For example, centralized, decentralized, or hybrid solutions seem feasible as every single approach has advantages and disadvantages. Whether one of those architectures is strongly superior or not has to be researched. Those decisions might also be influenced by the actual supply chain that is supposed to be modeled. It could differ depending on the goods that are transported or on the composition of the supply chain. For example, in this paper, we chose ocean-going ships as an example, but the situation might differ for entirely continental transport or transport chains, including transportation by air. Another aspect that has to be considered in more detail possible in a testbed are costs of the DSCT and precise benefits that can be generated from its use, and whether the benefits can outweigh the costs. Lastly, the adoption of DSCT will also greatly depend on the acceptance of the different market players and the impact on the market in general. On the one hand, some or many players can benefit greatly from a DSCT, but on the other hand, there might be players who lose the foundation of their business. The different market players' interests have to be researched in detail, and the effects have to be weighted.

Author Contributions: Conceptualization, A.B., B.G., J.C.L., P.P., J.W. and S.Z.; methodology, A.B., B.G., J.C.L., P.P., J.W. and S.Z.; software, not applicable.; validation, A.B., B.G., J.C.L., P.P., J.W. and S.Z.; formal analysis, not applicable; investigation, A.B., B.G., J.C.L., P.P., J.W. and S.Z.; resources, not applicable; data curation, not applicable; writing–original draft preparation, A.B., B.G., J.C.L., P.P., J.W. and S.Z.; writing–review and editing, A.B., B.G., J.C.L., P.P., J.W. and S.Z.; visualization, B.G., J.C.L., P.P., J.W. and S.Z.; supervision, not applicable; project administration, not applicable; funding acquisition, not applicable. All authors have read and agreed to the published version of the manuscript.

Funding: This research received no external funding.

Institutional Review Board Statement: Not applicable.

Informed Consent Statement: Not applicable.

Data Availability Statement: Not applicable.

Conflicts of Interest: The authors declare no conflict of interest.

References

1. Pfohl, H.C. *Logistiksysteme: Betriebswirtschaftliche Grundlagen. 9., neu bearb. u. aktual. Aufl.*; Springer: Berlin, Germany, 2018.
2. Marmolejo-Saucedo, J.A. Design and Development of Digital Twins: A Case Study in Supply Chains. *Mob. Netw. Appl.* **2020**, *25*, 2141–2160. [CrossRef]
3. Straube, F. *e-Logistik: Ganzheitliches Logistikmanagement*; Springer: Berlin/Heidelberg, Germany, 2004. [CrossRef]
4. Straube, F.; Reipert, J.; Schöder, D. City-Logistik der Zukunft—Im Spannungsfeld von Elektromobilität und Digitalisierung. *Wirtsch. Manag.* **2017**, *9*, 28–35. [CrossRef]
5. Nitsche, B.; Straube, F. Efficiently managing supply chain volatility—A management framework for the manufacturing industry. *Procedia Manuf.* **2020**, *43*, 320–327.
6. Reifsnider, K.; Majumdar, P. Multiphysics Stimulated Simulation Digital Twin Methods for Fleet Management. In Proceedings of the 54th AIAA/ASME/ASCE/AHS/ASC Structures, Structural Dynamics, and Materials Conference, Boston, MA, USA, 8–11 April 2013. [CrossRef]
7. Majumdar, P.K.; FaisalHaider, M.; Reifsnider, K. Multi-physics Response of Structural Composites and Framework for Modeling Using Material Geometry. In Proceedings of the 54th AIAA/ASME/ASCE/AHS/ASC Structures, Structural Dynamics, and Materials Conference, Boston, MA, USA, 8–11 April 2013. [CrossRef]
8. Hevner, A.; Chatterjee, S. Design Science Research in Information Systems. In *Design Research in Information Systems: Theory and Practice*; Springer: Boston, MA, USA, 2010; pp. 9–22. [CrossRef]
9. Peffers, K.; Tuunanen, T.; Rothenberger, M.; Chatterjee, S. A Design Science Research Methodology for Information Systems Research. *J. Manage. Inf. Syst.* **2007**, *24*, 45–77. [CrossRef]
10. Straube, F.; Pfohl, H.C. *Trends und Strategien in der Logistik-Globale Netzwerke im Wandel. Umwelt, Sicherheit, Internationalisierung, Menschen*; Technical Report; Darmstadt Technical University, Department of Business Administration; Bundesvereinigung Logistik (BVL) e.V.: Bremen, Germany, 2008.
11. Serdarasan, S. A review of supply chain complexity drivers. *Comput. Ind. Eng.* **2013**, *66*, 533–540. [CrossRef]
12. Marinekommando. Fakten und Zahlen zur maritimen Abhängigkeit der Bundesrepublik Deutschland: Jahresbericht 2019. Technical Report 32, Deutsche Bundeswehr, 2019. Available online: https://www.bundeswehr.de/resource/blob/156014/fa1039c05301b9c63ad642c683880778/jahresbericht-marinekommando-2019-data.pdf (accessed on 16 February 2021).
13. Jahn, C. Seeschiffsgüterverkehr. In *Verkehrs- und Transportlogistik*; Springer: Berlin/Heidelberg, Germany, 2013; pp. 203–215. [CrossRef]

14. Poschmann, P.; Weinke, M.; Balster, A.; Straube, F.; Friedrich, H.; Ludwig, A. Realization of ETA Predictions for Intermodal Logistics Networks Using Artificial Intelligence. In *Advances in Production, Logistics and Traffic*; Clausen, U., Langkau, S., Kreuz, F., Eds.; Springer International Publishing: Cham, Switzerland, 2019; pp. 155–176.
15. Atzori, L.; Iera, A.; Morabito, G. The Internet of Things: A survey. *Comput. Netw.* **2010**, *54*, 2787–2805. [CrossRef]
16. Andrews, J.G.; Buzzi, S.; Choi, W.; Hanly, S.V.; Lozano, A.; Soong, A.C.K.; Zhang, J.C. What Will 5G Be? *IEEE J. Sel. Areas Commun.* **2014**, *32*, 1065–1082. [CrossRef]
17. Mell, P.M.; Grance, T. *SP 800-145. The NIST Definition of Cloud Computing*; Technical Report; National Institute of Standards & Technology: Gaithersburg, MD, USA, 2011.
18. Hentschel, R.; Leyh, C. Cloud Computing: Status quo, aktuelle Entwicklungen und Herausforderungen. In *Cloud Computing: Die Infrastruktur der Digitalisierung*; Springer Fachmedien Wiesbaden: Wiesbaden, Germany, 2018; pp. 3–20. [CrossRef]
19. Weber, M.; Burchardt, A. Entscheidungsunterstützung mit Künstlicher Intelligenz: Wirtschaftliche Bedeutung, Gesellschaftliche Herausforderungen, Menschliche Verantwortung. Technical Report, Bitkom e.V. and Deutsches Forschungszentrum für Künstliche Intelligenz (DFKI), 2017. Available online: https://www.bitkom.org/sites/default/files/file/import/171012-KI-Gipfelpapier-online.pdf (accessed on 16 February 2021).
20. Kreutzer, R.T.; Sirrenberg, M. Was versteht man unter Künstlicher Intelligenz und wie kann man sie nutzen? In *Künstliche Intelligenz Verstehen: Grundlagen—Use-Cases—Unternehmenseigene KI-Journey*; Springer Fachmedien Wiesbaden: Wiesbaden, Germany, 2019; pp. 1–71. [CrossRef]
21. Reinsel, D.; Gantz, J.; Rydning, J. The Digitization of the World: From Edge to Core. Technical Report US44413318, IDC, 2018. Available online: https://www.seagate.com/files/www-content/our-story/trends/files/idc-seagate-dataage-whitepaper.pdf (accessed on 24 February 2021).
22. Borgi, T.; Zoghlami, N.; Abed, M. Big data for transport and logistics: A review. In Proceedings of the 2017 International Conference on Advanced Systems and Electric Technologies (IC_ASET), Hammamet, Tunisia, 14–17 January 2017; pp. 44–49. [CrossRef]
23. Yaga, D.; Mell, P.; Roby, N.; Scarfone, K. *Blockchain Technology Overview*; Technical Report NISTIR 8202; National Institute of Standards and Technology (NIST): Gaithersburg, MD, USA, 2018. [CrossRef]
24. Zheng, Z.; Xie, S.; Dai, H.N.; Chen, W.; Chen, X.; Weng, J.; Imran, M. An overview on smart contracts: Challenges, advances and platforms. *Future Gener. Comput. Syst.* **2020**, *105*, 475–491. [CrossRef]
25. The Privacy Preserving Techniques Task Team. *UN Handbook on Privacy-Preserving Computation Techniques*; Technical Report; UN Global Working Group on Big Data: 2019. Available online: http://publications.officialstatistics.org/handbooks/privacy-preserving-techniques-handbook/UN%20Handbook%20for%20Privacy-Preserving%20Techniques.pdf (accessed on 24 February 2021).
26. Gerlach, B.; Zarnitz, S.; Straube, F. Digital Twins in Logistics and Supply Chain Management – Conceptual Clarification, Use Cases and Potentials of "Digital Supply Chain Twins". Unpublished work.
27. Srai, J.; Settanni, E.; Tsolakis, N.; Aulakh, P. Supply Chain Digital Twins: Opportunities and Challenges Beyond the Hype. In Proceedings of the 23rd Cambridge International Manufacturing Symposium, Cambridge, UK, 26–27 September 2019. [CrossRef]
28. Ivanov, D.; Dolgui, A. A digital supply chain twin for managing the disruption risks and resilience in the era of Industry 4.0. *Prod. Plan. Control* **2020**, 1–14. [CrossRef]
29. Park, K.T.; Son, Y.H.; Noh, S.D. The architectural framework of a cyber physical logistics system for digital-twin-based supply chain control. *Int. J. Prod. Res.* **2020**, 1–22. [CrossRef]
30. Miller, J.; Nie, Y.; Liu, X. Hyperpath Truck Routing in an Online Freight Exchange Platform. *Transp. Sci.* **2020**, *54*, 1676–1696. [CrossRef]
31. Hausladen, I. *IT-Gestützte Logistik: Systeme-Prozesse-Anwendung*, 4th ed.; Springer Gabler: Wiesbaden, Germany, 2020. [CrossRef]
32. Gutenschwager, K.; Rabe, M.; Spieckermann, S.; Wenzel, S. *Simulation in Produktion und Logistik: Grundlagen und Anwendungen*, 1st ed.; Springer Vieweg: Wiesbaden, Germany, 2017. [CrossRef]
33. Korth, B.; Schwede, C.; Zajac, M. Simulation-ready digital twin for realtime management of logistics systems. In Proceedings of the 2018 IEEE International Conference on Big Data (Big Data), Seattle, WA, USA, 10–13 December 2018; pp. 4194–4201. [CrossRef]
34. Bradfield, R.; Wright, G.; Burt, G.; Cairns, G.; Van Der Heijden, K. The origins and evolution of scenario techniques in long range business planning. *Futures* **2005**, *37*, 795–812. [CrossRef]

Article

An Analytical Approach for Facility Location for Truck Platooning—A Case Study of an Unmanned Following Truck Platooning System in Japan

Daisuke Watanabe [1,*], Takeshi Kenmochi [2] and Keiju Sasa [3]

1. Department of Logistics and Information Engineering, Tokyo University of Marine Science and Technology, 2-1-6 Etchujima, Koto-ku, Tokyo 135-8533, Japan
2. Transport and Socioeconomic Research Division, The Institute of Behavioral Sciences, 2-9 Ichigayahonmura-cho, Shinjuku-ku, Tokyo 162-0845, Japan; tkenmochi@ibs.or.jp
3. Urban and Regional Planning Research Division, The Institute of Behavioral Sciences, 2-9 Ichigayahonmura-cho, Shinjuku-ku, Tokyo 162-0845, Japan; ksasa@ibs.or.jp
* Correspondence: daisuke@kaiyodai.ac.jp; Tel.: +81-3-5245-7367

Citation: Watanabe, D.; Kenmochi, T.; Sasa, K. An Analytical Approach for Facility Location for Truck Platooning—A Case Study of an Unmanned Following Truck Platooning System in Japan. *Logistics* **2021**, *5*, 27. https://doi.org/10.3390/logistics5020027

Academic Editor: Benjamin Nitsche

Received: 8 March 2021
Accepted: 29 April 2021
Published: 7 May 2021

Publisher's Note: MDPI stays neutral with regard to jurisdictional claims in published maps and institutional affiliations.

Copyright: © 2021 by the authors. Licensee MDPI, Basel, Switzerland. This article is an open access article distributed under the terms and conditions of the Creative Commons Attribution (CC BY) license (https://creativecommons.org/licenses/by/4.0/).

Abstract: Truck platooning involves a small convoy of freight vehicles using electronic coupling as an application in automated driving technology, and it is expected to represent a major solution for improving efficiency in truck transportation in the near future. Recently, there have been several trials regarding truck platooning with major truck manufacturers and logistics companies on public roads in the United States, European countries and Japan. There is a need to locate a facility for the formation of truck platooning to realize the unmanned operation of trucks following in a platoon. In this study, we introduce the current status of truck platooning in Japan and present the optimal location model for truck platooning using the continuous approximation model with a numerical experiment, considering the case in Japan. We derived the optimal locational strategy for the combination of the long-haul ratio and the cost factor of platooning. With parameters estimated for several scenarios for the deployment of truck platooning in Japan, the numerical results show that the optimal locational strategy for a platoon of manned vehicles and a platoon with unmanned following vehicles is the edge of the local region, and that for a platoon of fully automated vehicles is the center of the region.

Keywords: truck platooning; facility location; continuous approximation

1. Introduction

In the context of the current global trend toward sustainable development, sustainability is becoming more important in supply chain management (SCM) and for the natural environment. Green SCM has become one of the significant issues in the global logistics system, and efforts have been made to reduce the emissions of environmental burdens and greenhouse gas (GHG) emissions in supply chains [1]. Additionally, in Japan, various sectors, including freight transportation, face labor shortages under the condition of a declining and aging population with a low birthrate. As the insufficiency caused by this labor shortage in supply side has not caught up with increasing demand on the consumer side, such as in e-commerce, home-delivery, etc., some action needs to be taken to maintain balance in freight transportation.

One of the possible countermeasures for sustainable and efficient SCM is automation in freight transportation. In recent years, the development of various new technologies related to automation has progressed rapidly around the world to improve labor-savings and efficiency in freight transportation. Among the recent key trends and innovations in SCM, one of the technologies with the highest impact is self-driving vehicles (SDVs) [2]. In order to implement SDVs, it is necessary to integrate new technologies, such as Artificial Intelligence (AI) and the Internet of Things (IoT), as well as to comply with laws and regulations focusing on safe driving in each country. In the logistics industry, SDVs are expected to be used in a variety of transportation, from long-distance trucking to last-mile delivery. Fully automated vehicles (FAVs) are already being used in completely closed environments such as mines and ports, while on public roads, demonstration tests are still being conducted in limited areas under legal restrictions. As a major solution for improving the efficiency of long-haul trucking, truck platooning, which involves a small convoy of freight vehicles using electronic coupling with semi-automated driving, has been under technological development since the early 2000s [3]. Truck platooning is expected to reduce environmental burdens by reducing the air resistance of following trucks and could be a possible solution for the labor shortage problem.

In this decade, several trials have been conducted for truck platooning with major truck manufacturers and logistics companies on the public roads in the United States, European countries and Japan. In Europe, the Netherlands is taking the initiative to conduct large-scale field operational tests for the cross-border transportation [4] and R&D related to the development of inter-manufacturer-standard specifications by six major truck manufacturers [5]. In Germany, a field operational test of truck platooning on an expressway has been conducted with the involvement of logistics companies [6]. In the UK, the world's first platooning trials took place in a commercial operating environment to quantify real-world benefits [7]. The deployment of multi-brand platooning with unmanned following vehicles is assumed to be part of the roadmap for truck platooning in Europe by the end of 2021 [8]. In the United States, the key performance measures for evaluating truck platooning field deployments have been proposed by the government [9], and the operational tests of truck platooning with unmanned following vehicles have recently made steady progress in some commercial services [10]. In Japan, field operational tests on expressways have been conducted with manned following vehicles since 2017 and unmanned following vehicles since 2018 [11]. The trials in Europe mainly focus on manned operations, but those in the United States and Japan intend to include unmanned operations.

For the introduction of unmanned truck platooning, infrastructure improvement, laws and regulations and commercialization have been discussed. In particular, the truck platooning trials conducted in Japan revealed some issues related to infrastructure. For example, there is a need for a dedicated or prioritized lane for truck platooning and a facility for the formation of truck platooning to switch the drivers in the following truck in the platoon. Bhoopalam et al. [12] provided a framework to classify various new transportation planning problems that arise in truck platooning, as well as surveying relevant operational research models for these problems in the literature. In an overview of previous optimization studies of truck platooning schemes, literature on the planning, scheduling and routing of the operational side of truck platooning has been proposed, but research on facility locations on the strategic side has been quite limited. Therefore, this research focuses on facility locations for the formation of truck platooning for unmanned truck platooning. Continuous approximation (CA) is an efficient and effective technique for modeling complex and uncertain logistics problems, especially in the areas of facility locations [13]. In this study, we introduce the current status of truck platooning trials in Japan and summarize the related plan of truck platooning formation. Considering the case of the unmanned truck platooning system in Japan, we present an optimal location analysis to minimize the total operation cost of truck platooning using the CA model and discuss the implications of the computational results with a numerical experiment of the case of Japan.

2. Literature Review

In the formation of platoons, complex planning problems may arise, and sophisticated decision support models and tools are required in the planning, such as the scheduling and routing of platoons. Bhoopalam et al. [12] provided a framework to classify various new transportation planning problems that arise in truck platooning and surveyed relevant operations research models for these problems in the literature. For the scheduling problem,

Larsson et al. [14] presented a mathematical framework to formulate and analyze the platoon coordination and departure time scheduling problems under the condition of travel time uncertainty. Larsen et al. [15] presented a model for optimizing truck platoons formed at a platooning hub—that is, a fixed location—using a dynamic programming-based local search heuristic. In the factors of fuel consumption, Zhang et al. [16] summarized the methodologies about fuel savings for truck platooning, the coordination methods to improve the platooning rate and the look-ahead control strategies to generate fuel-efficient speed profiles for each vehicle driving in a platoon over different road conditions.

As a case study for truck platooning operation in a specific region, some simulation models that consider the regional logistics system have been proposed. Gerrits et al. [17] presented the design and implementation of an agent-based simulation model based on the Port of Rotterdam in the Netherlands and its surrounding expressways to study the potential benefits of truck platooning. The results showed that the most influential factors in platoon formation and the total platoon profitability are wage savings and the possibility of different truck brands platooning together. Jo et al. [18] analyzed the influence of truck platooning on the performance of freeway networks in terms of travel time savings based on the integration of a microscopic and macroscopic approach in Korea and observed that truck platooning would result in annual benefits of travel time savings corresponding to approximately USD 167.7 million in 2020. Paddeu et al. [19] investigated the potential for truck platooning to reduce carbon emissions from road freight in UK, presenting a series of scenarios that varied by adoption rates, operational models and platoon sizes. The result showed that there is a potential for small reductions in polluting emissions due to truck platooning. These simulation models based on case studies in each country require detailed data on freight demand and costs in the operation of truck platooning to simulate the potential future scenarios, but there is an inherent uncertainty in forecasting the future deployment of truck platooning.

To design logistics networks with the unmanned operation of following trucks in a platoon, there is a need to locate a facility for the formation of truck platooning. The facility location decision is classified into strategic planning for solid long-term decision-making in logistics problems. Laporte et al. [20] provided some guidelines on how location decisions and logistics functions can be integrated into a single mathematical model to optimize the configuration of a logistics network. Facility location problems can be categorized according to the location space into continuous and discrete with a network. The continuous approximation (CA) model can approximate the objective into localized functions that can be optimized by relatively simple analytical operations and widely applied to various logistics problems including facility location, inventory management and vehicle routing [13]. The formation center for truck platooning is considered as a platooning hub and can be formulated by the hub location problems (HLPs), and there are a large number of related studies for the optimization of hub location for logistics operations, mainly using a discrete model with a fixed set of candidate facility locations, discrete time periods and discrete customer demand points. Since future forecasting for truck platooning operation is quite difficult due to the restrictions and uncertainty of the detailed demand volume data and operational assumption, it is quite difficult to obtain exact solutions with a discrete model; however, it is suitable for discussing the basic characteristics of a facility location for truck platooning with the CA model. The developments in the CA model are strongly related to computational geometry and geometric probability considering the continuous location space [20,21]. In the case of many-to-many distribution with hubs for time-definite freight transportation carriers, Campbell [22] formulated hub location models without the consideration of service hubs to minimize transportation costs. As an integrated location-routing problem, Xie and Ouyang [23] studied the optimal spatial layout of transshipment facilities and the corresponding service regions on an infinite homogeneous plane that minimizes the total cost for facility set-up, outbound delivery and inbound replenishment transportation.

3. Current Status of Truck Platooning in Japan

3.1. Field Operational Tests on Public Road

In Japan, truck platooning has developed within a national intelligent transport systems (ITS) project named "Energy ITS" in 2008, focusing on energy saving and environmental protection in addition to safety and aiming at introduction in the near future, and the operational tests in this project were mainly conducted in limited areas such as test tracks [24]; in particular, unmanned operational tests directly connected with the solution for the current serious lack of truck drivers were conducted. Now, the field operational tests have been conducted by the Ministry of Economy, Trade and Industry (METI) and Ministry of Land, Infrastructure, Transport and Tourism (MLIT) mainly on expressways from fiscal year (FY) 2017 to 2020 [11]. The tests were conducted step-by-step under the conditions shown in Table 1. The control direction included the longitudinal direction only (CACC: Cooperative Adaptive Cruise Control, equivalent to Autonomation Level 1) and driving including the horizontal direction (CACC and LKA: Lane Keeping Assist, equivalent to Autonomation Level 2). Driver types in following vehicles include manned (equivalent to Autonomation Level 1 or 2) and unmanned (equivalent to Autonomation Level 4). The inter-vehicle distance and time were 35 m (70 km/h, 1.6 s), 20 m (70 km/h, 1 s), 10 m (70 km/h, 0.5 s) and 10 m (80 km/h, 0.4 s). In addition, the safety equipment included the monitoring system of the following vehicle with a Human–Machine Interface (HMI) and the Minimum Risk Maneuver (MRM); more advanced damage reduction methods, such as braking and Emergency Driving Stop, were installed in the trial in 2019.

Table 1. Field operational tests of truck platooning in Japan.

FY	Period	Location	No. of Vehicles	Control Direction *	Driver on Following Vehicle	Inter-Vehicle Time	Loading Condition/Time
2017	January–February 2018	Shin-Tomei Expressway	3 Multi-brand	CACC	Manned	1.6 s (70 km/h)	None/daytime
		Kita-Kanto Expressway	4 Multi-brand	CACC	Manned	1.6 s (70 km/h)	None/daytime
2018	November	Joshin-Etsu Expressway	4 Multi-brand	CACC	Manned	1.6 s (70 km/h)	Loading/daytime
	December	Shin-Tomei Expressway	4 Multi-brand	CACC + LKA	Manned	1.6 s (70 km/h)	None/daytime
	January–February 2019	Shin-Tomei Expressway (15 km)	3 Mono-brand	Electronic towing	Unmanned	0.5 s (70 km/h)	None/daytime
2019	June 2019–February 2020	Shin-Tomei Expressway (140 km)	3 Mono-brand	Electronic towing + MRM	Unmanned	0.5 s (80 km/h)	None/day and night
2020	May 2020–February 2021	Shin-Tomei Expressway (140 km)	3 Mono-brand (3 sets)	Electronic towing + MRM	Unmanned	0.5 s (80 km/h)	None/day and night

* CACC: Cooperative Adaptive Cruise Control; LKA: Lane Keeping Assist; MRM: Minimum Risk Maneuver.

The government's strategy "Public–Private ITS Initiative/Roadmaps" related to ITS/automated driving has been updated every year since its original publication in FY2014 [25]. The 2018 version provided the roadmap to achieve truck platooning with unmanned following vehicles on the Shin-Tomei Expressway in 2020 and the commercialization of manned following vehicle platooning in 2021. For commercialization in 2021, four major truck companies (ISUZU, HINO, Mitsubishi Fuso and UD) in Japan are developing products equipped with ACC and LKA [26]. The 2019 version clearly defines the approaches to realize the practical use of truck platooning with unmanned following vehicles in the target year of 2020, presenting the development phases shown in Table 2. For truck platooning with unmanned following vehicles, it is explicitly stated that a platoon should be formed and deformed outside the main lane of an expressway.

Table 2. Development phases of truck platooning in Japan.

	Truck Platooning with Manned Following Vehicles	Truck Platooning with Unmanned Following Vehicles
Target year	By 2021	After 2022
Driving technology	Following the vehicle in front using CACC + LKA technology	Following the vehicle in front using CACC + LKA technology
Control of following vehicles	The following vehicles follow the leading vehicle and support the driving of the following vehicles' drivers by automatically keeping the inter-vehicle distance, controlling the speed and remaining in the lane	The following vehicles are electronically towed and run unmanned by controlling their speed, keeping the inter-vehicle distance, staying in lane and changing lane
Driving steps	1. Start on the main lane (follow the vehicle in front) 2. The platoon can be deformed at any time and stops when the leading vehicle/the vehicle itself changes lane/enters a branch lane	1. The platoon is formed outside the main lane to start platooning (consisting of up to three vehicles) 2. Enter the main lane 3. Enter a branch lane 4. The platoon is deformed outside the main lane to stop platooning

In Europe, the project "ENabling SafE Multi-Brand pLatooning for Europe" (ENSEMBLE) suggested the pre-standards for interoperability between trucks, platoons and logistics solution providers to speed up the actual market adoption of (sub)system development and implementation and to enable the harmonization of legal frameworks in the member states [5]. In ENSEMBLE, three different levels of platooning automation are anticipated: Level A for the first stage, Level B with an advanced automation level and Level C with FAVs. The current status of platooning automation levels in ENSEMBLE in Europe [27] and Japan [28] is almost the same, as shown in Table 3. However, there are differences in some aspects, such as vehicle gap distance, fallback, fail-safe and the number of vehicles in a platoon, and Japan adopts stricter standards than Europe. The commercialization of longitudinal/horizontal platooning (in the same lane) in the initial phase is planned in the same year of 2022. In Europe, the main purpose for truck platooning is to reduce drivers' labor loads and the burden on the environment. Therefore, they mainly study truck platooning with manned following vehicles rather than truck platooning with unmanned following vehicles. This reveals that Japan is ahead of Europe from the perspective of conducting field operational tests with unmanned following vehicles.

Table 3. Comparison of platooning automation levels between Europe and Japan.

Automation	Europe	Japan
Longitudinal/horizontal platooning (in the same lane)	Level A	I. Introduction type
Longitudinal/horizontal platooning (with lane changes)	Level B	II. Development type
Full automation	Level C	Unmanned platooning

3.2. Infrastructure Development for Truck Platooning

Traffic rules, commercialization and infrastructure development for truck platooning have been discussed in advance of the discussion of legislation. Major tasks for truck platooning in Japan include the legal requirements of truck platooning with an unmanned following vehicle, the development of rules for truck platooning, the development of rules for Vehicle-to-Vehicle (V2V) communication, special traffic rules for truck platooning and the required infrastructure such as the facility for the formation/deformation of truck platooning.

Three platooning formation concepts have mainly been considered [3]: (i) scheduled platooning, (ii) "on-the-fly" or self-organized platooning and (iii) orchestrated platooning facilitated by Platooning Service Providers (PSPs). In orchestrated platooning, the Platoon

Formation Center (PFC) is the facility or parking lot for platooning formation operated by PSPs. As shown in Figure 1, PFCs need to be equipped with several functions such as a matching/coordination system for the truck platoon, parking spaces for electronic coupling and decoupling of truck platoon, a cargo handling yard and a rest station for drivers [29].

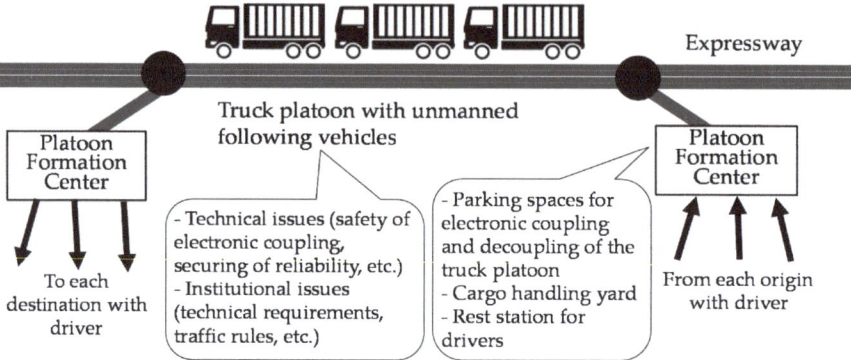

Figure 1. Truck platooning operation with Platoon Formation Centers.

3.3. Facility Location Plan for Platoon Formation Centers

Major cities and industries in Japan are geographically concentrated along the Pacific coast, especially between Tokyo, Nagoya and Osaka, as shown in Figure 2. The Shin-Tomei and Shin-Meishin expressways were opened in the 2010s with a high-standard design as an alternative route to the existing, dilapidated expressways between the three major cities. At first, the facility development plan for truck platooning was under discussion on the Shin-Tomei and Shin-Meishin expressways [29]. In this plan, the approximate candidate sites of three PFCs were proposed near the interchange of the major corridor and outer ring roads in the suburbs of three major cities, shown as the red circled areas in Figure 2.

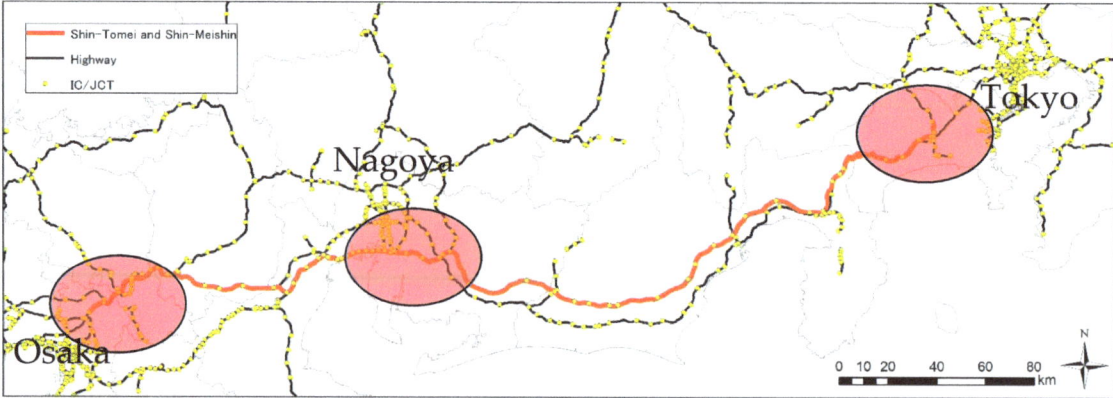

Figure 2. Facility development plan for Platoon Formation Centers for Tokyo–Nagoya–Osaka.

4. Formulation of Facility Location Model for Truck Platoon with Continuous Approximation

4.1. Model Description

We assume a simple route choice in the case of two trucks, as shown in Figure 3, to explain the effect of truck platooning formation. Both trucks need to make a detour to form a platoon, but this is a waste of time and cost for both trucks. To make the truck platooning more advantageous than the shortest route with a single truck trip, cost reduction on the platoon arc is quite an important factor, including saving fuel consumption and labor cost by platooning. Therefore, the cost factor of platooning (α) is adopted in the platoon arc.

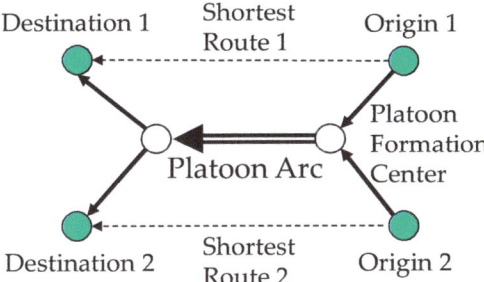

Figure 3. Routes with and without Truck platooning.

The formulation and assumption of this model are as follows. As shown in Figure 4, we consider the two circled regions A and B, whose radii are r, and the distance between two regions is l. The long-haul ratio x ($x > 2$) is deployed to consider the relationship between l and r as follows: in general, the long-haul ratio x becomes larger as the distance between two regions l becomes longer with a fixed radius r.

$$x = \frac{l}{r} \tag{1}$$

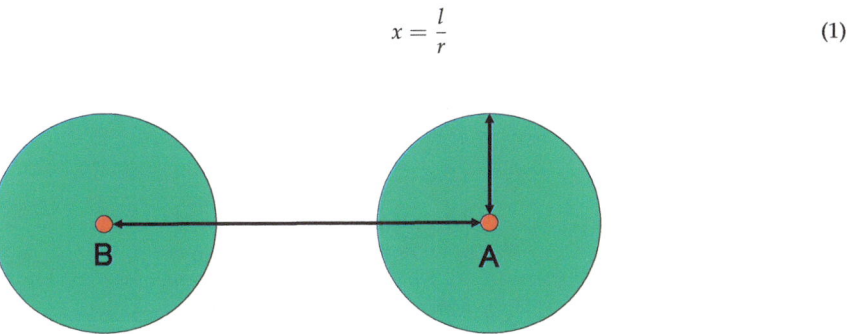

Figure 4. Two circled regions.

The travel demand between two regions is uniformly generated. As shown in Figure 5, travel cost is formulated as the average travel distance between two regions, and the scenarios for route choice are considered as follows:

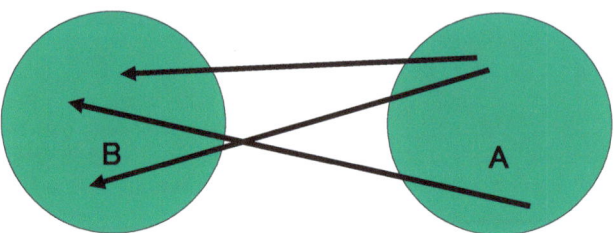

Case 1: Without platooning.

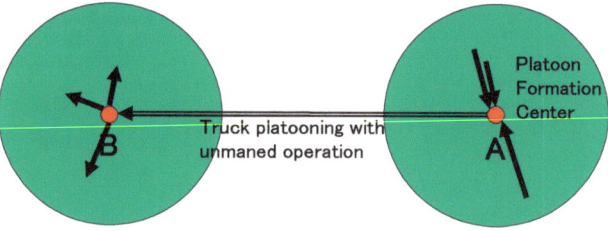

Case 2: With truck platooning, with platoon formation at the center of each region.

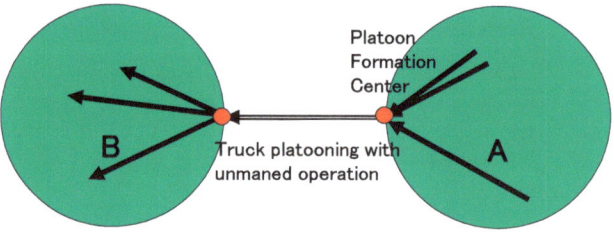

Case 3: With truck platooning, with platoon formation at the edge of each region.

Figure 5. Three scenarios with and without truck platooning.

Case 1: Without platooning;
Case 2: With truck platooning, with platoon formation at the center of regions;
Case 3: With truck platooning, with platoon formation at the edge of regions—i.e., the nearest location to another circle.

In Case 1, each truck travels alone and moves directly with the shortest distance from the origin to destination between two regions. The average travel distance is calculated using the approximate formulas of average distances between two points in two different coplanar regions [30]. The travel cost of Case 1 D_s is derived as follows:

$$D_s = l + \frac{r^2}{4l} \qquad (2)$$

In Case 2, the travel cost consists of the long-haul cost with platooning between the PFCs at the center of the region and the average travel cost in the local area of each PFC. In long-haul travel, the travel distance is l between two PFCs with the cost factor with platooning (α). In local access travel to each PFC, the average distance to the center of circle is $2/3r$ [21,31], and there are two circle regions for the origin and destination. The travel cost of Case 2 D_c is derived as follows:

$$D_c = \alpha l + 2\frac{2r}{3} \qquad (3)$$

In Case 3, the travel cost consists of the long-haul cost with platooning between the PFCs at the edge of the region and the average travel cost in the local area of each PFC. In long-haul travel, the travel distance is $l - 2r$ between two PFCs with the cost factor with platooning (α). In local access travel to each PFC, the average distance to the edge of the circle is $\frac{32r}{9\pi}$ [31,32], and there are two circle regions for the origin and destination. The travel cost of Case 3 D_e is derived as follows:

$$D_e = \alpha(l - 2r) + 2\frac{32r}{9\pi} \tag{4}$$

Figure 6 shows the comparison between the cost functions in cases 1, 2 and 3 with the change in the cost factor with platooning (α) using the long-haul ratio x as follows: for the low cost reduction scenario, $\alpha = 0.8$; for the middle cost reduction scenario, $\alpha = 0.5$; and for the high cost reduction scenario, $\alpha = 0.3$. We can observe that the travel cost in Case 3 is the cheapest case in scenarios where $\alpha = 0.8$ and 0.5, but not for $x = 2$, and the travel cost in Case 2 is the cheapest case in the scenario where $\alpha = 0.3$. Case 1 is the cheapest case in $\alpha = 0.8$ and 0.5 only where $x = 2$; i.e., the situation that two circles come into contact with each other. In conclusion, Case 2 is the optimal location as the cost factor with platooning (α) becomes smaller, but Case 3 is the optimal location for most scenarios. Case 1, without platooning, is the optimal route choice only in the special case that two regions are located close to one another.

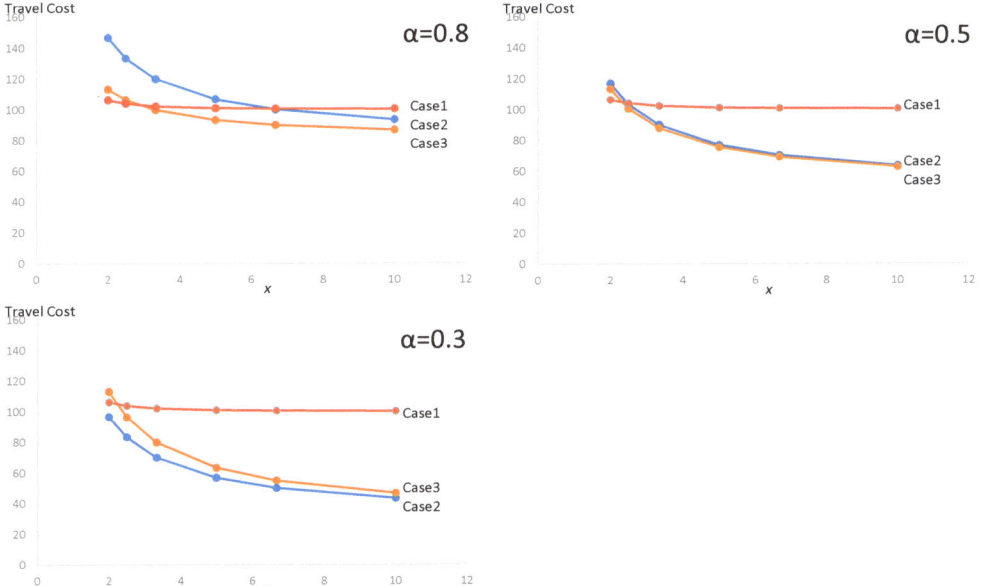

Figure 6. Travel cost with three scenarios of cost factors with platooning (α).

4.2. Optimal Location

In this section, the optimal locational strategy is discussed according to the analytical comparison among three cases. Solving the condition $D_s \geqq D_c$ from Equations (2) and (3) with the long-haul ratio x for the comparison between the travel Cost of Case 1 and 2, we can derive the following Equation:

$$\alpha \leqq 1 + \frac{1}{4x^2} - \frac{4}{3x} \tag{5}$$

Solving the condition $D_s \geqq D_e$ from Equations (2) and (4) with the long-haul ratio x for the comparison between the travel cost of Cases 1 and 3, we can derive the following equation:

$$\alpha \leqq \frac{4x^2 + \frac{256}{9\pi}x + 1}{4x(x-2)} \qquad (6)$$

Solving the condition $D_c \geqq D_e$ from Equations (3) and (4) with the long-haul ratio x for the comparison between the travel costs of cases 2 and 3, we can derive the following equation that is independent of the long-haul ratio x:

$$\alpha \geqq \frac{32}{9\pi} - \frac{2}{3} \qquad (7)$$

From Equations (5)–(7), we can obtain the results that show the dominant combination of x and the cost factor with platooning (α) for all three cases, as shown in Figure 7. The border of Case 1 and Case 2 is a quadratic function based on Equation (5), but the length of this border is quite short. The border of Case 1 and Case 3 is also a quadratic function based on Equation (6). The border of Case 2 and Case 3 is a constant value $\frac{32}{9\pi} - \frac{2}{3}$ to x based on Equation (7). Three borders meet at the point $\alpha = \frac{32}{9\pi} - \frac{2}{3}$ (=0.465) and $x = 2.284$.

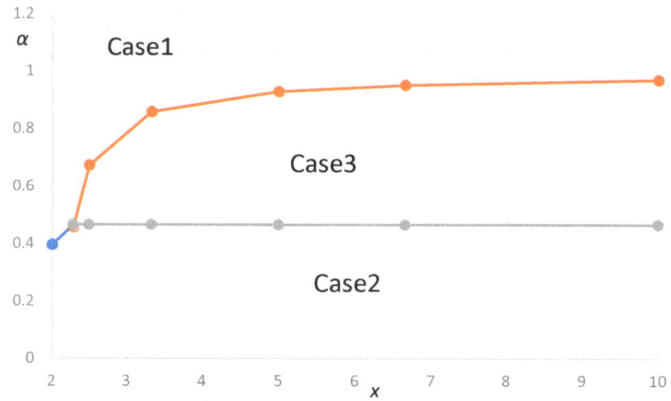

Figure 7. Optimal locational strategy for the combination of the long-haul ratio x and the cost factor with platooning (α).

5. Numerical Experiments Considering the Scenarios in Japan

5.1. Estimation of the Cost Factor with Platooning

In this section, we estimate the cost factor with platooning (α), which is the advantage of truck platooning considering the scenarios in Japan. The travel cost per vehicle is defined as follows: the single vehicle without platooning in Case 1 is s, the leading vehicle of the truck platoon in Case 2 and 3 is a, and the following vehicle of the truck platoon in Case 2 and 3 is b. The number of vehicles is n. The travel cost for a single vehicle without platooning in Case 1 is:

$$T_s = sn \qquad (8)$$

The travel cost for the platooning in Case 2 and 3 is:

$$T_p = a + (n-1)b \qquad (9)$$

The cost factor with platooning (α) is the ratio of the travel cost for the platooning to the travel cost for the single vehicle without platooning, and we can derive this as follows:

$$\alpha = \frac{T_p}{T_s} = \frac{a + (n-1)b}{sn} \quad (10)$$

To check the characteristics of Equation (10), the numerical experiment in the simple case ($s = 1$ and $a = 1$) is shown in Figure 8. As the number of vehicles in a platoon (n) increases, the cost factor with platooning (α) decreases. As the travel cost per vehicle following in the truck platoon (b) decreases, the cost factor with platooning (α) decreases.

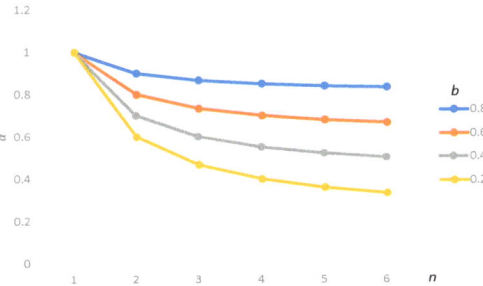

Figure 8. The cost factor with platooning (α) with the number of vehicles in a platoon (n) and travel cost per vehicle following in the truck platoon (b).

5.2. Optimal Locational Strategy for the Scenarios in Japan

Next, we estimate the parameter settings of several scenarios for the deployment of truck platooning in Japan. The ratio of labor costs in the trucking industry is around 40%, and this is related to the cost reduction for unmanned driving compared to manned driving. As regards the reduction in fuel consumption in a platoon, that of the leading vehicle is around 10% and that of the following vehicle is around 20%. In the scenario for platooning, these reduction factors are also considered both in leading and following vehicles. As for the total number of vehicles, the regulation limits the number of vehicles to three in a platoon.

We consider the following three scenarios that have not been discussed enough in Japan and derive the parameters as shown in Table 4. From Figure 7, we can derive the relationship between the cost factor with platooning (α) in three scenarios in Table 4 and the long-haul ratio x as shown in Figure 9.

Table 4. Calculation of parameters and the optimal locational strategy in three scenarios.

	Scenario	s	a	b	n	α	Optimal Location
I	Platoon of all manned vehicles	1	0.9	0.8	3	0.833	Case 3
II	Platoon with unmanned following vehicles	1	0.9	0.4	3	0.567	Case 3
III	Platoon of all fully automated vehicles (FAVs)	1	0.5	0.4	3	0.433	Case 2

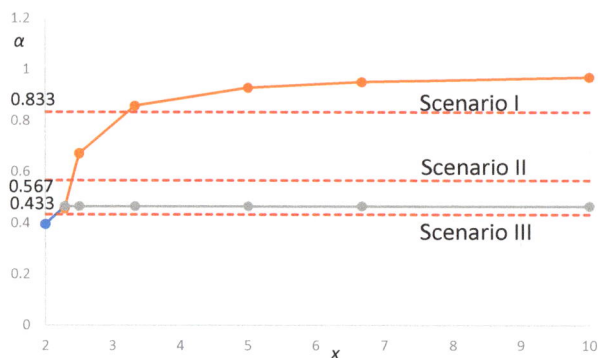

Figure 9. Optimal locational strategy for the combination of the long-haul ratio x and the cost factor with platooning (α) based on the parameters in Japan.

We choose the sections for scenario evaluation in Japan as shown in Table 5 and Figure 10. From Figure 9, we can derive the optimal locational strategy in the case of $x = 5$ as shown in the rightmost cell in Table 4. These results show that the optimal locational strategy for the platoon of all manned vehicles and the platoon with unmanned following vehicles is the edge of the circle region and that for the platoon of fully automated vehicles (FAVs) is the center of the circle region. As the candidate location for PFCs with unmanned following vehicles is around the suburbs of the metropolitan area near the outer ring road, as shown in Figure 2, we can conclude that the results from this analytical model are very close to this situation.

Table 5. Sections for the evaluation of scenarios in Japan.

Section	Distance l	Radius r	Long-Haul Ratio x
Tokyo-Osaka	500 km	100 km	5
Tokyo-Nagoya	300 km	60 km	5

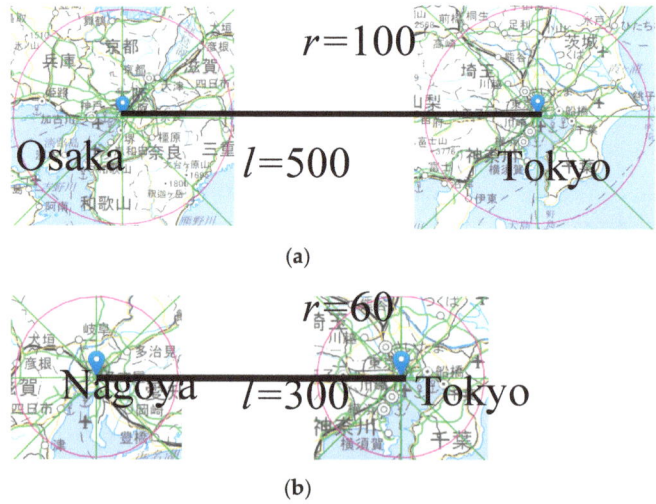

Figure 10. Sections for scenarios in Japan. (**a**) Tokyo-Osaka, (**b**) Tokyo-Nagoya

6. Implication

The results of this study have some implications both for logistics companies that may participate in truck platooning and for governments that implement road infrastructure investment and regulatory guidance measures.

First, logistics companies should adjust their truck transportation system to reduce the travel costs considering the deployment of truck platooning. From the numerical results using this continuous approximation model, it has been shown that logistics companies involved in long-haul transport could make their transportation system more efficient by participating in truck platooning based on the current cost structure. In addition, it is also shown that the travel distance of truck platooning is different depending on the scenarios of the platoon: (I) platoon of all manned vehicles, (II) platoon with unmanned following vehicles and (III) platoon of all fully automated vehicles (FAVs). Thus, the distance is between the fringes of the origin–destination regions for scenarios (I) and (II), while the distance is between the center of the origin–destination regions for scenario (III). Therefore, logistics companies should construct a desirable freight transportation system, considering the travel distance of their cargo and the advancement of truck platooning.

Next, the government has the role of developing infrastructure and regulatory guidance to support the freight transportation system of logistics companies. The numerical results of this study based on the current cost structure indicate that it is optimal to locate Platooning Formation Centers (PFCs) at the fringes of the origin–destination regions for scenarios (I) and (II), and at the center of the origin–destination regions for scenario (III). Therefore, the government should implement various policies, considering the advancement of truck platooning. In particular, for the future deployment of scenario (II) with unmanned following vehicles, the government should locate PFCs around the suburbs of the metropolitan area near the outer ring road. In addition, the government should secure land available for industrial uses where PFCs could be located among the optimal locations for PFCs and develop a road network infrastructure that allows truck platoon to travel safely.

In this decade, due to increasing freight transportation demands and a serious lack of drivers in Japan, efforts for the deployment of high-capacity vehicles (HCVs) are being made to improve the labor savings and efficiency of freight transportation. HCVs have been widely used in Europe and the U.S. for a long time, but the official introduction of 25 m long vehicles was only approved in 2019 on expressways along the Pacific coast from northern Japan (Tohoku) to western Japan (Kyushu) including the Shin-Tomei and Shin-Meishin expressways. As a supply chain in Japan, logistics between parts suppliers and assembly plants are linked by wide-area trunk transportation using expressways. In Japan, a production system based on the Just In Time (JIT) approach has been established, and it can be said that logistics is highly oriented toward high-frequency and low-volume transportation [33,34]. Considering the problems for the deployment of 25 m long vehicles, such as restrictions on the approved sections and the total weight of the vehicles, a collaborative distribution with HCVs is under operation among multiple logistics companies. An HCV with one tractor and one trailer can be considered as a convoy of two freight vehicles using a physical coupling, while truck platooning is a small convoy of multiple freight vehicles using electronic coupling. Therefore, the results of this research into Platoon Formation Centers (PFCs) are expected to be used to determine facility locations for the coupling and de-coupling of trailers in this collaborative distribution for HCVs.

7. Conclusions

In this study, we introduced the current status of truck platooning in Japan and presented the optimal location model for truck platooning using a continuous approximation model with a numerical experiment considering the case in Japan. Truck platooning has been under technological development since the early 2000s as a major solution for improving the efficiency of long-distance trucking. This research focused on the optimal locational strategy of Platoon Formation Centers (PFCs)—the facilities for the platoon formation of freight trucks for unmanned truck platooning—considering the facility development plan on major corridors between the major three metropolitan areas by the government. Continuous approximation (CA) is an efficient and effective technique for modeling complex and uncertain logistics problems, especially in the areas of facility locations. In this model, the travel cost is calculated as the average travel distance between two market areas and three cases—without platooning/with platooning via PFCs at the center/edge of each market area—are considered. We derived the optimal locational strategy of PFCs for the combination of the long-haul ratio and the cost factor with platooning. With the estimated parameters of several scenarios for the deployment of truck platooning in Japan, the numerical results show that the optimal locational strategy of PFCs for the platoon of all manned vehicles and the platoon with unmanned following vehicles is the edge of the local region and that for the platoon of FAVs is the center. Especially for PFCs with unmanned following vehicles, we can conclude that the results from this continuous approximation model based on the current cost structure are very close to the facility development plan by the government.

For future study, we need to consider the optimal location model inside a region and formulate this with a discrete network model for actual transport demand and road networks.

Author Contributions: Conceptualization, D.W.; methodology, D.W.; software, D.W.; validation, D.W., T.K. and K.S.; formal analysis, D.W.; investigation, T.K. and K.S.; resources, D.W., T.K. and K.S.; data curation, D.W.; writing—original draft preparation, D.W., T.K. and K.S.; writing—review and editing, D.W., T.K. and K.S.; visualization, D.W., T.K. and K.S.; supervision, D.W.; project administration, D.W.; funding acquisition, D.W. All authors have read and agreed to the published version of the manuscript.

Funding: This research was partially funded by the Institute of Behavioral Sciences (IBS Fellowship) and the Japan Society for the Promotion of Science (JSPS KAKENHI), grant number 19H02255.

Institutional Review Board Statement: Not applicable.

Informed Consent Statement: Not applicable.

Data Availability Statement: Not applicable.

Conflicts of Interest: The authors declare no conflict of interest.

References

1. Upadhyay, A. Antecedents of green supply chain practices in developing economies. *Manag. Environ. Qual. Int. J.* **2020**. [CrossRef]
2. DHL: Logistics Trend Ladar, 5th edition. Available online: https://www.dhl.com/global-en/home/insights-and-innovation/insights/logistics-trend-radar.html (accessed on 27 February 2021).
3. Janssen, R.; Zwijnenberg, J.; Blankers, I.; Kruijff, J.D. *Truck Platooning-Driving the Future of Transportation*; TNO 2014 R11893. 2015. Available online: https://www.semanticscholar.org/paper/Truck-platooning%3A-driving-the-future-of-Janssen-Zwijnenberg/8c06e8e2b7c15e9e186a254bda6c6adad83bad61 (accessed on 29 April 2021).
4. Aarts, L.O.; Feddes, G.E. European Truck Platooning Challenge-Creating next generation mobility. In Proceedings of the HVTT14: International Symposium on Heavy Vehicle Transport Technology, The Dutch Ministry of Infrastructure and the Environment, Rotorua, New Zealand, 15–18 November 2016.
5. Willemsen, D.; Schmeitz, A.; Fusco, M.; Jan van Ark, E.; van Kempen, E.; Soderman, M.; Atanassow, B.; Sjoberg, K.; Nordin, H.; Dhurjati, P. "Requirements Review from EU Projects", D2.1 of H2020 Project ENSEMBLE. 2018. Available online: https://platooningensemble.eu/storage/uploads/documents/2021/03/24/ENSEMBLE-Deliverable-2.1-StateOfTheArt_EUProjects_Final.pdf (accessed on 29 April 2021).
6. Hochschule Fresenius, DB Schenker and MAN Truck & Bus SE, "EDDI: Electronic Drawbar-Digital Innovation", Project Report-Presentation of the Result. 2019. Available online: https://www.deutschebahn.com/resource/blob/4136372/d08df4c3b97b7f8794f91e47e86b71a3/Platooning_EDDI_Project-report_10052019-data.pdf (accessed on 29 April 2021).
7. UK Heavy Goods Vehicle Platooning Project. Available online: http://www.helmuk.co.uk/ (accessed on 27 February 2021).
8. *EU Roadmap for Truck Platooning*; European Automobile Manufacturers' Association: 2017. Available online: https://www.acea.be/publications/article/infographic-eu-roadmap-for-truck-platooning (accessed on 29 April 2021).
9. *Truck Platooning Early Deployment Assessment–Independent Evaluation: Performance Measures for Evaluating Truck Platooning Field Deployments*; The United States Department of Transportation: Washington, DC, USA. 2020. Available online: https://rosap.ntl.bts.gov/view/dot/50551 (accessed on 29 April 2021).

10. Bishop, R. New Moves, New Markets for Truck Platooning Revealed at AVS2020. Available online: https://www.forbes.com/sites/richardbishop1/2020/09/27/new-moves-new-markets-for-truck-platooning-revealed-at-avs2020/?sh=9eb2c6a62974 (accessed on 27 February 2021).
11. Truck Platooning Initiative. Available online: https://truck-platooning-initiative.com/ (accessed on 27 February 2021).
12. Bhoopalam, A.K.; Agatz, N.; Zuidwijk, R. Planning of truck platoons: A literature review and directions for future research, *Transp. Res. Part B* **2018**, *107*, 212–228. [CrossRef]
13. Ansari, S.; Başdere, M.; Li, X.; Ouyang, Y.; Smilowitz, K. Advancements in continuous approximation models for logistics and transportation systems: 1996–2016. *Transp. Res. Part B Methodol.* **2018**, *107*, 229–252. [CrossRef]
14. Larsson, E.; Sennton, G.; Larson, J. The vehicle platooning problem: Computational complexity and heuristics. *Transp. Res. Part C Emerg. Technol.* **2015**, *60*, 258–277. [CrossRef]
15. Larsen, R.; Rich, J.; Rasmussen, T.K. Hub-based truck platooning: Potentials and profitability. *Transp. Res. Part E Logist. Transp. Rev.* **2019**, *127*, 249–264. [CrossRef]
16. Zhang, L.; Chen, F.; Ma, X.; Pan, X. Fuel Economy in Truck Platooning: A Literature Overview and Directions for Future Research. *J. Adv. Transp.* **2020**, *2020*, 1–10. [CrossRef]
17. Gerrits, B.; Mes, M.; Schuur, P. Simulation of Real-Time and Opportunistic Truck Platooning at the Port of Rotterdam. In Proceedings of the 2019 Winter Simulation Conference (WSC), 2019 Winter Simulation Conference (WSC), National Harbor, MD, USA, 8–11 December 2019; Institute of Electrical and Electronics Engineers (IEEE): Piscataway, NJ, USA, 2019; pp. 133–144.
18. Jo, Y.; Kim, J.; Oh, C.; Kim, I.; Lee, G. Benefits of travel time savings by truck platooning in Korean freeway networks. *Transp. Policy* **2019**, *83*, 37–45. [CrossRef]
19. Paddeu, D.; Denby, J. Decarbonising road freight: Is truck automation and platooning an opportunity? *Clean Technol. Environ. Policy* **2021**, 1–15. [CrossRef]
20. Laporte, G.; Nickel, S. *Location Science*; Springer: Cham, Switzerland, 2015.
21. Larson, R.; Odoni, A. *Urban Operations Research*, 2nd ed.; Dynamic Ideas: Charlestown, MA, USA, 2007.
22. Campbell, J.F. A continuous approximation model for time definite many-to-many transportation. *Transp. Res. B* **2013**, *54*, 100–112. [CrossRef]
23. Xie, W.; Ouyang, Y. Optimal layout of transshipment facility locations on an infinite homogeneous plane. *Transp. Res. Part B Methodol.* **2015**, *75*, 74–88. [CrossRef]
24. Tsugawa, S. An Overview on an Automated Truck Platoon within the Energy ITS Project. *IFAC Proc. Vol.* **2013**, *46*, 41–46. [CrossRef]
25. Strategic Conference for the Advancement of Utilizing Public and Private Sector Data and Strategic Headquarters for the Advanced Information and Telecommunications Network Society: Public-Private ITS Initiative/Roadmaps. 2019. Available online: http://japan.kantei.go.jp/policy/it/2019/2019_roadmaps.pdf (accessed on 29 April 2021).
26. Japan Automobile Manufacturers Association: Press Release on 20 July 2020. Available online: http://release.jama.or.jp/sys/news/detail.pl?item_id=1930 (accessed on 27 February 2021). (In Japanese).
27. Vissers, J.; Banspach, J.; Liga, V.; Tang, T.; Nordin, H.; Julien, S.; Martinez, S.; Villette, C. V1 Platooning Use-Cases, Scenario Definition and Platooning Levels, D2.2 of H2020 project ENSEMBLE. 2018. Available online: https://platooningensemble.eu/storage/uploads/documents/2021/03/24/ENSEMBLE-D2.2_V1-Platooning-use-cases,-scenario-definition-and-platooning-levels_FINAL.pdf (accessed on 29 April 2021).
28. *An Interim Report of the Joint Public-Private Sector Council for Commercialization of Truck Platooning*; The Joint Public-Private Sector Council for Commercialization of Truck Platooning: Tokyo, Japan, 2019. (In Japanese)
29. *The Reports of the Study Group on Utilization of Expressway Infrastructure Corresponding to New Logistics System*; The Ministry of Land, Infrastructure, Transport and Tourism: Tokyo, Japan, 2019. (In Japanese)
30. Koshizuka, T.; Kurita, O. Approximate formulas of average distances associated with regions and their applications to location problems. *Math. Program.* **1991**, *52*, 99–123. [CrossRef]
31. Vaughan, R. *Urban Spatial Traffic Patterns*; Pion Publication: London, UK, 1987.
32. Mathai, A.M. *An Introduction to Geometrical Probability: Distributional Aspects with Applications*; CRC Press: Boca Raton, FL, USA, 1999.
33. Kaneko, J.; Nojiri, W. The logistics of Just-in-Time between parts suppliers and car assemblers in Japan. *J. Transp. Geogr.* **2008**, *16*, 155–173. [CrossRef]
34. Guerrero, D.; Itoh, H. Ports, regions and manufacturing systems: Automobile manufacturing in Kyushu, Japan. *Case Stud. Transp. Policy* **2017**, *5*, 332–341. [CrossRef]

Article

Human Factors Influencing the Implementation of Cobots in High Volume Distribution Centres

Wim Lambrechts, Jessica S. Klaver, Lennart Koudijzer and Janjaap Semeijn *

Department of Marketing & Supply Chain Management, Faculty of Management, Open Universiteit, PB 2960 Heerlen, The Netherlands; wim.lambrechts@ou.nl (W.L.); jessica.klaver@ou.nl (J.S.K.); len_koudijzer@hotmail.com (L.K.)
* Correspondence: janjaap.semeijn@ou.nl

Abstract: Order picking is a logistics component of warehouse operations where substantial productivity gains are possible. In this study, we investigate implementation processes of collaborative order picking robots (cobots) and focus on the influence of human factors on their implementation in high volume distribution centres. These human factors are: resistance to change; organisational culture; communication on change; and leadership. Four case companies were selected that have experience with testing and introducing several types of cobot and have successfully implemented (at least) one type of cobot over an extended period. In-depth interviews with operational decision-makers led to the identification of 66 critical incidents related to human factors. The results demonstrate the importance of planning the implementation process in phases. Employees are hesitant or resistant to the change due to a lack of information, experience, and communication. The decisive role of the team leader is crucial to implement cobots successfully, and here the individual character traits (e.g., the variance in commitment, character, and motivation) influence the process as well. Although the introduction of cobots is not yet widespread, and the negative impact on the workforce (i.e., concerning job loss) is currently low, one should be aware of the possible future implications when robotisation becomes structurally embedded. Therefore, this article calls for a stronger link between human factors and the future of work, with a specific focus on reskilling and upskilling of logistics professionals in light of robotisation, rather than binary approaches in which robots are primarily seen as a threat to the current workforce.

Keywords: human factors; cobot; collaborative robot; distribution centres; warehousing

Citation: Lambrechts, W.; Klaver, J.S.; Koudijzer, L.; Semeijn, J. Human Factors Influencing the Implementation of Cobots in High Volume Distribution Centres. *Logistics* **2021**, *5*, 32. https://doi.org/10.3390/logistics5020032

Academic Editor: Benjamin Nitsche

Received: 4 March 2021
Accepted: 11 May 2021
Published: 31 May 2021

Publisher's Note: MDPI stays neutral with regard to jurisdictional claims in published maps and institutional affiliations.

Copyright: © 2021 by the authors. Licensee MDPI, Basel, Switzerland. This article is an open access article distributed under the terms and conditions of the Creative Commons Attribution (CC BY) license (https://creativecommons.org/licenses/by/4.0/).

1. Introduction

Robotisation will increase rapidly in (internal) logistics processes. Whether robots and other fully automatic systems are also the correct answer to future challenges from a business strategy perspective is debatable. Discussions about the human race, subject to slow change, and computers and robots, evolving at a rapid pace [1], lead to tensions and binary interpretations of one *versus* the other, which inevitably leads to discussions about the influence of robotisation on the future of work. Our study focuses on collaborative order-picking robots and aims to investigate the impact of human factors on their successful implementation in high-volume distribution centres. The order-picking process is essential to warehouse operations and consists of collecting (order picking) items for a specific order. When the items are collected, the order is prepared and sent to the customer. Order picking is an essential process but also a labour-intensive and capital-intensive one [2]. It is estimated that the order-picking costs comprise up to 55% of the total cost of warehousing [3].

Order picking has a significant impact on supply chain productivity, and it is seen as the logistics component where most productivity improvements are possible [4]. This study investigates whether these improvements can be realised by supporting the human operator with a robot during the task and which (human) factors must be considered in robot implementation processes. Collaborative robots are also known as cobots; they come in different versions and are programmed with a computer to perform certain actions automatically. Sensors enable the cobot to detect humans and their environment. The cobot communicates with the human operator, allowing the operator to adjust programming if necessary [1].

Currently, eighty percent of all warehouses operate entirely with people. Fifteen percent of the warehouses are partly automated and only five percent to a large extent. According to ABI Research [5], the collaborative robotics sector was expected to increase roughly tenfold between 2015 and 2020, reaching over $1 billion. The rise of robotisation seems irreversible [6,7].

Multinationals such as Amazon and Google take the lead and invest heavily in robotisation [8]. In 2012, Amazon claimed to have implemented 30,000 robots in 13 fulfilment centres [9]. At the start of 2019, Amazon announced that they had already deployed more than 100,000 robotic systems in more than 25 fulfilment centres across the United States. In June 2019, the company even indicated that this number has grown to 200,000 automated drive robots worldwide [10]. ABI research states that by 2025 more than four million commercial robots will be installed in more than 50,000 warehouses: the need for flexible, efficient, and automated e-commerce fulfilment will drive the rapid increase of cobots as same-day delivery becomes the norm: "Global adoption of warehouse robotics will also be spurred by the increasing affordability and Return on Investment (ROI) of a growing variety of infrastructure-light robots, as they are an attractive and versatile alternative to traditional fixed mechanical automation or manual operations" [11].

An inefficient order-picking process can lead to high operational costs and dissatisfaction among employees and customers. More and more logistics companies are taking the step to (partially) automate the order-picking process. For example, since November 2017, a Dutch logistics company was the first in the world to provide their distribution centre with the iGo Neo from Still [12]. This order-picking cart automatically follows his owner, the human, when collecting orders.

Several challenges can be identified in the rapid evolution of robotisation. First, the implementation requires organisational change (e.g., adjustments in operations). A solid implementation plan should be developed for the machines to work together successfully with the human warehouse operator. Second, employees might be hesitant or resistant to these changes. Robots can support humans in several tasks, but that requires trust and cooperation from the operator [13,14]. Third, increased robotisation impacts the workforce and leads to fears of job loss, thereby negatively affecting the motivation of employees. The existing literature on cobot implementations mainly sets focus on technical issues and success factors (e.g., related to human-robot interaction), and a detailed view on the role of human factors (such as resistance to change) is currently lacking.

Therefore, this study aims to analyse the human factors at play in the implementation of cobots in high volume distribution centres, with a specific focus on resistance to change, organisational culture, communication on change, and leadership. The remainder of this article presents the literature review (Section 2), with a focus on collaborative robots, their application in order picking processes, and issues of Human-Cobot Collaboration. Section 3 provides the materials and methods of our study, thereby highlighting the specificities of the human factors approach in organisational change processes. Detailed information about the critical incidents, which form the basis for our data analysis, is provided in the appendix. Section 4 presents the results, with a specific focus on the cobot implementation process: its drivers and barriers, and the specific human factors influencing this change process. In Section 5, the results of our study are framed within the existing body of knowledge, with specific and critical reflection on the influence of cobot introduction on the future of work and skill requirements. Section 6 concludes our study with the main insights of our research, recommendations for successful cobot implementation, limitations, and recommendations for further research.

2. Literature Review

Interaction between humans and robots is referred to in the literature as Human-Robot Interaction (HRI) or Human-Robot Collaboration (HRC) [15]. According to Sheridan, ref. [1] HRI can be categorized into four areas of application:

1. Human supervisory control of robots in the performance of routine tasks. These include handling parts on manufacturing assembly lines and accessing and delivering packages, components, mail, and medicines in warehouses, offices, and hospitals.
2. Remote control of space, airborne, terrestrial, and undersea vehicles for non-routine tasks in hazardous or inaccessible environments. Such machines are called "teleoperators". They perform manipulation and mobility tasks in the remote physical environment in correspondence to the remote human's continuous control movements. A computer that a human supervisor intermittently reprograms to execute pieces of the overall task is a "telerobot".
3. Automated vehicles in which a human is a passenger, including automated highway and rail vehicles and commercial aircraft.
4. Human-robot social interaction, including robot devices that provide entertainment, teaching, comfort, and assistance for children, elderly, and disabled persons.

Our study focuses on the human supervisory control of robots in their performance of routine tasks, as this fits with the order picking process in high volume distribution centres.

2.1. Collaborative Robots

A "cobot" is a collaborative robot used to assist human users at the workplace. It is introduced to ease the work of the employee. In logistics, this can mean that the cobot picks heavy packages, takes on repetitive actions simultaneously, or travels long distances to reduce human walking [8]. For example, Amazon employees walked 18km in the order picking process during a shift. After introducing cobots, the performance improved which led to a reduction of the employees' walking distance by 40–70% [16].

The principal difference between cobots and industrial robots is the shared workspace. Extensive fencing surrounds a traditional industrial robot so that the human operator cannot get close to the machine. These robots switch off when a person is detected. Collaborative robots, on the other hand, can work safely with people. The human operator is generally "in charge" and can tune the cobot through a programmed computer system. The cobots can detect the presence and movements of people so that they can adjust their behaviour accordingly to prevent accidents. This feature allows collaborative robots to collaborate safely with people [17].

This study focuses on cobots that support the order-picking process. De Weerd [18] concludes that the most significant advantage of working with cobots during order picking is that they take the most arduous work out of the hands of human order pickers, for example, because the cobots move the collected orders into crates themselves. Once an order has been completed, the order picker ensures that the trolley travels to its final destination with a single charge. A new robot then registers with the order picker to maintain continuity in the order picking process.

The automotive industry has been increasingly implementing cobots on assembly lines, but also other industries explore cobots and how they can collaborate with humans [19]. This change is not surprising because cobots offer various advantages to existing industrial robots. A cobot can be placed next to people in small areas. Additionally, they are more programmable than industrial robots and can be used flexibly for repetitive, ergonomically challenging tasks [20].

2.2. Cobots in Order Picking Operations

The order picking process is found in warehouses and consists of collecting (order picking) items for a specific order. When the items are collected, the order is prepared and sent to the customer. Order picking is a basic warehouse process, but it is estimated that picking costs participate with 55% of the total cost of warehousing [3]. Robots are no longer solely used in factory environments; they are also gradually moving to human-populated warehouses. Cobots may prove to be a valuable addition to the order picking process since cost reduction in that area would substantially impact the cost of the entire warehouse process [21,22].

In typical warehouse functions and flows within high volume distribution centres, the main activities include receiving, reserve storage & order picking, accumulation/sortation packing, and shipping [2]. Cobots may provide solutions to different categories of order picking:

1. Broken-case or piece-picking is a type of order picking where the individual responsible for picking would pick all the necessary items for one order. They might pick it from the same place or a combination of different shops based on their requirement. The item order picking process is often very repetitive. It is difficult for employers to find upstanding and motivated staff.
2. Case-picking is the order-picking of boxes or crates. This picking method is standard in warehouses, especially with retailers; most logistics operations consist of this method of order picking. Case-picking is often performed by a human operator with a pallet truck or roll container. Concerning case-picking, there is generally little diversity in products. The boxes often contain the same products.
3. Full-pallet picking is also known as unit-load picking. A pallet is loaded with various items so that the operator can move many items in one go. Picking with a full pallet is often done with different types of (lift) trucks, making pallet picking less labour-intensive than case-picking or piece-picking.

2.3. Human-Cobot Collaboration

Robinette, Wagner, and Howard [23] conclude that robots have incredible potential to assist humans in everyday tasks such as cleaning floors, but also in emergency tasks such as heart surgery and bomb disposal. Although the logistics sector is one of the fastest-growing sectors for robotics [24], many operations still occur manually in this sector. Automation is repeatedly proven difficult by the multitude of variations that have to be taken into account. Cobots should be able to take over the manual activities of man, but the warehouse staff must trust their new helper, and the environment must be ready as well. Hancock et al. [25] presented factors of trust development in human-robot interaction, based on human-related, robot-related, and environmental dimensions. Human-related factors include engagement, expertise, and comfort to work with robots.

Working with cobots is new to many people and, therefore, out of their comfort zone. As shown in studies focusing on automation, trust in HRI is an essential human factor that influences successful implementation [26]. More and more people are open to robotisation. One in three employees is willing to work together with a "robot colleague". No fewer than 42% of the respondents see a robot as an added value to the work process. The research shows that "time savings" is a major advantage of automation. Of course, some employees do not want to collaborate with robots. For example, in their Global Talent Trends Report, consultancy firm Mercer [27] concludes that 29% of respondents fear job loss. They see the robots as competition. Commitment among human staff will not arise immediately. The time factor likely plays a vital role in the development of engagement. Robots can support humans in several tasks, but many users do not trust them and have a negative prejudice [13]. Such attitudes can subsequently lead to the disuse of these valuable tools [28].

Ogawa et al. [29] analysed to what extent staff is comfortable with teleoperated robots. They received mixed reactions, including fear. People preferred to communicate with a human colleague than a teleoperated robot. Another teleoperated robot study showed that most robot operators reported that they could share their intentions to a reasonable extent. Most people who interacted with the robot saw the behaviour as fairly social [30]. However, robots can also appear threatening. Since the robot already looks different and people are not used to communicating with it, operators may feel uncomfortable if the robot is not doing what is expected of it [31]. Research by Hancock et al. [25] showed that the robot's performance had more influence on human trust. The better the robot does its job, the more confidence it generates with the user.

Other human factors (also labelled "environmental" factors in the study of Hancock et al. [25]) include 'communication and culture' and 'team collaboration'. The culture and communication within an organisation are also crucial in the implementation of robots. The following example clearly demonstrates this. The SWORD system (Special Weapons Observation Reconnaissance Detection System) was developed by the US Army in Iraq in 2007 to support combat [32]. Although the system worked well, the soldiers never used SWORD because they did not trust the system to safely function as it made unexpected movements due to technical malfunctions [32]. If there is no trust in a company's culture, the cobot will not be optimally used. "Trust, specifically, has been identified as an important facet in facilitating the correct and appropriate use of a robotic system" [33].

Communicating openly and honestly with the human operators and adequately informing them of the changes that are to come is a key driver for successful implementation processes. With every organisational change process, the team's willingness to engage in the change process itself is ultimately decisive. Every change brings tension and resistance to change, especially in the beginning phases of the process [34,35].

According to Maurtua et al. [36,37], human-robot collaboration can potentially contribute to the realization of factories of the future. They see these shared workspaces as places where people work together with the robot as a team. The cobots perform repetitive and risky tasks, while the human operators can focus on the critical tasks in the work process, which require their expertise.

3. Materials and Method

This research investigates the role of human acceptance on the cobot implementation process in high-volume distribution centres and is based on multiple case studies. These are most suitable for exploratory research [38] and make it possible to analyse phenomena requiring interaction between investigator and informant, and numerous information sources. Qualitative research is particularly suitable for analysing and comparing different practices in a real-life context. This study contributes to the knowledge gap in the literature concerning human factors influencing the implementation of cobots in logistics and warehousing environments.

Cases were selected based on several criteria: (1) organisation is or has a high-volume distribution centre; (2) organisation is located in the Netherlands; (3) organisation has tested more than one type of collaborative robots in their distribution centre; (4) organisation has successfully introduced at least one type of collaborative robot in their distribution centre. The third criterion was used to select cases that show a certain level of maturity and experience in the introduction of the cobot. The fourth criterion differs from the third. This criterion is focused upon the actual (long-term) implementation and use of cobots in the distribution centre of the case organisation. Both the third and fourth selection criteria proved useful yet strict to find suitable cases for our research. Four case companies were found that met our criteria and were willing to participate in the study. Referring to an earlier study, estimating that only 1 or 2 percent of a sample of 1000 companies had invested in robots [39], our sample seems to fit the qualitative approach and purposes of our research. The general characteristics of the selected cases are presented in Table 1. Due to privacy reasons, the information is anonymised, and so is the link between companies and the specific type of cobots tested and implemented.

Table 1. Overview of cases.

Case Company	Type	Number of Employees
A	Logistics service provider	>100,000
B	Fruit and vegetable company	>1000
C	Manufacturer automotive industry	>500
D	Logistics service provider	>20,000

At least three different types of cobots have been tested and implemented at these case companies, and these have been discussed and focused upon in our study: (1) OPX-L 12 iGo neo (producer: Still); (2) YuMi®—IRB 14,000 (producer: ABB); (3) LOCUSBOTS™ (producer: Locus).

Data was gathered at these four case companies engaged in cobot implementation processes through (1) open and reflective interviews with key stakeholders (with project managers; innovation leads); (2) desk research of relevant documents regarding the implementation process; (3) observations regarding cobot implementation in the respective organisations. Figure 1 presents the research model of this study, which guides the development of the semi-structured interviews (Appendix A). The model is based on previously validated models focusing on human factors in organisational change processes [35,40] and represents the innovative change process (in this case: the introduction of cobots), surrounded by several influencing human factors (in this case: resistance to change; communication on changes; leadership; organisational culture). These human factors lead towards open and reflective vital questions to be used during the interviews.

The semi-structured interviews with experts and observations in case companies allow for analysis of the influence of human acceptance and the work environment on cobot implementation processes. Through the use of literature-based, semi-structured interview guidelines, internal and content validity is ensured. According to Qu & Dumay [41], semi-structured interviews involve consistent and systematic questioning guided by identified themes, interposed with probes designed to elicit more detailed responses. The schedule was used to interview the operational experts of the four case companies. These interviews were conducted in the respondents' environment, leading to minimal time investment and respondents feeling entirely at ease.

The collected data were analysed in Microsoft Excel. In an open coding approach, labels derived from the research model and related human factors were attached to the data, which lead to a structured overview of influencing factors in cobot implementation processes: culture, resistance to change, communication, and leadership. Regarding the organisational change process, the following issues received prime focus for the data analysis: (1) adjustments; (2) kick-off and instructions; (3) investment; (4) workforce; (5) preparation; and (6) productivity. Regarding human factors of stakeholders involved (both project managers and warehouse operators), particular attention was provided to the following issues: (1) prejudice; (2) unfamiliarity; (3) curiosity; (4) commitment; (5) character; and (6) motivation. Where possible, relationships between different influencing factors were outlined, clarified, and described (cf. the grey arrows in the research model, as presented in Figure 1), which altogether resulted in a data matrix with 66 critical incidents in the cobot implementation process and the influence of human factors. Appendix B, Tables A1 and A2 provide an overview of the identified critical incidents.

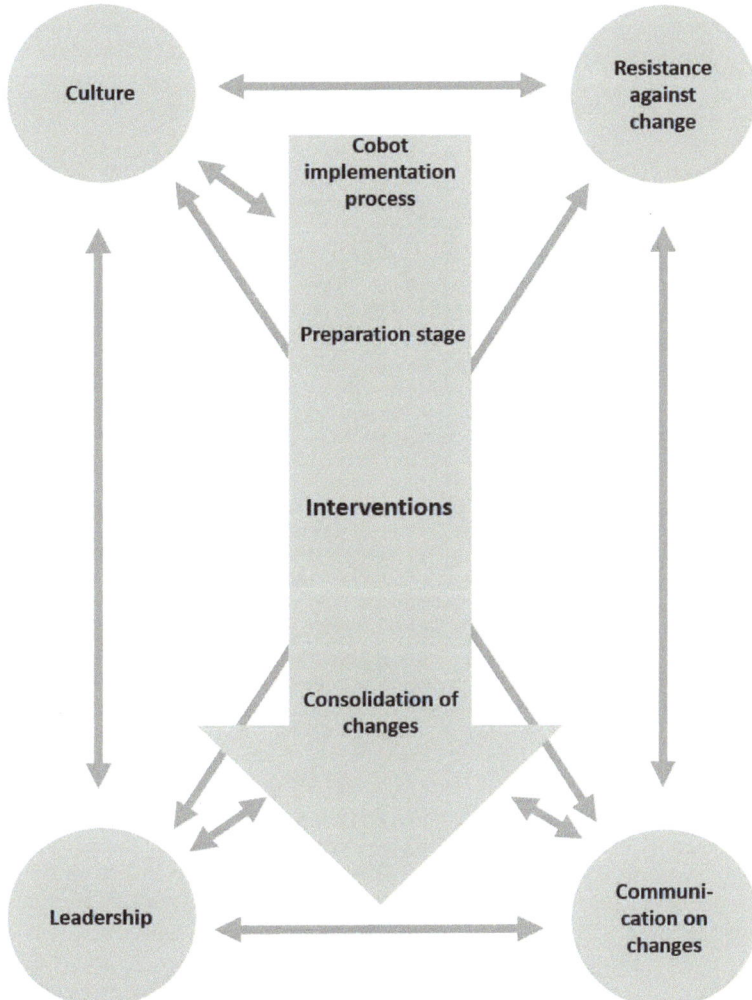

Figure 1. Human factors research model (based on [35,40]).

4. Results

4.1. The Cobot Implementation Process

The implementation of cobots requires innovative organisational changes. The critical incidents identified in the data of the four case companies show that the implementation process is a challenging and often complex process, both from the organisational and the individual perspective. Table 2 presents an overview of the critical incidents and human factors identified concerning the cobot implementation process, with a specific focus on adjustments made, kick-off and instructions, and preparation.

Table 2. Critical incidents and human factors identified related to adjustments; kick-off; and preparation of the implementation process.

Theme	Critical Incidents	Human Factor Identified
Facilitation of cobot introduction (adjustments)	The infrastructure for the supply and removal of materials has been adjusted (Case A) Now we think that the cobots work better in an isolated part of the warehouse, which requires adjustment (Case B) An emergency button had to be made to stop the cobot when needed. This was a big adjustment, according to the technicians (Case D)	Resistance to change Culture
Adhering to business-as-usual (adjustments)	But the current process must continue (Case A) No, the current process should preferably continue (Case B) No major adjustments were made; that was a requirement from the management (Case C)	Resistance to change Culture
Information sharing (kick-off & instructions)	Team leaders were trained by the [cobot] supplier, who had to explain the work with the cobots to their team (Case A) We ensured that all layers of the organisation were aware of the development. Step-by-step, person-by-person, employees were informed. We set up an information corner. There was also a monthly meeting (Case B) We did not inform everyone in advance. The preparation could have been much better. We did set up the test phase well enough (Case C) A project team was set up and we took several operators to another company to look at operative cobots (Case D) In retrospect, it turned out that we could have involved more employees (Case D)	Leadership Communication Resistance to change Culture
Decisive role of team leader (preparation)	The team leader is there to guide the operators where necessary. We informed them in advance and took them to another company (Case A) It is their job to explain it to the operators (Case A) The team leaders were closely involved in the design phase. It is important for them to feel that they contribute to the success (Case B)	Leadership

To facilitate cobot implementation, adjustments need to be made in the warehouse or operations. The type of cobot will influence the number of adjustments needed, yet in all cases, we identified resistance to far-reaching adjustments, mainly spurred by management demands or expectations. Minor adjustments are acceptable, to the extent that they do not disrupt the existing processes:

> "No, the current process should preferably continue" (Case B)

> "Now we think that the cobots work better in an isolated part of the warehouse, which requires adjustment" (Case B)

> "An emergency button had to be made to stop the cobot when needed. This was a big adjustment according to the technicians" (Case D)

> "No major adjustments were made; that was a requirement from the management" (Case C)

This adherence to business-as-usual and hesitancy to fully adopt cobots in the warehousing operations is in contract with the innovation aspirations as expressed by the respondents. They see innovation as a way to create new opportunities for the organisation to improve its operations and shared various arguments for their choice of cobots:

1. Regarding process improvement: by using cobots, goods for multiple customers can be "picked" at the same time so that more orders can be processed.
2. Regarding flexibility: organisations requiring a necessary adjustment in the work process can become more flexible. Cobots are mobile and can be deployed in the departments wherever they are most needed.

3. Regarding ergonomic development and absenteeism: the introduction of cobots allows for approaches in which warehouse employees are physically relieved. The cobot follows the employee, and the operator can collect the orders. With this development, the organisation tries to reduce the high absenteeism due to illness and physical injuries.
4. Regarding scarcity in the labour market: this factor can also be linked to absenteeism. A high-quality workforce with the right skills is hard to find and retain, and cobot implementation can potentially relieve issues related to scarcity on the labour market.

In light of these arguments, it is not surprising that the focus is set on innovation, nor is it strange that this innovation is being sought in robotisation. Causes of hesitancy to fully engage in cobot innovation processes can be found in the financial consequences and investments needed. Yet, the cases in our sample are pioneers, as one expert declared:

"You can keep consulting and calculating, but you just have to start!" (Case B)

According to the experts, a decisive factor during implementation is a clear and solid preparation and instruction (e.g., in a "kick-off & instruction"). By engaging everyone in the process from the start, enthusiasm is created and prejudice reduced. Suppose only a few higher positions are informed, who have to instruct and motivate the other employees. In that case, scepticism arises among the operators, and it will be much more challenging to motivate the employees to work with the cobot. One of the case organisations ensured that all layers of the organisation were aware of the development: from management to the operators, up to the works council. Step by step, person-by-person, employees were informed. The organisation set up an information corner where the project and related technology were explained, which led to an initial "meeting" and familiarisation with the cobots. There was also a monthly meeting where the operators were informed about working with the cobots, and there was time to share experiences. Every operator received training and was rewarded with a certificate if they had mastered the work with the cobot, which made the work with the cobot a fun challenge.

One of the experts admits that his organisation could have included more employees in the preparation. He was confronted by the fact that employees were not open to working with cobots, had much prejudice, and lagged in productivity. Other experts had arranged the preparation very precisely. At the respective companies under their responsibility, the implementation was structured in phases, all layers of the organisation were extensively instructed, and key users were involved in creating support. At these organisations, employees were enthusiastic from the start. Through this way of working, the employer developed trust among the operators and thus tackled issues of resistance to change, a factor that also emerges from our literature study as an indispensable part of an implementation process:

"We ensured that all layers of the organisation were aware of the development. Step-by-step, person-by-person were informed. We set up an information corner. There was also a monthly meeting" (Case B)

"We could have prepared the operators even better" (Case D)

Table 3 presents the critical incidents and human factors identified concerning investments, workforce, and productivity. Regarding the facilitation of cobots in the organisation, both costs and investments are critical organisational factors. Although this study does not explicitly focus on cobot implementations from a financial perspective, this factor cannot be wholly disregarded. According to the experts, cobots are currently an expensive investment. Hence, while there is increased interest, at this moment only a few organisations work with these machines.

Table 3. Critical incidents and human factors identified related to investments, workforce, and productivity during the implementation process.

Theme	Critical Incidents	Human Factor Identified
Costs and investments related to cobot introduction	It is a major investment, which means that we do not purchase multiple cobots (Case A) You actually have to work in two or three shifts for a proper return on investment. That is why I think the deployment of cobots will develop faster at production companies that can produce day and night (Case B) Standing still is going backwards. You can keep consulting and calculating, but you just have to start (Case B) A cobot is a big investment (Case C) Cobots will really have to become cheaper in the coming years to become attractive to a bigger audience (Case C) A cobot costs a lot of money, so after a few months we opted for a different robot solution (Case D)	Culture Resistance to change
Influence of cobot introduction on the workforce	The cobots do not influence the workforce, but people don't believe that, so it does affect the culture (Case A) Not yet, the amount of work is increasing and the use of cobots is not yet large enough (Case B) No jobs were lost, there is sufficient work (Case C) Still ... the economy is now growing, so the workforce is growing. But if the economy slows down, it may indeed be that a cobot is more attractive and cheaper to keep in service than a human operator (Case C) Replacing jobs is not going that fast, maybe in five or ten years, but fear among staff rules (Case D)	Culture Resistance to change
Influence of cobot introduction on productivity	There is a lot of difference in motivation and character among the team leaders. This means that one team may work very well with the cobot, while the other does not (Case A) Since we instructed the team leaders properly, the operators work correctly with the cobots. However, we are not achieving the productivity that we had in mind (Case B) Less commitment from the team leader means less commitment from the operators and ultimately less productivity overall (Case C) All cobots have been implemented, but productivity is not being achieved at this time because the preparation should have been better (Case C) The productivity that can be achieved with cobots has not been achieved (Case C) That also depends on whether the productivity is high enough for a good return on investment (Case C) You see that if the motivation of a team leader weakens, the results plummet (Case D) The cobot did not give us the desired result (Case D)	Resistance to change Leadership Culture

Moreover, the number of cobot experts in the Netherlands remains limited. Cobots are seen as an expensive form of innovation. Depending on its features, a cobot costs between €40–90k:

> "You actually have to work in two or three shifts for a proper return on investment. That is why I think the deployment of cobots will develop faster at production companies that can produce day and night" (Case B)

The robots earn themselves back sooner in a three- or five-shift operation than in a one-shift operation. Most organisations work with a limited number of cobots. The investment for every cobot is a large one and must be calculated with great care. It is therefore questionable whether the number of cobots will increase spectacularly in the coming years, as mentioned by one of the experts:

> "Cobots will really have to become cheaper in the coming years to become attractive for a bigger audience" (Case C)

With a strong focus on the economic dimension of cobot introduction, respondents highlight the importance of checking whether the initial cost of cobot implementation can deliver the desired productivity and output. However, this demands a deeper understanding of the human factors which can aid or hinder cobot implementation.

The use of cobots in logistics is a relatively new development, and not every implementation, so far, has been successful. Since only a few logistics organisations in the Netherlands use cobots, the implementation of these machines is custom-made. During the implementation, technical adjustments are needed before the cobot does precisely what the organisation has in mind. However, the organisation also has to deal with human staff and their emotions, trust, and patience. When the human operator does not fully support the cooperation with the cobot, and the cobot does something different from expected, the operator might become demotivated; this makes the implementation process vulnerable. Here we see how the various human factors influence each other, driving or hindering successful implementation processes.

Regarding the impact of cobot implementation on the workforce, cobots are seen as a relevant supplement to human operators. For example, cobots are used for repetitive order picking work, which is tedious and physically demanding for human operators. Cobots have been purchased to work together with humans, and the experts believe there to be enough work to keep both "in service":

"Still (. . .) the economy is now growing, so the workforce is growing. However, if the economy slows down, it may indeed be that a cobot is more attractive and cheaper to keep in service than a human operator. That also depends on whether the productivity is high enough for a good return on investment" (Case C)

Regarding the impact of cobot implementation on productivity, the four case companies show mixed results. It is expected that cobots increase the quality of (repetitive) work: they can be switched on and off depending on the workload at that particular moment. Being able to scale up and down flexibly is a crucial issue in logistics. Additionally, the quality of the work that the cobot carries out does not diminish as time goes on. The machine can continue to do the repetitive work in the same way as long as necessary. A human operator is influenced by other factors such as concentration, commitment, and fatigue.

Cobots reduce the workload of the human operator but can also ease the work by taking on heavy and repetitive work, making the order picking work lighter for the operator, resulting in fewer injuries, fitter staff, and lower absenteeism. In turn, the operators can focus on more important and complex work activities in the workplace.

Regarding the link with human factors, it becomes clear from the critical incidents that successful implementation largely depends on the commitment of the operators and team leaders. However, successful implementation processes have not been yielding the expected impact on productivity:

"Because we have instructed the team leaders properly, the operators work correctly with the cobots. However, we are not achieving productivity that we had in mind" (Case B)

"The cobot did not give us the desired result" (Case D)

The logistics supply chain requires distribution centres for flexibility, as it can be hectic in the inbound department while not in other departments. Moreover, this can be completely different the next day. Logistics organisations must deal with this, and cobots allow them to be stationed where they are needed most, making the organisation more flexible when an adjustment to the work process is necessary. However, it appears that this is a bit more complicated in real life since a key user must move the cobot. One of the experts tested this with his staff through a feedback form. It was stated that the moment the cobot is "in the way", and there is no key user, it cannot be moved, thereby negatively impacting productivity.

4.2. Resistance to Change

Organisational change processes will always cause commotion and fear among employees. Cobots are new and unknown to the people who have to work with them for the first time. Table 4 provides an overview of the results concerning prejudice, unfamiliarity, and curiosity among employees.

Table 4. Critical incidents and human factors identified related to prejudice, unfamiliarity, and curiosity among employees during the implementation process.

Theme	Critical Incidents	Human Factor Identified
Scepticism among employees (prejudice)	The first employees to use the cobot were sceptical (Case A) There was certainly some turmoil when we announced that we would focus on robotisation (Case B) The level of trust was not very high. The first employee was very sceptical (Case C) I was surprised to see how much resistance there was, also among the technicians (Case D) The amount of resistance that arises when people only hear the word "robot" or "cobot" was unprecedented (Case D)	Resistance to change Culture
Lack of experience (unfamiliarity)	The use of cobots was a real culture shock for our employees (Case A) Due to unfamiliarity, the cobots are used too little (Case C) It seems that people are really afraid of the cobots (Case D)	Resistance to change Culture Communication
Gaining experience with cobots (curiosity)	Some operators were experimenting, for example, unexpectedly standing in front of the cobot to find out how the cobot would react (Case B) The employees were triggered by the lights and the bells on the cobot (Case C) There was more fear than curiosity (Case D)	Resistance to change Culture

One of the experts indicates that this resistance surprised him (in a negative sense) during his implementation process. The majority of employees are sceptical and often hesitant or resistant when a change is occurring. The role of staff members involved in the implementation process is also important. According to the experts, team leaders were more open to cobots than the average operator because they experience daily problems in staff shortages, process issues, and absenteeism and are jointly responsible for tackling these problems. The decisive role of the team leader is thus highlighted in all cases:

"I was surprised to see how much resistance there was, also among the technicians" (Case D)

"The amount of resistance that arose when people only hear the word "robot" or "cobot" was unprecedented" (Case D)

Some of the experts indicated they had underestimated the difficulty of motivating people. Their organisation's kick-off program consisted of twenty team leaders, trained by the supplier, who had to explain the work with the cobots to their team. They experienced differences in motivation and character among the team leaders, leading to mixed results in the team performance. The character and the willingness for people to get involved are important factors, and the kick-off must be geared towards motivating all involved team members. Of course, a radical change, such as the implementation of a cobot, has consequences for the work environment. A much-discussed consequence is a change in the workforce, as reflected in professional logistics magazines: will robots take over our jobs in the future? The experts strongly reject this statement:

"There has certainly been some turmoil when we announced that we would focus on robotisation" (Case B)

One of the most important, and at the same time, most difficult objectives mentioned in the various cases is human operators' acceptance of and their willingness to engage in the introduction of cobots. According to the experts, you gain the acceptance of employees through good preparation and extensive instruction:

"The level of trust was not very high. The first employee was very sceptical" (Case C)

"The character and the will[ingness] of the people are important factors. The kick-off must be effective to motivate all those different characters" (Case B)

"Certain people refuse to work with the cobot" (Case C)

"The amount of resistance that arose when people only hear the word "robot" or "cobot" was unprecedented" (Case D)

These quotes suggest the importance of thoroughly preparing the change process to create support and trust, and lower the resistance to change. Team leaders play a decisive role in these processes, and the cases have even shown differences at team level in the implementation success of cobots.

4.3. Leadership during Cobot Implementation

Table 5 presents the results concerning the commitment, character, and motivation of employees during cobot implementation processes. These constructs all play a role in the human factors occurring and influencing the cobot implementation process and specifically point toward the importance of leadership.

Several experts mentioned that the role of operational manager/supervisor/team leader consists mainly of guiding and motivating the operators. The organisations train these team leaders during implementation to immediately support their team, which makes their role crucial both during and after the implementation phase. A team leader must continue to motivate because:

"Negativity sneaks into a team if a cobot does not work perfectly in one go (. . .). A test/implementation of a cobot is custom-made and requires many new insights. You need the team leaders to keep on motivating and to really take on their leadership role!" (Case D)

Another expert pointed toward the importance of commitment in light of successful implementation:

"He/she signals the first impressions and feedback. Less commitment from the team leader means less commitment from the operators and ultimately less productivity" (Case C)

When you work with people, you have to deal with differences in character. Operator A may be more open to change than operator B. One operator is more interested in technology than the other, and there is always a difference in willingness to learn something new. One of the key features noticed by the experts is that employees involved are generally curious about cobots. Survey results among their employees (e.g., warehouse operators; order pickers) show that the lights and signals do "trigger" the employees to further explore possibilities to include cobots in their work. Some employees want to test machines by standing in front of them to see how the cobot reacts. It is also important to examine to what extent the human operator is committed to working with the cobot. For example, a temporary worker experiencing a cobot for a day will probably be less committed to the machine than a permanent employee who experiences the benefits in daily operations. To illustrate, one of the experts said:

"It is difficult to motivate people to use the cobots properly. Especially since we also have to deal with new people every day who work for us as flex workers and sometimes do not even speak the Dutch language" (Case C)

"Character plays a major role here too. You see a huge difference in motivation between the team leaders, which also makes the difference in the teams visible. One team leader finds technology and innovation more fun and interesting than the other team leader" (Case D)

Table 5. Critical incidents and human factors identified related to the commitment, character, and motivation of employees during the implementation process.

Theme	Critical Incidents	Human Factor Identified
(Lack of) Committed employees	We should have involved more people from the start (Case A) The results became worse because the employees did not work with the cobot (Case A) The employees would like to work with the cobots, but we notice that the speed is not yet high enough to make it profitable (Case B) We have to deal with new people every day who work for us as flex workers. They are less committed and sometimes do not even speak the Dutch language (Case C) We could have prepared the operators even better (Case D) The support was not ample, but due to the failure of the cobot the commitment was quickly gone (Case D)	Communication Culture Leadership Resistance to change
Differences in character among employees	The willingness of employees [to work with the cobot] depends on their character (Case A) The character and the will[ingness] of the people are important factors (Case B) Certain people refuse to work with the cobot (Case C) Character plays a major role here too. You see a huge difference in motivation between the team leaders, which also makes the difference in the teams visible. One team leader finds technology and innovation more fun and interesting than the other team leader (Case D)	Resistance to change Culture Leadership
(Lack of) motivated employees	You see a huge difference in motivation between the team leaders, which also makes the difference in the teams visible (Case A) I underestimated how difficult it is to motivate employees. There is a lot of difference in motivation among the team leaders; with the result that one team works very well with the cobot and the other much less (Case A) The team leader must be convinced of the cobots, because he/she must create support (Case B) The operators were enthusiastic to get started (Case B) The team leader reports about the first signals and feedback. You see a lot of differences between team leaders (Case C) Negativity sneaks into a team if a cobot does not work perfectly in one go. A test/implementation of a cobot is custom-made and requires many new insights (Case D) Proactivity from the team leaders is so important! You see that if the motivation weakens, the results plummet. As an organisation you have to spend time on this. That really is a learning point for our organisation (Case D) You need the team leaders to keep on motivating and to really take on their leadership role (Case D)	Resistance to change Leadership Culture Communication

Preparation and instructions in advance are necessary to transfer the information to the operators properly. It is also essential that the team leader is convinced and will create support. Every decision made in such a process can be crucial and must be included in the design from the onset and be taken seriously. The team leader should feel that he/she is contributing to and has an influence on these developments. To illustrate, one expert took his team leaders to another company that was already working with robots to create awareness of the possibilities. Character, motivation, and proactivity are essential factors in leadership during cobot implementation:

> "Proactivity from the team leaders is so important! You see that if the motivation weakens, the results plummet. As an organisation you have to spend time on this. That really is a learning point for our organisation" (Case D)

These results highlight the pivotal role of motivated, committed, and proactive team leaders in the cobot implementation process; team leaders can ultimately aid or inhibit this process. Thus, it is the organisation's responsibility to include them in the initial phase of implementation and instruction.

5. Discussion

Our research is an addition to the existing literature on cobot implementations. It aims to fill the gap in the literature on the influence of human factors on cobot implementation processes in high volume distribution centres. Previous research has focused on the technical aspects and possibilities of the implementations, thereby largely ignoring the importance of human factors in these processes. In Section 5.1, we will further elaborate on a specific issue related to these processes, i.e., trust. Section 5.2 provides critical reflections about the influence of robotisation on human factors and the future of work.

5.1. Trust

The results confirm that organisations that start a cobot implementation process are confronted with resistance to change, caused by prejudice, scepticism, and unfamiliarity among staff. Our human factors approach confirms earlier research from Sanders et al. [13] into trust and prior experience in HRI. Despite their curious nature, the staff's trust must be gained before they are willing and confident to work with cobots. Moreover, trust is also linked to the individual characteristics of operators, as they might be sceptical, hesitant, or resistant to change. The lack of experience in working with cobots is also a critical influencing factor in the implementation process. According to the experts, a temporary employee is less committed to the cobot than an operator with a permanent contract. These findings are in line with those of Tsui et al. [42], who state: "Not only does experience lead to increased use, but higher levels of experience also engender more positive attitudes toward robots."

The results of our study demonstrate that a good instruction plan and the associated kick-off are essential for a successful implementation process. The better the preparation is arranged (structured in phases, all layers of the organisation extensively instructed and key users deployed to create support), the more enthusiastic the employees are about the cobots, hence tackling barriers caused by lack of trust and resistance to change. Central to this is information sharing, communication, and gaining the trust of the operators. According to Maurtua et al. [36,37], employees will only accept a cobot if they feel confident and safe with the cobot and can communicate well with the machine. As confirmed by our results, the interaction between the robot and the employee is crucial.

This study also demonstrates that human acceptance cannot be viewed separately from the work environment during the implementation process of cobots in high-volume distribution centres. Although the physical environment hardly needs adapting to implement a cobot and these "new employees" currently have no direct influence on the workforce, information sharing is an essential success factor for the implementation process. Human factors related to the work environment, organisational culture, and communication need to be taken into account and their interaction and changing nature. This is in line with earlier studies on the changing nature of influencing factors in organisational change processes (e.g., [40]).

A clear and structured instruction contributes to the operator's trust and increases the chance of acceptance and commitment. Kessler, MacArthur, & Hancock [33] propose a different explanation for this result. In their research, they conclude: "trust has specifically been identified as an important facet in facilitating the correct and appropriate use of a robotic system, which is a defining factor of successful interaction". Our research has demonstrated that good preparation and instruction can increase trust. Human factors such as resistance to change, prejudice, and unfamiliarity can then be positively influenced, which increases human acceptance. We can conclude from these results that well-prepared operators are more committed to working with cobots than those without any knowledge of the cobots.

5.2. Future of Work

Our results demonstrate that organisational culture is of great importance to the success of an implementation process. Other human factors can influence the culture within an organisation: the behaviour of colleagues (e.g., a lack of trust; resistance to change), but also whether and how team leaders take up their commitment and leadership role. If employees are not open to cooperation, innovation, and new ways of working, there is a low chance of successful implementation [25]. It is plausible that an organisation with a positive culture of improvement is more likely to achieve a successful implementation than an organisation where the culture can be labelled as conservative.

The operational managers, but especially the team leaders, play an important role as they are the ones who have to motivate and guide people, but also because they receive the first signals and feedback. Motivating and involving people in advance and during the process is essential for successful implementation. Calitz et al. [20] declare this in their research into the type of communication required to implement changes. A manager must recognise that human-cobot collaboration requires a different approach than human-human collaboration and that people need the motivation to develop trust in cooperation with cobots. Our results show that in the four case companies at hand, the impact of cobot implementation processes on the workforce has been underestimated. In contrast, its impact on productivity has been overestimated. On the one hand, the impact on the workforce was minimised, yet as case C clearly outlined, its future effects cannot be underestimated. Further research is necessary on how to organize the different elements of work based on whether they are better served by robots or humans (e.g., routinized tasks vs critical thinking). Consequently, this could increase autonomy and satisfaction and, as a result of this, well-being in the workplace, which, in return, could further increase intrinsic motivation and productivity [43,44].

Far-reaching and rapidly changing robotisation processes inevitably influence the future of work. Today's workforce is insufficiently prepared, affecting employees' feelings of fear of losing their job and fear of working together with a non-human/non-communicative partner, which is further provoked by binary position-taking (human versus computer) by the management. Such adverse effects on organisational processes have also been documented in other contexts, pointing toward the effect of vicious cycles that hinder innovation [45]. Instead of focusing on job loss and thus encouraging vicious cycles of resistance to change, one should critically reflect on the role of human factors in the future of work. Such a message inevitably includes dimensions of upskilling and reskilling of the workforce to be ready for the future [46]. Further research can address the link between human factors and the future of work, including dimensions of individual resilience, empowerment, and flourishing e.g., [47,48]. Such connections have been laid within the context of education and professionalisation and could inspire business and industrial change as well.

6. Conclusions

This study has shown that different human factors influence the cobot implementation processes and lead to recommendations for the successful implementation of cobots in order picking processes. Resistance to change appeared a crucial human factor and can be divided into three items: (1) Prejudice: pointing to the importance of overcoming initial prejudices and deferring judgment until sufficient information is available; (2) Scepticism: the majority of people is sceptical by nature and often goes into resistance when a change is applied; (3) Unfamiliarity: because most operators are working with a cobot for the first time. These factors show that it is crucial to engage the employees in the changes in advance to turn resistance to change into more trust and willingness to be involved.

Leadership as a human factor plays a decisive role in the implementation process. Team leaders have the responsibility to inform and encourage employees to work with the cobot successfully. Commitment and engagement are needed to get used to the cobot. Our results show that team leaders were more open to cobots than the average operator because they experience daily problems in terms of staff shortages, process issues, and absenteeism, and they are jointly responsible for tackling these problems. Both leadership and resistance to change are inevitably influenced by the other human factors at play: organisational culture and communication on changes.

The results demonstrate, however, two issues that are underexposed within the current debate around robotisation. On the one hand, trust is being viewed from a reductionist and linear perspective from a point where there is a lack of trust, which is then 'solved' by interventions to increase productivity. On the other hand, the role of robotisation in the future of work is being interpreted as inevitably requiring different and new skills, causing a skills gap in the current workforce. Both issues (trust and/in future of work) are closely related to each other. The expression "robot automation" can evoke feelings of fear in a facility, and employees will be afraid of losing their job. Implementing cobots requires investments that—from the management viewpoint—must be earned back by saving on staff. Such binary interpretations are not only detrimental for human factors in an organisation (leading to vicious cycles with more resistance; thus less productivity), they also neglect the importance of human-robot interaction and the need for re- and upskilling for the future of work.

Our study also has its limitations which lead to recommendations for further research. First, the specific selection criteria have led to a relatively small sample of four case companies. It was important to select only companies with a certain level of maturity in cobot implementation to achieve rich results (as reflected in the 66 identified critical incidents). Although the small sample is in line with recommendations for qualitative research [49], further research with a larger sample and quantitative approaches could lead to other insights into the role and (whether vicious or not) dynamics of human factors in robotisation processes. Second, our choice for the human factors resistance to change, communication, organisational culture, and leadership was informed by earlier research following the human factors approach. Yet, we are aware that more human factors are at play (e.g., as identified by [25]) that could be analysed in-depth, such as empowerment, competence, and mindsets.

Author Contributions: Conceptualization, W.L., L.K. and J.S.; methodology, L.K. and J.S.; validation, W.L. and J.S.; formal analysis, W.L., L.K. and J.S.; investigation, W.L., L.K. and J.S.; writing—original draft preparation, W.L., L.K. and J.S.; writing—review and editing, W.L., J.S.K. and J.S.; supervision, W.L. and J.S. All authors have read and agreed to the published version of the manuscript.

Funding: This research received no external funding.

Institutional Review Board Statement: The study was conducted according to the guidelines of the Declaration of Helsinki, however Institutional Review Board approval was not requested for this data collection.

Informed Consent Statement: Informed consent was obtained from all subjects involved in the study.

Data Availability Statement: Due to the nature of this research, the participants of this study did not agree for their data to be shared publicly.

Conflicts of Interest: The authors declare no conflict of interest.

Appendix A. Interview Guidelines

General information	Could you tell me about your function and you role in the implementation process? What is the role of your organisation/department in the logistics supply chain?
Current order picking process and the choice for robotisation	Order picking is a basic warehousing process, but has an important influence on supply chain's productivity. Which order picking system types can be found in your warehouse? What made your organisation decide to implement cobots in the order picking process? Which cobot did your organisation choose? Why this cobot? What improvements does this cobot make to the process?

Human factors	How did the warehouse employees react to the collaboration with cobots? How would you describe the trust level of warehouse employees during the collaboration with cobots? Do you think that trust influenced the outcomes of the implementation? How? Which factors influenced the trust of the human operator during the implementation of order picking cobots? Has the working environment been adapted for implementation? How? Was a kick-off program initiated at the start of the implementation process? How? Which organisational requirements have been fulfilled during the implementation process? Was there a clear responsibility for each stakeholder in the process? Was this the appropriate way for this implementation process in your opinion? To what extent do you think the operations manager is essential during the implementation of cobots? Why? Can you tell which critical decisions were made during the process? What made these decisions so important? Which factors can be positively influenced by a team leader during the implementation? To what extent have your operations manager succeeded in properly preparing the staff? How did he/she achieve this?
Results of the cobot implementation process	Are you satisfied with the outcomes? Why? What were the main learnings from this project? Have jobs been lost as a result of the implementation of cobots? What went well? What should have been done differently/better?

(Source: based on [35,40,50]).

Appendix B. Critical Incidents Identified in the Data

Table A1. Critical incidents related to the organisational change process.

Case Company	Critical Incident	Quote Interview	Data Label	Human Factor Identified
A	1. Facilitation of cobot introduction	The infrastructure for the supply and removal of materials has been adjusted	Adjustments	Resistance to change
	2. Adhering to business-as-usual	But the current process must continue	Adjustments	Resistance to change
	3. Communication and information	Team leaders were trained by the [cobot] supplier, who had to explain the work with the cobots to their team	Kick-off & instructions	Leadership
	4. Costs and investments related to cobot introduction	It is a major investment, which means that we do not purchase multiple cobots	Investment	Culture
	5. Influence of cobot introduction on the workforce	The cobots have no influence on the workforce, but people don't believe that, so it does affect the culture	Workforce	Culture
	6. Decisive role of team leader	The team leader is there to guide the operators where necessary. We have informed them in advance and have taken them to another company	Preparation	Leadership
	7. Decisive role of team leader	It is their job to explain it to the operators	Preparation	Leadership
	8. Influence of cobot introduction on productivity	There is a lot of difference in motivation and character among the team leaders. Which means that one team works very well with the cobot, and the other much less	Productivity	Resistance to change Leadership
B	9. Adhering to business-as-usual	No, the current process should preferably continue	Adjustments	Culture Resistance to change

Table A1. *Cont.*

Case Company	Critical Incident	Quote Interview	Data Label	Human Factor Identified
	10. Facilitation of cobot introduction	Now we think that the cobots work better in an isolated part of the warehouse, which requires adjustment	Adjustments	Resistance to change Culture
	11. Communication and information	We ensured that all layers of the organization were aware of the development. Step-by-step, person-by-person were informed. We set up an information corner. There was also a monthly meeting.	Kick-off & instructions	Communication
	12. Communication and information	The character and the will[ingness] of the people are important factors. The kick-off must be effective to motivate all those different characters	Kick-off & instructions	Resistance to change Communication
	13. Communication and information	Every operator received training and was rewarded with a certificate if they had mastered the work with the cobot	Kick-off & instructions	Resistance to change Communication Culture
	14. Costs and investments related to cobot introduction	You actually have to work in two or three shifts for a proper return on investment. That is why I think the deployment of cobots will develop faster at production companies that can produce day and night	Investment	Culture
	15. Costs and investments related to cobot introduction	Standing still is going backwards. You can keep consulting and calculating, but you just have to start	Investment	Resistance to change Culture
	16. Influence of cobot introduction on the workforce	Not yet, the amount of work is increasing and the use of cobots is not yet large enough	Workforce	Resistance to change Culture
	17 Decisive role of team leader	The team leaders were closely involved in the design phase. It is important that they feel that they contribute to success	Preparation	Leadership
	18. Influence of cobot introduction on productivity	Because we have instructed the team leaders properly, the operators work correctly with the cobots. However, we are not achieving productivity that we had in mind	Productivity	Leadership Culture
C	19. Adhering to business-as-usual	No major adjustments were made, that was a requirement from the management	Adjustments	Resistance to change
	20. Communication and information	We have not informed everyone in advance. The preparation could have been much better. We have not set up the test phase well enough	Kick-off & instructions	Communication
	21. Costs and investments related to cobot introduction	A cobot is a big investment	Investment	Resistance to change Culture
	22. Costs and investments related to cobot introduction	Cobots will really have to become cheaper in the coming years to become attractive for a bigger audience	Investment	Resistance to change Culture
	23. Influence of cobot introduction on the workforce	No jobs were lost, there is sufficient work	Workforce	Culture

Table A1. *Cont.*

Case Company	Critical Incident	Quote Interview	Data Label	Human Factor Identified
	24. Influence of cobot introduction on the workforce	Still ... the economy is now growing, so the workforce is growing. But if the economy slows down, it may indeed be that a cobot is more attractive and cheaper to keep in service than a human operator.	Workforce	Resistance to change Culture
	25. Decisive role of team leader	The team leaders are trained by the [cobot] supplier. They had to introduce the cobot and explain it to the employees	Preparation	Leadership
	26. Influence of cobot introduction on productivity	Less commitment from the team leader means less commitment from the operators and ultimately less productivity	Productivity	Resistance to change Leadership
	27. Influence of cobot introduction on productivity	All cobots have been implemented, but productivity is not being achieved at this time because the preparation should have been better	Productivity	Culture
	28. Influence of cobot introduction on productivity	The productivity that can be achieved with cobots is not achieved	Productivity	Culture
	29. Influence of cobot introduction on productivity	That also depends on whether the productivity is high enough for a good return on investment	Productivity	Culture
D	30. Facilitation of cobot introduction	An emergency button had to be made to stop the cobot when needed. This was a big adjustment according to the technicians	Adjustments	Resistance to change
	31. Communication and information	A project team has been set up and we have taken a number of operators to another company to look at operative cobots.	Kick-off & instructions	Communication
	32. Communication and information	In retrospect it turned out that we could have involved more employees	Kick-off & instructions	Resistance to change Communication
	33. Costs and investments related to cobot introduction	A cobot costs a lot of money, so after a few months we opted for a different robot solution	Investment	Culture
	34. Influence of cobot introduction on the workforce	Replacing jobs is not going that fast, maybe in five or ten years, but fear among staff rules	Workforce	Resistance to change Culture
	35. Decisive role of team leader	The location manager has given a presentation. A project team with operators and team leaders was then established	Preparation	Leadership
	36. Influence of cobot introduction on productivity	You see that if the motivation of a team leader weakens, the results plummet	Productivity	Resistance to change Leadership
	37. Influence of cobot introduction on productivity	The cobot did not give us the desired result.	Productivity	Resistance to change

Table A2. Critical incidents related to scepticism, (lack of) commitment and motivation.

Case Company	Critical Incident	Quote Interview	Data Label	Human Factor Identified
A	1. Skepticism among employees	The first employees to use the cobot were skeptical	Prejudice	Resistance to change
	2. Lack of experience/gaining experience with cobots	The use of cobots was a real culture shock for our employees	Unfamiliarity	Resistance to change
	3. (Lack of) Committed employees	We should have involved more people from the start	Commitment	Communication
	4. (Lack of) Committed employees	The results became worse because the employees did not work with the cobot	Commitment	Communication Culture
	5. Differences in character among employees	The willingness of employees [to work with the cobot] depends on their character	Character	Resistance to change
	6. (Lack of) motivated employees	You see a huge difference in motivation between the team leaders, which also makes the difference in the teams visible	Motivation	Resistance to change
	7. (Lack of) motivated employees	I underestimated how difficult it is to motivate employees. There is a lot of difference in motivation among the team leaders; with the result that one team works very well with the cobot and the other much less	Motivation	Resistance to change Leadership Culture
B	8. Skepticism among employees	There has certainly been some turmoil when we announced that we would focus on robotisation	Prejudice	Resistance to change
	9. Lack of experience/gaining experience with cobots	Some operators were experimenting, for example, unexpectedly stand in front of the cobot, in order to find out how the cobot would react	Curiosity	Resistance to change Culture
	10. (Lack of) Committed employees	The employees would like to work with the cobots, but we notice that the speed is not yet high enough to make it profitable	Commitment	Culture Leadership
	11. Differences in character among employees	The character and the will[ingness] of the people are important factors. The kick-off must be effective to motivate all those different characters	Character	Resistance to change
	12. (Lack of) motivated employees	The team leader must be convinced of the cobots, because he/she must create support	Motivation	Resistance to change Leadership
	13. (Lack of) motivated employees	The operators were enthusiastic to get started	Motivation	Resistance to change Culture Leadership
C	14. Skepticism among employees	The level of trust was not very high. The first employee was very skeptical	Prejudice	Resistance to change
	15. Lack of experience/gaining experience with cobots	Due to unfamiliarity, the cobots are used too little	Unfamiliarity	Resistance to change Culture Communication
	16. Lack of experience/gaining experience with cobots	The employees were triggered by the lights and the bells on the cobot	Curiosity	Resistance to change Culture

Table A2. Cont.

Case Company	Critical Incident	Quote Interview	Data Label	Human Factor Identified
	17. (Lack of) Committed employees	We have to deal with new people every day who work for us as flex workers. They are less committed and sometimes do not even speak the Dutch language	Commitment	Resistance to change Culture
	18. Differences in character among employees	Certain people refuse to work with the cobot	Character	Resistance to change
	19. (Lack of) motivated employees	The team leader reports about the first signals and feedback. You see a lot of differences between team leaders	Motivation	Leadership
D	20. Skepticism among employees	I was surprised to see how much resistance there was, also among the technicians	Prejudice	Resistance to change
	21. Skepticism among employees	The amount of resistance that arose when people only hear the word "robot" or "cobot" was unprecedented	Prejudice	Resistance to change Culture
	22. Lack of experience/gaining experience with cobots	It seems that people are really afraid of the cobots	Unfamiliarity	Resistance to change Culture
	23. Lack of experience/gaining experience with cobots	There was more fear than curiosity	Unfamiliarity Curiosity	Resistance to change Culture
	24. (Lack of) Committed employees	We could have prepared the operators even better	Commitment	Communication Culture
	25. (Lack of) Committed employees	The support was not large, but due to the failure of the cobot the commitment was quickly gone	Commitment	Resistance to change Culture
	26. Differences in character among employees	Character plays a major role here too. You see a huge difference in motivation between the team leaders, which also makes the difference in the teams visible. One team leader finds technology and innovation more fun and interesting than the other team leader	Character	Resistance to change Leadership Culture
	27. (Lack of) motivated employees	Negativity sneaks into a team if a cobot does not work perfectly in one go. A test/implementation of a cobot is custom-made and requires many new insights.	Motivation	Resistance to change Communication Culture
	28. (Lack of) motivated employees	Proactivity from the team leaders is so important! You see that if the motivation weakens, the results plummet. As an organisation you have to spend time on this. That really is a learning point for our organisation	Motivation	Resistance to change Leadership Culture
	29. (Lack of) motivated employees	You need the team leaders to keep on motivating and to really take on their leadership role	Motivation	Leadership

References

1. Sheridan, T.B. Human–robot interaction: Status and challenges. *Hum. Factors* **2016**, *58*, 525–532. [CrossRef]
2. Goetschalckx, M.; Ashayeri, J. Classification and design of order picking systems. *Logist. World* **1989**, *2*, 99–106. [CrossRef]
3. Anđelković, A.; Radosavljević, M. Improving order-picking process through implementation warehouse management system. *Strateg. Manag.* **2018**, *23*, 3–10. [CrossRef]
4. De Koster, R.; Le-Duc, T.; Roodbergen, K.J. Design and control of warehouse order picking: A literature review. *Eur. J. Oper. Res.* **2007**, *182*, 481–501. [CrossRef]
5. ABIresearch. Collaborative Robotics Market Exceeds US$1 Billion by 2020. Available online: https://www.abiresearch.com/press/collaborative-robotics-market-exceeds-us1-billion-/ (accessed on 17 April 2018).
6. Dijkhuizen, B. The advance of cobots logistics. *Logistic* **2017**, *12*, 6.
7. Dijkhuizen, B. Robots nemen tilwerk uit handen. *Logistiek* **2017**, 24–25. Available online: www.logistiek.nl (accessed on 10 July 2018).
8. Bonkenburg, T. Robotics in logistics. A DPDHL perspective on implications and use cases for the logistics industry. *Troisdorf DHL Trendrep.* **2016**. Available online: https://www.dhl.com/content/dam/downloads/g0/about_us/logistics_insights/dhl_trendreport_robotics.pdf (accessed on 20 May 2021).
9. Pepitone, J. Amazon Buys Army of Robots. Available online: https://money.cnn.com/2012/03/20/technology/amazon-kiva-robots/Protime (accessed on 10 July 2018).
10. Heater, B. Amazon Debuts a Pair of New Warehouse Robots. Available online: https://techcrunch.com/2019/06/05/amazon-debuts-a-pair-of-new-warehouse-robots/?guccounter=1 (accessed on 23 July 2019).
11. ABIresearch. 50,000 Warehouses to Use Robots by 2025 as Barriers to Entry Fall and AI Innovation Accelerates. Available online: https://www.abiresearch.com/press/50000-warehouses-use-robots-2025-barriers-entry-fall-and-ai-innovation-accelerates/ (accessed on 10 April 2019).
12. Weerd, P.D. Autonoom als opstap naar automatisering. *Logistiek* **2017**, *2017*, 52–53.
13. Sanders, T.L.; MacArthur, K.; Volante, W.; Hancock, G.; MacGillivray, T.; Shugars, W.; Hancock, P.A. Trust and Prior Experience in Human-Robot Interaction. In Proceedings of the Human Factors and Ergonomics Society 2017 Annual Meeting, Austin, TX, USA, 9–13 October 2017; pp. 1809–1810.
14. Vagaš, M.; Galajdová, A.; Šimšík, D. Techniques for Secure Automated Operation with Cobots Participation. In Proceedings of the 2020 21th International Carpathian Control Conference (ICCC), High Tatras, Slovakia, 27–19 October 2020; pp. 1–4.
15. Michaelis, J.E.; Siebert-Evenstone, A.; Shaffer, D.W.; Mutlu, B. Collaborative or Simply Uncaged? Understanding Human-Cobot Interactions in Automation. In Proceedings of the 2020 CHI Conference on Human Factors in Computing Systems, Honolulu, HI, USA, 25–30 April 2020; pp. 1–12.
16. Allen, V. Walk 11 Miles a Shift and Pick up An Order Every 33 Seconds: Revealed, How Amazon Works Staff 'to the bone' [Persbericht]. Available online: http://www.dailymail.co.uk/news/article-2512959/Walk-11-miles-shift-pick-order-33-seconds--Amazon-works-staff-bone.html (accessed on 12 June 2018).
17. Roehl, C. Know Your Machine: Industrial Robots vs. Cobots [Blogpost]. Available online: https://blog.universal-robots.com/know-your-machine-industrial-robots-vs.-cobots (accessed on 20 January 2019).
18. Weerd, P.D. Robots in De Logistiek: Dit is Er, Dit Kunnen Ze. Available online: https://www.logistiek.nl/warehousing/artikel/2018/01/robots-de-logistiek-dit-er-dit-kunnen-ze-101161844 (accessed on 26 June 2018).
19. Strohkorb, S.; Huang, C.M.; Ramachandran, A.; Scassellati, B. Establishing Sustained, Supportive Human-Robot Relationships: Building Blocks and Open Challenges. In Proceedings of the AAAI Spring Symposium on Enabling Computing Research in Socially Intelligent Human Robot Interaction, Palo Alto, CA, USA, 21–23 March 2016; pp. 179–182. Available online: https://www.aaai.org/ocs/index.php/SSS/SSS16/paper/.../11942 (accessed on 10 July 2018).
20. Calitz, A.P.; Poisat, P.; Cullen, M. The future African workplace: The use of collaborative robots in manufacturing. *SA J. Hum. Res. Manag.* **2017**, *15*, 1–11. [CrossRef]
21. Cao, H.L. A collaborative homeostatic-based behavior controller for social robots in human–Robot interaction experiments. *Int. J. Soc. Robot.* **2017**, *1*, 675–690. [CrossRef]
22. Cohen, Y.; Shoval, S.; Faccio, M.; Minto, R. Deploying cobots in collaborative systems: Major considerations and productivity analysis. *Int. J. Prod. Res.* **2021**, 1–17. [CrossRef]
23. Robinette, P.; Wagner, A.R.; Howard, A.M. Effect of Robot Performance on Human–Robot Trust in Time-Critical Situations—IEEE Journals & Magazine. Available online: https://ieeexplore.ieee.org/document/7828078 (accessed on 20 December 2020).
24. Francis, S. Fast-Growing Sectors within Robotics and Automation. Available online: https://roboticsandautomationnews.com/2018/01/12/fast-growing-sectors-within-robotics-and-automation/15656/ (accessed on 20 December 2018).
25. Hancock, A.; Billings, D.R.; Schaefer, K.E.; Chen, J.Y.C.; Visser, E.J.D.; Parasuraman, R. A meta-analysis of factors affecting trust in human-robot interaction. *Hum. Factors* **2011**, *53*, 517–527. [CrossRef]
26. Simões, A.C.; Soares, A.L.; Barros, A.C. Factors influencing the intention of managers to adopt collaborative robots (cobots) in manufacturing organizations. *J. Eng. Technol. Manag.* **2020**, *57*, 101574. [CrossRef]
27. Mercer. Global Talent Trends 2019 (Connectivity in the Human Age). Available online: https://www.mercer.com/content/dam/mercer/attachments/global/Career/gl-2019-global-talent-trends-study.pdf (accessed on 20 May 2021).
28. Parasuraman, R.; Riley, V. Humans and automation: Use, misuse, disuse, abuse. *Hum. Factors* **1997**, *39*, 230–253. [CrossRef]

29. Ogawa, K.; Nishio, S.; Koda, K.; Balistreri, G.; Watanabe, T.; Ishiguro, H. Exploring the natural reaction of young and aged person with telenoid in a real world. *J. Adv. Comput. Intell. Intell. Inform.* **2011**, *15*, 592–597. [CrossRef]
30. Sorbello, R.; Chella, A.; Calí, C.; Giardina, M.; Nishio, S.; Ishiguro, H. Telenoidandroid robot as an embodied perceptual social regulation medium engaging natural human humanoid interaction. *Robot. Auton. Syst.* **2014**, *62*, 1329–1341. [CrossRef]
31. Broadbent, E. Interactions with robots: The truths we reveal about ourselves. *Ann. Rev. Psychol.* **2017**, *68*, 627–652. [CrossRef] [PubMed]
32. Ogreten, S.; Lackey, S.; Nicholson, D. Recommended roles for uninhabited team members within mixed-initiative combat teams. In Proceedings of the 2010 International Symposium on Collaborative Technologies and Systems, Chicago, IL, USA, 17–21 May 2010; pp. 531–536.
33. Kessler, T.; Stowers, K.; Brill, J.C.; Hancock, P.A. Comparisons of human-human trust with other forms of human-technology trust. *Proc. Hum. Factors Ergon. Soc. Ann. Meet.* **2017**, *61*, 1303–1307. [CrossRef]
34. Langley, A.; Smallman, C.; Tsoukas, H.; Van de Ven, A.H. Process studies of change in organisation and management: Unveiling temporality, activity, and flow. *Acad. Manag. J.* **2013**, *56*, 1–13. [CrossRef]
35. Verhulst, E.; Boks, C. The role of human factors in the adoption of sustainable design criteria in business: Evidence from Belgian and Dutch case studies. *Int. J. Innov. Sustain. Dev.* **2012**, *6*, 146–163. [CrossRef]
36. Maurtua, I.; Ibarguren, A.; Kildal, J.; Susperregi, L.; Sierra, B. Human–robot collaboration in industrial applications. *Int. J. Adv. Robot. Syst.* **2017**, *14*. [CrossRef]
37. Maurtua, I.; Fernandez, I.; Tellaeche, A.; Kildal, J.; Susperregi, L.; Ibarguren, A.; Sierra, B. Natural multimodal communication for human–robot collaboration. *Int. J. Adv. Robot. Syst.* **2017**, *14*. [CrossRef]
38. Ghauri, P. Designing and Conducting Case Studies in International Business Research. In *Handbook of Qualitative Research Methods for International Business*; Marschan-Piekkari, R., Welch, C., Eds.; Edward Elgar: Cheltenham, UK, 2004; pp. 109–124.
39. Dekker, F. Robot—En ICT-Gebruik in Het Nederlandse Bedrijfsleven, *ESB, Jaargang 101, editie 4733*. 2016. Available online: https://fabiandekker.nl/_PDF_V2/312313_DEKKER%20(def).pdf (accessed on 10 July 2018).
40. Verhulst, E.; Lambrechts, W. Fostering the incorporation of sustainable development in higher education. Lessons learned from a change management perspective. *J. Clean. Prod.* **2015**, *106*, 189–204. [CrossRef]
41. Qu, S.Q.; Dumay, J. The qualitative research interview. *Qual. Res. Account. Manag.* **2011**, *8*, 238–264. [CrossRef]
42. Tsui, K.; Desai, M.A.; Yanco, H.; Cramer, H.; Kemper, N. Measuring attitudes towards telepresence robots. *Int. J. Intell. Control Syst.* **2011**, *16*, 1–11.
43. Hechanova, R.M.; Alampay, R.B.; Franca, E.P. Empowerment, job satisfaction and performance among Filipino service workers. *Asian J. Soc. Psychol.* **2006**, *9*, 72–78. [CrossRef]
44. Kasser, T.; Sheldon, K.M. Time affluence as a path toward personal happiness and ethical business practice: Empirical evidence from four studies. *J. Bus. Ethics* **2009**, *84*, 243–255. [CrossRef]
45. Schenkel, M.; Krikke, H.; Caniëls, M.C.; Lambrechts, W. Vicious cycles that hinder value creation in closed loop supply chains: Experiences from the field. *J. Cleaner Prod.* **2019**, *223*, 278–288. [CrossRef]
46. Abe, E.N.; Abe, I.I.; Adisa, O. Future of Work: Skill Obsolescence, Acquisition of New Skills, and Upskilling in the 4IR. In *Future of Work, Work-Family Satisfaction, and Employee Well-Being in the Fourth Industrial Revolution*; IGI Global: Hershey, PA, USA, 2021; pp. 217–231.
47. Lambrechts, W. *Learning 'For' and 'In' the Future: On the Role of Resilience and Empowerment in Education*; Paper Commissioned for the UNESCO Futures of Education Report; UNESCO: Paris, France, 2020.
48. Vallor, S. Moral deskilling and upskilling in a new machine age: Reflections on the ambiguous future of character. *Philos. Technol.* **2015**, *28*, 107–124. [CrossRef]
49. Creswell, J.W. *Qualitative Inquiry & Research Design: Choosing among Five Approaches*, 3rd ed.; Sage: Thousand Oaks, CA, USA, 2013.
50. van Keulen, F.; Ahsmann, B.; van den Akker, E.; Habraken, M.; Burghardt, P.; Jayawardhana, B.; Van Lente, H.; Meinders, T.; Thuis, B. Smart industry roadmap: Onderzoeksagenda voor HTSM en ICT en routekaart voor de NWA. *Smart Ind.* **2018**. Available online: http://pure.tudelft.nl/ws/portalfiles/portal/71932725/Smart_Industry_Roadmap_2018.pdf (accessed on 20 May 2021).

MDPI
St. Alban-Anlage 66
4052 Basel
Switzerland
Tel. +41 61 683 77 34
Fax +41 61 302 89 18
www.mdpi.com

Logistics Editorial Office
E-mail: logistics@mdpi.com
www.mdpi.com/journal/logistics

www.ingramcontent.com/pod-product-compliance
Lightning Source LLC
LaVergne TN
LVHW070000100526
838202LV00019B/2592